ne Rene   0

INTERNATIONAL BOOK OF DYSLEXIA
A CROSS-LANGUAGE COMPARISON AND PRACTICE GUIDE

Edited by **Ian Smythe**, **John Everatt** and **Robin Salter**

PART I: LANGUAGES
PART II: COUNTRIES

John Wiley & Sons, Ltd

Other Wiley Editorial Offices

John Wiley & Sons Inc., 111 River Street, Hoboken, NJ 07030, USA

Jossey-Bass, 989 Market Street, San Francisco, CA 94103-1741, USA

Wiley-VCH Verlag GmbH, Boschstr. 12, D-69469 Weinheim, Germany

John Wiley & Sons Australia Ltd, 33 Park Road, Milton, Queensland 4064, Australia

John Wiley & Sons (Asia) Pte Ltd, 2 Clementi Loop #02-01, Jin Xing Distripark, Singapore 129809

John Wiley & Sons Canada Ltd, 22 Worcester Road, Etobicoke, Ontario, Canada M9W 1L1

Wiley also publishes its books in a variety of electronic formats. Some content that appears in print may not
be available in electronic books.

Library of Congress Cataloging-in-Publication Data

British Library Cataloguing in Publication Data

A catalogue record for this book is available from the British Library

ISBN 0-471-49841-6

Typeset in 10/12pt Times by SNP Best-set Typesetter Ltd., Hong Kong
Printed and bound in Great Britain by Antony Rowe, Chippenham SN14 6LH
This book is printed on acid-free paper responsibly manufactured from sustainable forestry in which at least
two trees are planted for each one used for paper production.

CONTENTS

PART I: LANGUAGES

Part II: Countries

Note: These chapters can be found online at www.wileyeurope.com/go/dyslexia

Introduction: Dyslexia – different contexts, same problems
Ian Smythe and Robin Salter

Dyslexia in Argentina
Maria Jose Quintana

Dyslexia in Australia
Paul Whiting

Dyslexia in Austria
Maria Götzinger-Hiebner and Michael Kalmár

Dyslexia in Bahrain
Haya Al-Mannai

Dyslexia in Belgium
Elena Grammaticos and Anny Cooreman

LIST OF CONTRIBUTORS

Salim Abu-Rabia, University of Haifa, Faculty of Education, Haifa, Mount Carmel, 31905, Israel.

Mikko Aro, Agora Child Research Centre, PO Box 35, University of Jyväskylä, 40014, Jyväskylä, Finland.

Marta Bogdanowicz, Polski Towarzystwo Dysleksji, Pomorska 68, 80343, Gdansk, Poland.

Alessandra G.S. Capovilla, PSE-IP, Cidade Universitaria, Av. Prof. Mello Moraes 1721, São Paulo, SP 05508-900, Brazil.

Fernando C. Capovilla, PSE-IP, Cidade Universitaria, Av. Prof. Mello Moraes 1721, São Paulo, SP 05508-900, Brazil.

John Everatt, Dept of Psychology, University of Surrey, Guildford, Surrey, GU2 5XH, UK.

Kaveh Farrokh, Langara College, 100 West 49th Avenue, Vancouver, BC, V5Y 2Z6, Canada.

Esther Geva, Department of Human Development and Applied Psychology, The Ontario Institute for Studies in Education, University of Toronto, 252 Bloor West, Toronto, M5S IV6, Canada.

Almudena Giménez de la Peña, Facultad de Psicologia, University of Malaga, 29071, Malaga, Spain.

Usha Goswami, Faculty of Education, University of Cambridge, Shaftesbury Road, Cambridge, CB2 2BX, UK.

Éva Gyarmathy, Veresegyhaz, Galagonya u.33, H-2112 LE, Hungary.

Dorthe Haven, Dansk Videnscenter for Ordlindhed, Kongevejen 256A, st., Virum, DK 2830, Denmark.

Leena Holopainen, Niilo Maki Institute, Jyväskylä, Finland.

Olga Inshakova, Logopedia Department of Defectologica, Moscow State Pedagogical University, Moscow, Russia.

Birgit Dilling Jandorf, Dansk Videnscenter for Ordlindhed, Kongevejen 256A, st., Virum, DK 2830, Denmark.

Mark Leikin, Faculty of Education, Haifa University, Haifa, Mount Carmel, 31905, Israel.

Ingvar Lundberg, Department of Psychology, Goteborg University, Haraldsgatan 1, S-41314, Goteborg, Sweden.

Heikki Lyytinen, Agora Child Research Centre, PO Box 35, University of Jyväskylä, 40014, Jyväskylä, Finland.

Helen Nielsen, Dansk Videnscenter for Ordlindhed, Kongevejen 256A, st., Virum, DK 2830, Denmark.

Costas D. Porpodas, Laboratory of Cognitive Analysis of Learning, Language and Dyslexia, Faculty of Humanities and Social Sciences, Department of Education, University of Patras, 26500, Patras, Greece.

Pieter Reitsma, PI Research, Vrije Universiteit, Rijksstraatweg 145, 1115 AP, Duivendrecht, Amsterdam, The Netherlands.

Gerd Schulte-Körne, Dyslexia Research Group, Department of Child and Adolescent Psychiatry and Psychotherapy, Philipps-University Marburg, Hans-Sachs-Strasse 6, 35039, Marburg, Germany.

David L. Share, Faculty of Education, Haifa University, Haifa, Mount Carmel, 31905, Israel.

Ian Smythe, 34 Collingwood Road, Sutton, Surrey, SM1 2RZ, UK.

Patrizio Tressoldi, Dipartimento di Psicologia Generale, Università di Padova, Via Venezia, 8, 35131, Padua, Italy.

Lesly Wade-Woolley, Cognitive Studies and Educational Psychology, Faculty of Education, Duncan McArthur Hall, Room A208, Queen's University, Kingston, K7L 3N6, Ontario, Canada.

Brendan Weekes, Laboratory of Experimental Psychology, School of Biological Sciences, University of Sussex, Falmer, Brighton, BN1 9QG, UK.

Jun Yamada, Faculty of Integrated Arts and Sciences, Hiroshima University, 1-7-1 Kagamiyama, Higashi Hiroshima, 739-8521, Japan.

Wengang Yin, Institute of Psychology, Chinese Academy of Sciences, Beijing, 100101, China.

PREFACE

Today nothing is new, and that is as true in dyslexia as much as it is in many other spheres. When Confucius (551–479 BC) said, 'I hear and I forget, I see and I remember, I do and I understand', he was talking about multi-sensory teaching. It is said that he observed his students to understand how each learned, and taught with respect to their strengths and weaknesses, so that whatever he taught was suited to their learning style. And of course it is this approach that is at the heart of teaching the dyslexic individual. So, to quote another great teacher, 'Most ideas about teaching are not new, but not everyone knows the old ideas' (Euclid *c*. 300 BC).

This is the second version of the *International Book of Dyslexia*, and we are delighted to have expanded so much upon the first one. The book now consists of Part 1 that is dedicated to considering the effects of language on dyslexia, and Part 2, available electronically on www.wileyeurope.com/go/dyslexia, that has greatly increased the number of countries that were included in the first version. And there is so much to celebrate in terms of advance even in those few short years, not only in terms of research, as demonstrated in Part 1, but also in progress made in the many countries as reported in Part 2.

But let us not forget that in many places there has not been a great advance. We should not rest on our successes to date. Without doubt, during the past six years it is the Internet that has opened up so much in the dyslexia community, whether it is through access to information, distribution of resources, or just people being able to communicate so much more easily across vast distances. But there is still, for example, a shortage of dyslexia provision in most of Africa. And few countries in central America have a dyslexia network, even though there is information on dyslexia in the Spanish language.

Sadly, Marion Welchman, the inspiration for the original version, passed away just three weeks after the first book was published. For those readers not familiar with her work, she was a pioneer in the UK, and an inspiration to many around the world including those in the 18 countries who specifically mentioned her contribution to their dyslexia work. She loved the first version. She would have been delighted in seeing the advances in this second

International Book of Dyslexia: A Cross Language Comparison Guide. Edited by Ian Smythe, John Everatt and Robin Salter. ISBN 0471498416 © 2004 John Wiley & Sons, Ltd.

version. And she would have been the first to celebrate the diversity of approaches not only in this book, but also in dyslexia assessment and teaching throughout the world.

We have moved away from the idea that we all learn the same way. We are now beginning to understand that the underlying difficulties of the individual will vary not only from individual to individual, but also from language to language. So all we have to do now is ensure the resources for identification and teaching of these individuals are available, to suit their learning style, and in their preferred language.

To use a phrase usually attributed to Harry Chasty: 'If they cannot learn the way we teach, can we teach the way they learn?'

Ian Smythe, John Everatt and Robin Salter
September 2003

DYSLEXIA
A cross-linguistic framework

Ian Smythe and John Everatt

INTRODUCTION TO PART I

Part 1 of this book is devoted to issues related to the potential effects of different languages on the diagnosis/assessment of dyslexia and the teaching/support of individuals identified as dyslexic. Each of the languages covered in Part 1 is presented in a separate chapter that provides the author's personal review of current knowledge. The coverage includes a discussion of the difficulties that a dyslexic individual may experience with the language's orthography (i.e., the writing system, including the written symbols that represent a language) and phonology (i.e., the basic units of sound in the language). Chapter 20 focuses on specific issues related to multilingualism, i.e., situations in which the individual is required to learn several languages and/or scripts. Clearly, it is not possible to include a chapter on every language currently used in the world. Part 1, therefore, focuses on those languages for which there was an available body of research that authors could use to discuss a range of issues. Authors were given the liberty to discuss those issues that they felt were important within the language within which they were working. Many, therefore, concentrated on the development of literacy skills. Given that most definitions of dyslexia (see section on Dyslexia definitions and related terminology on p. 3) have the common element of literacy acquisition difficulties, this was an obvious point of commonality for the following chapters. Some authors, however, also discussed other aspects that are associated with dyslexia, particularly when this was pertinent to specific features of the language or theoretical perspective outlined.

A second topic discussed by many authors was the transparency of the language. Transparency refers to the relationship between the written symbol of the script and its associated sound in speech. Some languages have a more regular script (i.e., a high correspondence between written symbols and speech sounds), alternatively referred to as

International Book of Dyslexia: A Cross-Language Comparison and Practice Guide. Edited by Ian Smythe, John Everatt and Robin Salter.   ISBN 0471498416   © 2004 John Wiley & Sons, Ltd.

a transparent/shallow orthography (see, for example, Chapters 18 and 13 on Spanish and Italian). Other languages have a much more inconsistent (irregular) correspondence between symbols and sounds, and are often referred to as non-transparent or deep orthographies, of which English is the most quoted example. However, some authors discuss other language features that might affect the development of literacy skills and/or the manifestation of dyslexia. For example, difficulties have been encountered when trying to fit Chinese and Japanese scripts into the simple transparent/non-transparent continuum (see Chapters 3 and 14). The more logographic (or morphographic) Chinese characters do not allow a simple decoding of alphabetic elements that has been seen as the main benefit of a transparent script. However, the logographic symbol represents both a concept and a sound relatively regularly. In these languages, therefore, other issues (such as the number of symbols to be learnt or the ability to rapidly access such symbols) may be of greater importance than the processes used in decoding alphabetic symbols.

Chapter 11 on Hebrew discusses another factor that may lead to differences between languages. In some language contexts, the transparency provided by the script varies with literacy learning. At some point in learning, the markers that once precisely specified a sound are removed. It is assumed that more experienced readers do not require these markers and should have learned to access a word and its meaning from other sources of information. In such cases, an assessment of the influence of context, meaning and/or morphological derivation may be seen as fundamental to our understanding of literacy acquisition and literacy deficits. Morphemic awareness (i.e., an understanding of the basic units of a word that convey meaning) has been hypothesized as important in several language contexts. For example, Hungarian has been described as a regular script, but an agglutinal language (see the discussion Chapter 12). This latter feature leads to very long words being common, produced as additional morphological units are combined with a root word to vary its meaning. Even a child with a perfect understanding of the rules associating graphemes and phonemes may require considerable cognitive resources in the areas of auditory short-term memory, auditory perception and discrimination, as well as access to the morphologic lexicon, to spell such words correctly. The ability to identify morphological compounds may be one way of supporting learning by reducing processing load. Alternatively, morphemic derivation may only be vital for learning when the association between grapheme and phoneme becomes irregular. The agglutinal nature of the language may be less vital in learning literacy as long as the letter sequence can be used to decode into an accurate sound-form. Comparisons of English, Hungarian and Hebrew may clarify the relative importance of these language features.

The following chapters will therefore contain common elements, but will vary in style and emphasis. The editors provided the basis from which the authors developed their contribution, but made every effort to avoid biases that may have led to issues being neglected that should be discussed in language contexts. Contributions were requested from authors working in the language discussed in that chapter. This ensured a local perspective was given to the issues related to that language. For this reason, many of the papers/books referenced in chapters were written in the language discussed and may be new to the English literature – many were new to the editors. The presentation of this work was, the editors felt, an important function of such a book. However, the number and variation of the works referenced have led to differences between authors in the terminology used. Where these differences in terminology reflect the work discussed, they have been retained. Where differences between authors led to potential confusion between chapters, further clarification was requested. As editors, we felt that such variations in perspective required both an introduction to these differences in viewpoints and a framework in which to view the work presented. The aim of this introduction is to present such a framework while outlining the background to dyslexia research and theory. The framework discussed was developed from the cross-language work of Smythe and Everatt who have found it useful for these comparative purposes. It should be read as an aid to comparison, rather than as a definitive model of dyslexia across different languages.

The following sections start with some background information on dyslexia, its definition and related terminology. Subsequent sections briefly discuss the theoretical positions that have dominated work in this area, contrasting unitary and sub-type perspectives, as well as touching on issues specific to cross-language investigations. The introduction then moves on to discuss the proposed framework, the evidence that has inspired this viewpoint and findings that indicate the necessity for modification and further work.

THE CONCEPT OF DYSLEXIA

In his discussion of the classical theory of 'concepts', Wittgenstein (1953) looked at the concept of games, and how it changes with different uses of the term. He realized that there were similarities and relationships, but nothing common to all of its uses. Board games, card games, team ball games or just throwing a ball against a wall – all can be thought of as games. However, there were no defining features, or common characteristics, that specified these as games. As a result, Wittgenstein referred to a 'family resemblance' rather than specific properties to denote a concept. This was a significant shift away from the classical theory of concepts, which was required to be clearly defined by specific properties. For example, the classical perspective may describe a square as having four properties: (1) being a closed figure; (2) having four sides; (3) having sides equal (in length); and (4) having equal angles. All squares must have those properties. Historically, much of the work on dyslexia has been approached from this 'classical concept' perspective. That is, an assumption that there must be a core deficit common to all dyslexic individuals. However, the approach of Wittgenstein, which would see the concept of dyslexia as a 'network of overlapping and criss-crossing similarities' (McShane, 1991, p. 128), may be more appropriate.

In line with Wittgenstein's theory of concepts, no universal criteria have been produced that may be used to identify dyslexia across different language contexts. Terminology and criteria for both classification and investigation/assessment have regularly been disputed, even within the English language context (Rutter, 1978; Smythe and Everatt, 2000; Stanovich and Siegel, 1994; Vellutino, 1978). Furthermore, theorists have differed about the cognitive processes that lead to the behavioural outcomes associated with dyslexia and which require investigation and assessment (Bruck, 1990; Olson *et al.*, 1989; Stanovich, 1986; Tallal, 1984; Wolf and O'Brien, 2001). While reductionism might lead to the acceptance of particular cognitive functions as fundamental to dyslexia, until a consensus has been reached, in terms of both definition and methodologies, comparative research, particularly that which requires cross-language referents, will continue to be problematic (see the first edition of this book: Salter and Smythe, 1997).

DYSLEXIA DEFINITIONS AND RELATED TERMINOLOGY

Do definitions of dyslexia show evidence of the necessary consensus? At present, the answer must be no. In order to comprehend the demands made upon a definition, it is necessary to understand why particular individuals/groups have used the terminology. Stanovich (1992) noted that definitions of dyslexia have served many different purposes. He conceptualized the differences as: (1) for scientific purposes, whereby assumptions may be judged by research criteria; (2) for school personnel, whereby additional services may be provided for low achievers; and (3) for parent groups, who will use a definition for advocacy in resource allocation within the legislation. Each particular group (researchers attempting to identify causes, educators allocating resources, employers providing support, parents seeking support or dyslexic individuals who want a label that confirms they are not stupid) will have a reason for their interest in dyslexia and their requirements of a definition. Such a diversity of influences has led to a diversity of definitions within the English-language literature.

Tönnessen (1995) categorized definitions of dyslexia and specific learning difficulties into three principal types: symptom-based, causal-based and prognosis-based. The symptom-based definition has been the most frequently used. In these cases, dyslexia has been identified by characteristics that could be seen as defining properties. According to Tönnessen, these characteristics need to have been shown to be observable and measurable. However, many definitions have been hindered by a list of characteristics that were poorly defined and difficult to measure. Additionally, no single characteristic has been found to be common to all dyslexics, meaning that lists have been presented as potential rather than necessary symptoms.

The causal definition, on the other hand, avoids the problem of producing lists of potential characteristics by requiring a necessary causal factor to be identified. However, an understanding of the underlying cause of dyslexia is required. The difference here is that a characteristic that is not a cause may be included in the symptom viewpoint, but would not be included in a causal theory. At present, causal viewpoints have been mainly restricted to research-based theories and require further empirical evidence for their acceptance (see the section, Hypotheses of specific learning difficulties on p. 8). Such causal viewpoints may be better seen as working hypotheses that are open to scrutiny and disproof.

Tönnessen (1995) referred to a final category as the prognosis-based definition. In these cases, dyslexia would need to be defined, at least in part, on the basis of successful treatment. Tönnessen suggested that the persistence of difficulties/characteristics could be included in both symptom-based and prognosis-based definitions. However, the prognosis approach was rarely used in the literature, probably because the rationale for assessment has been to provide the appropriate treatment, rather than the treatment determining the appropriateness of assessment.

The Health Council of the Netherlands produced a series of criteria to determine the acceptability of a definition of dyslexia (Gersons-Wolfensberger and Ruijssenaars, 1997). The criteria used were:

(a) It should be descriptive with no explanatory elements.
(b) It should be specific enough to identify dyslexia within the whole of reading and spelling problems.
(c) It should be general enough to allow for various scientific explanatory models and any developments those models might undergo.

(d) It should be operationalizable for the purposes of research into people and groups.
(e) It should be directive for statements concerning the need for intervention.
(f) It should be applicable to the various groups involved.

With these criteria in mind, the committee produced the following 'working definition':

> Dyslexia is present when the automatization of word identification (reading) and/or spelling does not develop or does so very incompletely or with great difficulty.

This definition was free from any constraints of the language or script involved, acknowledging that as some children may do very well at these skills, others will do poorly. Thus, in principle, it could be adopted for all countries and cultures. The Council acknowledges that the elimination of exclusionary factors has widened the catchment area and therefore increased the numbers of people who may be defined as dyslexic. However, having freed itself from including a causal element in the definition, it is difficult to see how it could be used to differentiate the dyslexic individual from those with global learning difficulties. As such, this definition could be argued to have failed to be *specific enough to identify dyslexia within the whole of reading and spelling problems* (criterion (b)).

The Health Council of the Netherlands definition became the basis for that proposed by the Working Party of the Division of Educational and Child Psychology of the British Psychological Society (British Psychological Society, 1999) who presented the view that 'Dyslexia is evident when accurate and fluent word reading and/or spelling develops very incompletely or with great difficulty.'

The British Psychological Society Working Party definition avoids causal viewpoints and exclusionary criteria and, therefore, could be argued to be non-specific, as in the case of the Health Council of the Netherlands' definition. Both these definitions were derived with educational practitioners in mind, hence they focused on the most obvious education-related behavioural outcome of dyslexia, i.e., literacy acquisition problems. Given that dyslexia has often been equated with reading/writing deficits, and that this would be the feature that most individuals working with dyslexics would be aware of, these definitions may appear to have fulfilled their purpose. However, if additional features of dyslexia led to large variations in these same behavioural outcomes (i.e., reading/writing performance), then they may be seen as having failed. An example of this problem was the potential for the behavioural outcome criteria to mask the abilities of the gifted dyslexic. Such a gifted dyslexic individual may have overcome their immediate dyslexia difficulties (i.e., literacy problems) by the use of alternative strategies that have been explicitly taught (e.g., an intensive phonics programme), or through alternative strategies that might invoke other intellectual domains. Problems would be encountered when assessing a child who was found to be working at reading and spelling levels commensurate with their peer group and, therefore, would be considered as having achieved age-appropriate automatization, but who would be doing even better if the teaching methods were more closely matched to their specific cognitive profile. Similar difficulties would arise when assessing an adult dyslexic who overcomes their childhood literacy learning difficulties by a combination of hard work and compensatory strategies. A strict interpretation of the above definitions might conclude that these individuals are now no longer dyslexic.

Tönnessen (1995) also raised the question of whether a child may be referred to as dyslexic if they have not yet started reading. Under the Health Council of the Netherlands and the British Psychological Society Working Party definitions, if reading and/or writing difficulties cannot be demonstrated, then the child should not be considered dyslexic. However, if the child shows signs that research has identified as significant correlates of the later development of dyslexia, it would seem reasonable to say that the child was 'at risk of dyslexia'. That is, if the child were to be taught following the usual curriculum and methods, there would be a (measurable) probability that the child would develop reading and writing difficulties. Under such circumstances, it would be indefensible to delay support until failure has been evidenced.

An alternative to the behavioural outcome approach has been to provide additional features in the dyslexia definition. An example of this approach was that used by the British Dyslexia Association definition (Peer, 2001):

> Dyslexia is best described as a combination of abilities and difficulties which affect the learning process in one or more of reading, spelling, writing and sometimes numeracy/language. Accompanying weaknesses may be identified in areas of speed of processing, short-term memory, sequencing, auditory and/or visual perception, spoken language and motor skills.

One of the aims of such a definition was to use more accessible language demanded by parents and teachers. The use of the term 'abilities' also allowed the distinction to be made between those with specific deficits and those with more general difficulties. However, this definition failed to differentiate difficulties at the behavioural level from the underlying processing deficits. The use of the term 'accompanying' avoided the issue of stating whether the weaknesses were causes of the reading and writing difficulties or additional symptoms. Such a definition, therefore, would have been more likely to be classed as a symptom-based definition. However, as indicated above, in the absence of a clear idea of what constitutes dyslexia, a consistent list of core symptoms has yet to be developed. For example, contrast this UK-based viewpoint with that proposed by the International Dyslexia Association (quoted in Masland, 1997) which states that dyslexia is: 'characterized by difficulties in single word decoding, usually reflecting insufficient phonological processing abilities'. This definition can be seen to share features with that of the British Dyslexia Association; however, fundamental differences can also be seen. Although the British Dyslexia Association definition suggested a list of accompanying features, the International Dyslexia Association focused on a core, potentially, causal factor underlying the dyslexic's difficulties in reading and writing. This phonological deficit has become a dominant hypothesis in the field, although its generality across all language contexts can be questioned (see the section, Hypotheses of specific learning difficulties on p. 8).

A slightly different alternative has been the criteria-led definition. This has been used in research and where practitioners have needed to identify the level of difficulties for the allocation of resources. One of the most often quoted criteria-led symptom definitions, and one used in many countries, has been the ICD-10 'Diagnostic Criteria for the Diagnosis of Specific Reading Disorder' (Diagnostic Criteria for Research) (World Health Organisation, 1993):

> A score on reading accuracy and/or comprehension that is at least 2 standard errors of prediction below the level expected on the basis of the child's chronological age and general intelligence, with both reading skills and IQ assessed in an individually administered test standardized for the child's culture and educational system.

The criterion in this case was two standard errors and was used to provide a cut-off point for identification purposes. This had the advantage of specifying the level of difficulty quantitatively and, hence, avoid criticisms about the lack of specificity of terms such as 'very incompletely' and 'great difficulty'. Definitions such as those of the ICD-10 were seen as leading to more objective criteria. However, as argued by Snowling (2000), statistically 2.28 per cent of any given population would be two standard deviations or more below the mean in a normal distribution. This will occur whether we want to call these individuals dyslexic or not. Indeed, it will occur with any normally distributed population of scores, be they a population of scores on a reading test, footballing skills or the height of crops in a field. The results from dyslexia-related studies that use discrepancy criteria seem to reflect this figure derived from statistical theory. Rodgers (1983) reported a figure remarkably close to the statistical theoretical figure (2.29 per cent) using reading measures purported to be an improvement over those used by Yule *et al.* (1974); although see Miles and Haslum (1986). Similarly, Shaywitz *et al.* (1992) used a criterion of 1.5 standard deviations from the norm and reported figures of 5.6 per cent in the first grade, 7 per cent in the third grade and 5.4 per cent in the fifth grade, which were approximately those predicted on the basis of a normal distribution. The obvious problem with these methods was the determination of the appropriate cut-off. Given that 'such cut-offs may have no biological validity' (Shaywitz *et al.*, 1992, p. 150), should we have more confidence in the ICD-10 criteria than in that used by Shaywitz *et al.* (1992)? A rationale for the use of one cut-off point over another needs to be provided, rather than trusting to the vagaries of tradition. An argument presented in Ellis (1984) associated these criteria-based definitions to those used in certain areas of medicine, such as when determining a cut-off point to diagnose obesity. Here the cut-off is determined by the potential for over-weight leading to health problems (heart problems, diabetes, cancer, etc.). Use of this perspective in the dyslexia field would seem to lead to the determination of literacy problems leading to educational/employment problems. If a 1.5 standard deviation criterion did not lead to major educational/employment problems, but the 2 standard deviation criteria did, then the use of the ICD-10 criteria is justified. An additional difficulty for this justification is that it may vary across languages and cultures. A 1.5 SD criterion may indicate major problems and a restriction of opportunity in one language but not in another.

A second issue related to the ICD-10 criteria that has been deliberated was the use of a discrepancy between actual literacy attainment and IQ-based predictions of expected literacy attainment. Although many methods of identification have used some form of discrepancy criteria, even if comprised of a difference (discrepancy) between the individual and other members of the particular population, most discussions of discrepancy models for reading and writing difficulties have been based on the discrepancy between reading and intelligence. Tönnessen (1995) concluded that a discrepancy can be informative when suggestive of a specific difficulty, but that absence of a discrepancy should not be used to preclude the possibility of a difficulty. He also presented the view that, as well as there being a necessity to determine the nature of intelligence, the discrepancy model would only make sense if there was a strong correlation between IQ and reading. However, Stanovich (2000) noted that the correlation found between IQ and reading varies from study to study, depending upon the measures used.

Further difficulties with the discrepancy model were noted by Lyon *et al.* (2001). First, they pointed out that criteria such as those proposed by the ICD-10 contained an implicit assumption of failure. Educationalists have to wait until a discrepancy has been established before they can say that the difficulty exists. Second, IQ measures have been shown to be somewhat unreliable under the age of nine, which suggested that reliable assessments would have to be delayed until further failure has been experienced.

A final difficulty with the IQ-based discrepancy position was the lack of evidence for differences between groups of high IQ and low IQ children with reading deficits in all except the measures on which the IQ score was derived (see Ellis *et al.*, 1996; Share, 1996; Siegel, 1988). Such findings have questioned the logic of definitions that have separated these subgroups. Such a viewpoint has led to the development of definitions, such as those of the Health Council of the Netherlands and the British Psychological Society that avoid the distinction between children with specific reading problems and those with more general learning difficulties. If this approach is taken, then dyslexics would comprise both children with specific difficulties in literacy and those with more general problems in learning. If the IQ-based discrepancy position is taken, then those children with more general learning difficulties will not be included among the dyslexics. Variations between practitioners, and countries, will inevitably occur with such differing positions.

However, variations between countries in the use of the term dyslexia need not be confined to the inclusion/exclusion of those with general learning difficulties. Similarly, differences are not confined to dyslexia, but may also occur with other terms used within the specific learning difficulties field. A comparison of terminology usage across Europe provides a glimpse of the potential problem. In the UK, the term dyslexia has been used for both reading and writing difficulties (see British Psychological Society definition above). In Russia, however, the term dyslexia has referred to reading difficulties only, while dysgraphia has been used to mean writing difficulties, including spelling and handwriting skills (Inshakova and Boldyreva, 1997). This can be contrasted with Italy where dysgraphia has been used for motor skill deficits, whilst dysorthographia has referred to spelling difficulties (Biancardi and Milano, 1999). In Poland, the term dysautographia has been used to describe the difficulty in the acquisition of the automated kinaesmotor skills derived from practice that allow handwriting to develop in a consistent and legible fashion (Bogdanowicz, 1999). Each of these terms may be used by practitioners in different countries to describe slightly different though related populations of children and adults with learning difficulties. Under such circumstances, terms such as dyslexia may be seen as useful when discussing issues with parents of individuals undergoing assessment, or with those individuals themselves, or when considering issues of policy, but their usefulness may be limited for research, and potentially for assessment procedures, particularly when cross-linguistic comparisons are considered.

HYPOTHESES OF SPECIFIC LEARNING DIFFICULTIES

An understanding of the cause(s) of dyslexia would obviously greatly improve the degree of consistency in viewpoints across individuals, organizations and nations. As indicated in the previous section, however, there have been numerous hypothesized causes of dyslexia. The principal hypothesis, derived mainly from research on reading and writing English, has been the phonological deficit hypothesis (see Stanovich, 1988). The sheer volume of research carried out in English has led to views of the reading process and, in particular, difficulties in acquiring literacy skills, being based on the English orthography. Furthermore, literacy acquisition research in non-English languages has been reported which has suggested that this viewpoint can be generalized to other languages (see Goswami, 2000). However, the phonological deficit perspective does not account for all of the literacy-related difficulties experienced by children, particularly when considered across different languages. An isolated phonological perspective may not provide a model that will work with the diverse nature of scripts found around the world, where the relationship between sound and graphical representation is completely different to that of English, such as found in Chinese. Similarly, phonologically based remediation programmes may be inappropriate for some children who come from a language background where the specific difficulties do not respond to that approach. Additionally, as will be seen from the various chapters in Part 1 of this book, the exact nature of what should be included within the term phonological, and the importance of those different sound-based elements, vary not only with age but also across languages. For these reasons, other areas (or causal viewpoints) have been proposed in the literature. These have included: basic perceptual and memory processes, both auditory (linguistic and non-linguistic) and visual; processes involved in the access of the semantic lexicon or morphemic units; speed of processing; sequencing/timing deficits; and factors related to working memory processes and attention or executive control. In addition, there have been views that have argued for a single underlying cause (e.g., the phonological deficit hypothesis: Stanovich, 1988) and those which have considered that there are several underlying causes that lead to distinct sub-types of dyslexia (e.g., dysphonetic and dyseidetic: Boder, 1973). Such divergent opinions about what constitutes dyslexia were one of the reasons why definitions such as those proposed by the Health Council of the Netherlands and the British Psychological Society avoided causal explanations. Given that these hypothesized causes may vary with language usage, the following provides a brief overview.

It was proposed above that the dominant single cause viewpoint was the phonological deficit hypothesis. This perspective has been derived from the substantial evidence that phonological skills form an integral part of the acquisition of word level literacy (Bryant and Bradley, 1985; Rack et al., 1994; Snowling, 2000; Stanovich, 1988). Difficulties in phonology have been a major distinguishing factor between dyslexics and non-dyslexics matched for age and reading level (Rack et al., 1992; Snowling, 1981), and these difficulties have been associated with dyslexia throughout development and into adulthood (Beaton et al., 1997; Bruck, 1993; Elbro et al., 1994). Relationships between phonological processing and literacy have been identified in languages other than English (see, for example, Alegria et al., 1982; Bentin et al., 1991; Lundberg et al., 1988; Torneus, 1984). Although there are fewer studies in non-alphabetic scripts, such as those used in Japanese and Chinese, there is evidence that phonological manipulation skills are related to the acquisition of literacy skills in these languages. Ho and Bryant (1997) found rhyming skills in young Chinese children predicted later literacy skills, and whereas Mann (1986) found that Japanese first-grade children were worse than first-grade American children in terms of phoneme deletion, many Japanese children were aware of phonemes by the fourth grade. Support for the cross-language generalization of the phonological perspective has come from studies which indicate that early phonological training (together with suitable linkage to early orthography and literacy experience) improves word literacy (see Bryant and Bradley, 1985; Cunningham, 1990; Elbro et al., 1996; Olofsson and Lundberg, 1985; Schneider et al., 1997).

However, despite the wealth of data supporting the phonological deficit hypothesis, it is not without its difficulties. First, there is a lack of clarity regarding what exactly should be included in a phonological-based theory. For example, there is disagreement as to the key features of phonology that are essential to early word reading: see discussions in Goswami and Bryant (1990), Muter et al. (1998), Bryant (1998) and Hulme et al. (1998) on whether English-speaking children progress through different levels of phonological skills, including an onset-rime level or syllable division, or whether they are able to work at a phoneme level immediately upon starting the process of learning to read. Also, the ability to decode written symbols into sounds, the ability to store and/or manipulate phonological forms and the ability to retrieve/produce verbal labels have all been associated with phonological processing. Yet these processes may add independent variance to literacy (see Wagner and Torgesen, 1987) questioning their inclusion within a unitary causal framework. Indeed, some of these 'phonological' processes have been incorporated in alternative causal positions. For example, differences in the speed of access of verbal labels have been used as evidence of speed of processing deficits among reading disabled children (see below). Similarly, explanations that propose deficits in short-term memory or working memory cite evidence that short-term recall of phonological information is a characteristic of dyslexia (see discussions in Hulme and Mackenzie, 1992; Mann and Liberman, 1984; Thomson, 1990).

Various studies, across different languages (see Gathercole and Baddeley, 1993; Wimmer et al., 1998), have suggested that children who experience difficulties with retaining sounds in short-term memory are likely to have problems with the acquisition of verbal vocabulary and development of stable graphic-sound associations. Such processes may be important in reading and listening comprehension, as well as in language acquisition (Daneman, 1991; Daneman and Carpenter, 1980; Gathercole et al., 1992). Catts (1989) showed that dyslexics have greater difficulty than non-dyslexics in the areas of short-term recall of letters, words, digits and sentences. Even tapping a rhythm by hand has been found to be a problem for dyslexic children (Wolff et al., 1990). However, it has been argued (Hulme and Roodenrys, 1995) that the direction of causality between short-term memory deficits and reading problems has not been demonstrated, i.e., reading problems may lead to poor short-term memory performance. Also explanations in terms of general short-term or working memory deficits have not been able to account for the equivalent performance of dyslexics and non-dyslexics on measures of short-term recall that do not require the processing of verbal (or auditory) information, nor can they account for the fact that not all poor readers/spellers show poor performance on measures of auditory (digit) span (see Everatt et al., 1999; Gathercole and Pickering, 2001). The alternative position has been to argue that phonological short-term memory is specifically impaired in dyslexics and that this leads to deficits in processing new language information, such as learning new letter strings or a new vocabulary (Gathercole and Baddeley, 1989; Gathercole et al., 1991). Such a phonological short-term memory position has been almost indistinguishable from the general phonological deficit viewpoint and, hence, has been subsumed under this perspective. However, this still presents the problem that phonological short-term memory and other measures of phonological processing (e.g., awareness of rime or phoneme units) have been found to be separable in terms of their explanation of variability in literacy ability.

Other theories that have been categorized within the general phonological deficit perspective have focused on auditory (perceptual-based) processes (e.g., Tallal, 1980; Tallal and Katz, 1989; Tallal et al., 1997). The work of Tallal is based on the idea that individuals with language-related literacy deficits have a problem processing rapidly changing auditory information – we will return to this view below. Consistent with the auditory deficit perspectives, there has been evidence that the ability to categorize speech sounds is more difficult for the dyslexic individual than the average reader (Serniclaes et al., 2001; Sutter et al., 2000). Sutter et al. (2000) argue that the dyslexic individual has greater difficulty constructing an auditory 'scene' than their non-dyslexic counterpart. Similarly, a number of researchers (Helenius *et al.*, 1999; Lorenzi *et al.*, 2000) have confirmed the role of auditory temporal processing in speech processing and argued that differences in such processes may be detectable at birth (Leppänen *et al.*, 1999). McCrory *et al.* (2000) found that dyslexics showed deficits specific to auditory repetition. However, there are inconsistencies in the auditory deficit perspective as a single cause interpretation. For example, a study by Cestnick and Jerger (2000) suggested that poor irregular word readers had difficulty recalling tones in a sequence only when they were presented rapidly, whereas poor non-word readers had difficulty across tone tasks, irrespective of speed of presentation or mode of recall. They propose that irregular word reading is associated with auditory sequencing, while non-word reading performance is associated with general auditory performance. Dissociations between verbal and non-verbal processing (i.e., sound-based processing which is language or non-language based) have been demonstrated by a number of researchers (Adlard and Hazan, 1998; McAnally and Stein, 1996), contrary to the view that all types of auditory presented information should show deficits. Furthermore, Heath *et al.* (1999) have argued that such auditory processing deficits cannot be the unitary cause of phonological and language deficits in disabled readers. Although auditory problems may lead to language and, hence, phonological deficits, the latter may occur independently of hearing difficulties. For example, the inability to translate a letter into a corresponding sound can occur without auditory processing deficits (see discussion in Snowling, 2000). Therefore, as with phonological awareness and phonological short-term memory, decoding skills and auditory processing may need to be considered separately.

Another difficulty for the phonological deficit perspective has been the reported cases of individuals who have experienced difficulties with reading, writing and spelling, without an accompanying phonological deficit. This has been found in relatively isolated cases in English (see Goulandris and Snowling, 1991; Howard and Best, 1997). However, such cases may be more frequent in other languages. Given that the phonological deficit viewpoint was derived from the perspective of dyslexia as a language-related disability, it could be argued that differences across languages would be expected. Similarly, such language-based differences need not be an indication of a different underlying cause. The same cause may be responsible for dyslexia, but the behavioural manifestation of dyslexia may, like literacy in general, vary across languages (see discussions in Goswami, 2000). However, without a precise indication of the effect of phonological units on literacy and how these are predicted to vary across language contexts, such variations cast doubt on the universality of the phonological deficit hypothesis. For example, evidence has been inconclusive about which features of phonology are essential to early word reading (compare Chapters 6, 10 and 18 on English, Greek and Spanish). Research in English has argued for the importance rhyme (or rime) sound units (Goswami and Bryant, 1990) in predicting the acquisition of literacy. However, in Portuguese, rhyming skills were not strongly related to literacy development in the work reported by Cardoso-Martins (1995). If rime processing were the unit of phonology that determined the incidence or level of dyslexia, then differences between English and Portuguese may be inevitable. Our own work has indicated that measures requiring the ability to identify the initial onset (alliteration tasks) or the final rime (rhyme tasks) within a word could distinguish groups of Grade 3 children with and without literacy deficits in English, but less reliably in Hungarian and not at all in Chinese. (See also Caravolas, 1993.)

Specification of the units of phonological processing responsible for dyslexia, and how these may lead to differing incidence/level, may prove vital for the identification of dyslexia across different countries, as well as for the development of effective literacy programmes in different languages. For example, English assessment tools (e.g., the Dyslexia Screening Test, Fawcett and Nicolson, 1996; the Phonological Assessment Battery, Frederickson *et al.*, 1997) that have incorporated measures of phonological processing that require children (and adults) to process information at the level of the rhyme may not be appropriate for an equivalent assessment in another language (such as Portuguese). Similarly, these language differences may impact on remediation strategies. If rime identification is shown to be important in one language (English), but not another (Chinese), or is shown to be important at one stage of development in one language and at another stage of development in another language, then remediation programmes should reflect these differences. An even stronger argument can be made for cross-language variations in remediation if it is assumed that the regularity of a language tempers the effect of a phonological deficit (see Spencer, 2000). If this is the case, and dyslexia is defined as caused by a phonological deficit, then dyslexics in a regular language should, on average, have more severe phonological deficits than their counterparts in a less regular language. Given that those with severe phonological deficits are typically those who show few gains from a phonologically mediated remediation programme (see Torgesen and Davis, 1996), then effective remediation may, in part, be determined by the language of instruction. Phonological remediation may be successful with some English dyslexics but not at all with individuals identified as dyslexic in a regular language. This argument does not indicate that phonological processing should not be taught in a regular language (the evidence above for its effectiveness in different languages contradicts this extreme perspective); however, it does highlight the need to consider the effectiveness of particular remediation programmes for different language contexts when specific definitions of cause are embraced.

A final area that requires clarification has been the evidence that some, if not all, dyslexics show deficits in areas that seem unrelated to phonological processing (see Nicolson and Fawcett, 1995). If phonological processing deficits have not accounted for all dyslexia-related learning difficulties across languages, alternative causal accounts may prove important for identification and remediation. Alternative single cause theories, however, suffer similar problems to those outlined above. Historically, the main alternative to the language-based, or phonological, theories have been the visual processing deficits theories (see Everatt, 1999). These have taken many forms, but the main single cause theories have argued for dyslexics having: (1) a dysfunctioning transient or magnocellular pathway that leads to blurred vision due to inappropriate interactions with a normally functioning sustained or parvocellular visual system (see Breitmeyer, 1993; Lovegrove, 1996); (2) poor eye movement control that leads to the eyes being inappropriately positioned during reading and, hence, numerous corrective eye movements or confused ordering when processing text (Pavlidis, 1981); or (3) interchangeable eye dominance that, due to the slight difference in positioning of the eyes when processing text, leads to blurred vision as the brain switches between dominant images (Stein, 1993; Stein *et al.*, 1989). Other visual-related theories have been either incorporated within multi-causal positions (see below) or were proposed as explanations of more than dyslexia – the view that reading problems derive from sensitivity to certain wavelengths of light (Irlen, 1991; Wilkins *et al.*, 1994) falls into this latter category and, therefore, lacks specification. Although none of the visual-based perspectives have been totally rejected, they suffer two main problems in their account of dyslexia (see reviews by Hogben, 1997; Everatt, 2002). First, they have failed to account for the finding that some individuals with dyslexia do not show deficits in non-literacy tasks that require the use of those processes associated with the theoretical cause. Some dyslexics with measurable literacy problems do not show transient/magno-cellular processing deficits (Everatt *et al.*, 1999), others do not show highly abnormal eye movements during reading (Rayner and Pollatsek, 1989) and still others do not show variations in eye dominance (Bishop, 1989; Goulandris *et al.*, 1998). Second, similar research has indicated that some normal readers show the same visual deficits as dyslexics yet present little evidence of literacy acquisition problems. As with the phonological deficit hypothesis, the visual deficit viewpoints have, so far, failed to account for all dyslexia-related difficulties (see also Skottun and Parke, 1999).

However, visual processes may help explain variability in literacy skills, particularly if a cross-language perspective is considered. For example, Ho (1994) found that visual dis-crimination skills (especially constancy of shape) and visual memory skills at three years old were, along with phonological awareness, significant predictors of reading Chinese at four and five years old. Similarly, McBride-Chang and Ho (2000) have suggested that speed and phonological awareness are important predictors of Chinese character recogni-tion, and that slow naming speeds are associated with poor visual attention as well as letter knowledge. Gupta and Garg (1996) found that dyslexic Hindi/English bilinguals produced poorer visual discrimination scores than non-dyslexic bilingual controls and a similar result was found by Everatt *et al.* (2000) with Sylheti/English bilinguals. Again, both groups of bilinguals also presented evidence of differences between good and poor readers in measures of phonological processing. Such evidence may, therefore, be consistent with combinations of visual and phonological deficits.

A single-causal perspective that has combined both visual and auditory system deficits has been proposed by proponents of the view that dyslexia is produced by a temporal processing deficit (see Stein, 2001). The origins of this perspective can be found in the work of Tallal and colleagues (see Tallal, 1980; 1984) on children with speech and language difficulties. In this work, children with speech and language difficulties failed to discriminate phonological forms that were separated by short millisecond gaps or which could only be distinguished by the initial few milliseconds after their onset. These findings locate problems in the area of processing rapidly changing temporal informa-tion. Although these findings have been difficult to replicate, particularly with children with specific reading difficulties (see Marshall *et al.*, 2001; Mody *et al.*, 1997), they are consistent with findings for deficits in the processing of rapidly changing visual informa-tion that have been used to argue for a transient or magnocellular deficit (e.g., Lovegrove, 1996). These commonalities have led theorists such as Stein (2001) to combine visual and auditory temporal processing deficits within the same theoretical framework. Such a deficit might lead to visual and/or auditory deficits and, thereby, explain the variations in difficulties evident in the visual and phonological literature described above. This framework may also combine with perspectives that have proposed timing and/or auto-maticity deficits related to the activity of the cerebellum (Fawcett and Nicolson, 2001) and, hence, explain the range of deficits found in the performance of English dyslexic chil-dren by Nicolson and Fawcett (1995). However, although grand theories such as those proposed by Stein (2001) have been valuable in terms of bringing together different find-ings, they often suffer from a lack of specification as to how the hypothesized cause leads to the identified behavioural difficulties. In this case, the question remains as to how the temporal deficit (or timing deficit) leads to literacy problems. Similarly, weaknesses in each element of the theory need to be resolved and the potential interactions between visual, auditory and motor factors need to be specified together with the consequences of these interactions.

Another theoretical position that may be related to the temporal processing theory stems from the differences between dyslexics and non-dyslexics in terms of the speeded retrieval of verbal labels. Such rapid naming deficits have been found in a multitude of conditions: with colours, line drawings/pictures of familiar objects, digits, letters, words and non-words (see Ben-Dror *et al.*, 1991; Bowers and Wolf, 1993; Denckla and Rudel, 1976; Spring and Capps, 1974; Wolf and Bowers, 2000; Wolf and O'Brien, 2001). Longitudinal studies have shown that, not only are such measures predictive of later reading perform-ance (Wagner *et al.*, 1994), but that naming deficits persist into adulthood (Felton *et al.*, 1990). Scarborough (1998) noted that while the literacy scores in Grade 2 were the best predictor of future reading and spelling outcomes, for those with reading disabilities, pre-diction of literacy skills was improved by the inclusion of rapid naming. Similarly, Meyer *et al.* (1998) found that rapid naming scores were predictive of literacy in a poor reading group, though not in an average reading group. Badian (1993) noted that naming speed for letters and pictured objects were the strongest differentiators, along with phonemic awareness and visual symbol processing, of adequate and poor readers. This research also indicated that letter naming speed was the best predictor of word recognition, whereas object naming speed was the best predictor of reading comprehension. Wimmer (1993) found that among German-speaking children, rapid naming of numbers was the largest predictor of variance in speed of reading text, reading high frequency words, and reading pseudowords. Relatively slow rapid naming speeds were characteristic of German dyslexic children, even though they generally do well on reading accuracy. Research in other alpha-betic transparent scripts shows similar results (Korhonen, 1995).

However, while Wolf (1997) clearly argues for speed of processing to be considered a dissociable process, others see it subsumed under phonological causes (Wagner and Torgesen, 1987). For example, naming deficits can be found in the number of errors produced by dyslexic individuals, particularly when objects with low frequency names are used (Swan and Goswami, 1997). These findings suggest that poor naming performance may not be due to a speed of processing deficit but to poor representations of the verbal labels. This interpretation is more consistent with a phonological deficit perspective (see Swan and Goswami, 1997). In order to explain problems specifically associated with phonological processing, while retaining the idea of a speed of processing deficit, Wolf and colleagues (Bowers and Wolf, 1993; Wolf and Bowers, 2000; Wolf and O'Brien, 2001) have proposed that there are distinct sub-types of dyslexia that are based on the occur-rence of phonological and/or speed of processing deficits. Hence, some poor readers are considered to have phonological processing deficits with no speed of processing problems, while others show the reverse symptomatology, and a third group shows problems in both areas. The latter double-deficit group is considered to show the most problems in literacy skills development. Consistent with this perspective, Cronin and Carver (1998) found that phonological and rapid naming tasks both predicted unique variance in reading attainment among first graders, suggesting that these measures should be considered as separate factors in the initial stages of reading development. Similarly, DeJong and van der Leij (1999) found that Dutch children, from kindergarten to second grade, showed independ-ent influences of rapid naming of objects and phonological awareness on reading achieve-ment. Finally, intervention programmes that train fluency in word identification strategies have been found to improve the exception word reading skills of reading disabled children, particularly those with specific naming deficits (Lovett et al., 1994; 2000; see also Wolf et al., 2000). Although it still needs to be shown that these interventions specifically targeted speed of processing, and that it was the improvements in this area that led to the identified literacy gains, such findings point to potential advantages for strategies that may improve rapid accessing processes.

However, despite recent interest in this view, the double-deficit hypothesis of phonological and speed deficits is not the only sub-type theory. Numerous other theories have postulated the existence of distinct sub-types in an attempt to understand the diverse symptomology found among dyslexics (for example, Bakker, 1979; Boder, 1973; Fletcher et al., 1997; Mattis, 1981; Satz and Morris, 1981; Seymour and MacGregor, 1984; Watson et al., 1983). Although views differ as to the number and characteristics of these sub-types, the majority of these alternatives have focused on the distinction between language-related and visual-related sub-types rather than phonological versus speed of processing. One of the rationales for this language/visual distinction has been the analogy with acquired dyslexia. This analogy has led to one of the most influential of sub-type perspectives being the distinction between surface and phonological sub-types. In terms of children with literacy acquisition problems, this surface/phonological classification has been most clearly demonstrated in the procedures of Castles and Coltheart (1993), which are often considered within the framework of the dual route model (see Ellis, 1984). The basic form of the dual route model has proposed reading to involve both sublexical and lexical procedures. The sublexical procedure decodes novel letter strings via grapheme/phoneme correspondence rules that exist in alphabetic writing systems. A dysfunction within this route results in phonological dyslexia. In this sub-type of dyslexia, individuals experience difficulties decoding unfamiliar words such as in non-word reading tasks ('pib', 'splab', 'norch'). In contrast, the lexical procedure treats written words as whole units. Visual or orthographic representations of words are used to access the pronunciation stored in the mental lexicon. A break within the lexical procedure results in surface dyslexia. In this sub-type of dyslexia, individuals have to rely on sublexical procedures to recover the pronunciation of a word. The large number of phonetically irregular words within the English language leads to pronunciation errors when relying on the sublexical route. For example, attempts to decode the irregular words 'pint', 'have' and 'yacht' via grapheme–phoneme correspondence rules would result in pronunciations that rhyme with 'mint', 'save' and 'patch'. It is hypothesized that such irregular words can only be read correctly by the lexical route.

Again, the phonological deficit hypothesis has provided an alternative explanation for this sub-typing proposal. Phonological dyslexics are consistent with the phonological deficits proposed by Stanovich (1988), and surface dyslexia has been argued as a milder form of phonological deficit together with exceptionally inadequate reading experience. As evidence for this alternative, Stanovich et al. (1997) compared phonological and surface dyslexic sub-types with reading age controls who were similar to the dyslexics in terms of reading experience. Castles and Coltheart's (1993) procedures used chronological age-matched non-dyslexics who may have had more reading experience than the dyslexics. Although Stanovich et al. (1997) found that the number of dyslexics presenting evidence of phonological difficulties remained consistent with those identified by Castles and Coltheart (1993), the incidence of surface dyslexia was virtually eliminated by the reading age comparative procedure. Based on these findings, phonological dyslexia has been called a developmental deviancy, while surface dyslexia has been referred to as a developmental delay or lag (see also Snowling and Nation, 1997). The hypothesis that phonological and surface dyslexia follow differential developmental sequences is corroborated by Manis *et al.* (1996). Again, phonological dyslexia is seen to represent a severe and specific phonological processing deficit. However, on this view, the surface dyslexic profile is believed to result from a global delay in word recognition together with impaired orthographic and phonological knowledge (see also Zabell and Everatt, 2002).

One of the earliest researchers to propose a sub-typing system involving similar processes to those outlined above was Boder (1973) who argued for two sub-types termed dysphonetic and dyseidetic. These sub-types reflect the possible failures of the two routes in a dual route model of reading. Again differences between these sub-types were hypothesized to be due to the systems that are disabled in the children with literacy difficulties. If the child is not able to use phonetic transcription (that is, a phoneme–grapheme correspondence system is incompletely developed), they would be classified as dysphonetic. If the child has problems with irregular words, such as 'yacht', then their orthographic lexicon is incomplete, and they are said to be dyseidetic. An alternative approach along similar lines to that of Boder (1973) was proposed by Bakker (1979). This sub-typing theory divided dyslexics into 'Linguistic' (L) and 'Perceptual' (P) sub-types, reflecting a distinction between a language and a visual deficit. Although it is not as widely accepted as Boder's system (Licht and Spyer, 1994), research has suggested that an analysis of reading errors may allow certain individuals to be classified in accordance with this theory, and that differential hemisphere stimulation may be used for remediation (Robertson, 1996). Such remediation processes are more consistent with the model underlying the Bakker system.

However, each of the above dichotomous sub-typing explanations requires the inclusion of a third, typically unclassified, group of individuals with literacy problems. For example, some 15 per cent of the dyslexic cohort tested remained unclassified following the procedures used by Castles and Coltheart (1993). Such additional sub-types often present evidence of a mixed profile and can make up a significant proportion of dyslexics. In the procedures used by Boder, 67 per cent of dyslexics could be categorized as dysphonetic and 10 per cent as dyseidetic; however, there was also a mixed group that represented 23 per cent of the cohort. The views of Bakker (see discussions in Licht and Spyer, 1994) also require the inclusion of a third sub-type that presents characteristics of both L and P sub-types. Alternative sub-typing procedures have been proposed to try to classify these 'unclassified' sub-types. Such alternatives have focused on statistical methods, such as cluster analysis (see, for example: Fletcher and Satz, 1985; Satz and Morris, 1981; Watson *et al.*, 1983), to try to separate sub-types of poor readers. However, these procedures have led to highly varying numbers of sub-types and very different classification systems. Additionally, the neuropsychological basis for such sub-types can be questioned, given that a clear distinction between sub-types has not been identified. The transition between good and bad performance in any sub-skill appears along a continuum, rather than as a simple dichotomy. Where one determines the cut-off may determine the incidence of different sub-types. Indeed, the very term dyslexia, as applied to a sub-type of readers, has been referred to as misguided and without a basis in cognitive theory (Stanovich and Siegel, 1994). Tönnessen (1995) suggested that much of the confusion over the existence of sub-types is a direct reflection of the lack of a clear and concise definition of dyslexia.

A good example of the problems encountered by sub-typing work, but which also shows the diversity of potential areas of dysfunction that can be related to literacy difficulties, is the work by Fletcher *et al.* (1997). They used statistical cluster techniques to identify seven sub-types of readers. These included two sub-types that were non-reading disabled and five reading disabled groupings. Such cluster analysis techniques can divide average readers into sub-types, even if this is not the main purpose of the procedure. Each individual in the data set was tested using a range of cognitive tasks that measured phonology, rapid naming, verbal short-term memory, visual tasks, speech production and visual attention. Each reading disabled individual was assigned to a sub-type that was a combination of specific deficits in these tasks. However, this classification procedure still required visual evaluation of sub-type profiles (Fletcher *et al.*, 1997). That is, human qualitative judgement was used to supplement statistical calculations. Again, where a cut-off is made is highly subjective. Although this research suffers from similar problems to that outlined above, it shows that a range of cognitive areas may need to be assessed to distinguish different groups of individuals with literacy problems and indicates that cognitive functions beyond phonology may usefully be included in assessment procedures. Despite the problems encountered, such differentiation of children by cognitive ability and style may be important as they have been related to beneficial remediation procedures (Brooks and Weeks, 1999; Lyon, 1985; Weeks *et al.*, 2002).

LITERACY AND LANGUAGE

According to Rack *et al.* (1993) any model of reading should (1) describe how reading develops; (2) examine skills needed for reading; (3) specify mental operations involved in reading; and (4) explain how this fits with current brain knowledge. Although this framework was constructed within the context of an alphabetic script, it is also valid for non-alphabetic systems such as Chinese, and mixed systems such as Japanese (the *kana* syllabaries and the *kanji* character writing). However, few models have been developed to accommodate the diverse linguistic characteristics necessary to account for literacy acquisition in every language. Theories derived from the dual route model (see discussion in the previous section) are a case in point. In assessing the ability of the dual route system to account for reading and dictation (spelling) in Chinese (Mandarin/Putongua), Olson and Caramazza (1994) concluded that while Chinese may be accommodated within a form of the dual route model, the linguistic rules for such languages are far more complex than in the alphabetic systems on which the model was based. Any perspective of dyslexia derived simply from the dual route viewpoint, therefore, may be inadequate to explain Chinese literacy difficulties. Seymour (1999) proposed a more complex model involving orthographic, morphographic and linguistic systems, analogous to orthographic, phonological and semantic lexicons, and incorporated developmental features that were not normally associated with the dual route concept. These lexicons have usually been hypothesized as a store of implicitly and explicitly acquired knowledge that may be accessed during the reading and writing process. Responses to literacy measures will depend upon the entries contained in those lexicons, and the ability to retrieve them. Gathercole *et al.* (1997) indicate that lexical knowledge is important for learning the sounds of new words and that children who become poor readers are better, at least to start with, in using unbound morphemes than younger children of the same reading level. Similarly, evidence indicates that semantic coding deficits accrue in older children (Vellutino *et al.*, 1995). In reviewing models of word reading, Raymer and Berndt (1996) suggested a need to incorporate lexical processes that derive from orthographic inputs and directly activate phonological output without semantic mediation. Finally, whereas Treiman and Cassar (1997) suggested that children do not make full use of morphological relations among words in English, Joanisse *et al.* (2000) suggested it was important, at least for the dyslexic individual.

Work with Alzheimer's Dementia patients has revealed a number of dissociations in the lexical system that may be relevant, though currently untested, in the dyslexia field. These include category-specific naming deficits (Crosson, 1999) and preserved reading skills in a patient with severely impaired semantic memory (Cipolotti and Warrington, 1995). Bushell and Martin (1997) also found a dissociation between word categories, specifically concrete nouns and motion verbs. Although not reported in the developmental literature, these results may provide clues as to word finding difficulties, including why some dyslexic children have problems with tasks such as rapid naming when certain types of words are involved. Nakamura *et al.* (1998) demonstrated that acquired language difficulties in the reading performance of Japanese Alzheimer's Dementia patients showed dissociations between *kanji* reading and comprehension, suggesting that *kanji* can be read without meaning, contrary to the more accepted notion that reading Chinese script is usually activated from orthography to phonological output via the semantic lexicon (Perfetti and Tan, 1998). Research with Alzheimer's Dementia patients has also demonstrated spelling and reading were critically dependent upon intact semantic memory in English (Graham *et al.*, 2000) and Chinese (Weekes, 2000).

The work reported in this and the previous section indicates the importance of incorporating various processes in a model of literacy, as well as dyslexia, if cross-language differences are to be accommodated. In a study of literacy difficulties experienced by children learning to read and write in Chinese, English and Hungarian, we found that good and poor literacy learners were differentiated by different cognitive factors across the three languages. Children with good and poor literacy skills in reading and writing single words were matched in terms of their age, sex, educational background, history of difficulties and non-verbal ability. In English, good and poor literacy children differed in measures of phonological processing; specifically, the ability to identify alliteration and rhyme, the ability to store phonological information that is known (words and digits) and unfamiliar (non-words), and the ability to access a known lexical representation rapidly (rapid naming of digits and objects). In Hungarian, a similar pattern of differences focused on phonological processing; however, the differences were apparent only in measures of alliteration, non-word sequences and rapid naming of digits. Although the same basic processes seem to distinguish groups of poor readers/writers from their able peers in both languages, the level and characteristics of the deficits seem to vary between the groups. One potential explanation may be the level of transparency of Hungarian (a highly regular language) compared to English (a relatively irregular language). However, the specific reason why this should lead to the results obtained requires further elaboration. For example, the data indicate that Hungarian is related to specific differences between good and poor literacy children in the recall of sequences of non-words, whereas English presented more general differences in sequence repetition between those with and without literacy difficulties (see Smythe *et al.*, submitted). Similarly, a simple transparency explanation also does not explain the lack of differences found between good and poor Chinese literacy children in phonological-based tasks. These groups differed on measures of visual processing and rapid naming only. Poor Chinese readers/writers were as able as their peers to identify rhyme and alliteration, and repeat sequences of familiar and unfamiliar phonemes. Although some level of phonological deficit at the point of representing words may have led to the literacy difficulties experienced by these Chinese speakers, an explanation that includes the processes required to rapidly access a known lexical item from its visual representation seems more consistent with the patterns of deficits presented. These findings lead to the general conclusion that literacy in different languages may require different processes for its successful acquisition. The recent brain-mapping research by Paulesu *et al.* (2000) is consistent with this perspective. This research suggests that English and Italian individuals process the same word (e.g., 'pizza') differently. On average, when processing such words, separate areas of the brains of English and Italian speakers were most activated.

There are numerous factors involved in the acquisition of reading and writing. It also seems logically plausible that failure in any one will result in reduced effectiveness in literacy acquisition. Given that different languages require different processes to be incorporated in the acquisition of literacy, or may require the application of the same processes but to different degrees, then it seems highly plausible that the underlying cognitive causes of dyslexia will vary across languages. As such, it may be possible that the same individual is found to be dyslexic in one language, but not in another. If any given individual uses two languages that have different cognitive demands, it is possible that they will demonstrate signs of dyslexia in one language but not in a second. Although relatively rare in the literature, there are studies of, what one might call, differential dyslexia. Leker and Biran (1999) described a patient with a particular acquired reading difficulty in Hebrew who showed no difficulties when reading in English. These researchers argue for the existence of a separate, language-associated, neuronal network within the right hemisphere, and propose that this system may be more important for certain languages/scripts. Similarly, there has been research showing that the two main types of Japanese script, *kanji* (Chinese characters) and *kana* (a syllabary) can be dissociated in Alzheimer's patients (Nakamura *et al.*, 1998), raising the possibility of a similar dissociation of the two scripts in a developmental context. Wydell and Butterworth (1999) reported the single case of a child who presented evidence of dyslexia in their first language (English) but not in their second language (Japanese). In a larger-scale study, Kline and Lee (1972) assessed a group of Canadian children who were learning to acquire literacy in both English and Chinese. Their data indicated that, while most children had no problems with reading and writing in either language, some had trouble with Chinese but not English, and others had trouble with English but not Chinese. Miller-Guron and Lundberg (2000) identified Swedish children who were demonstrating dyslexia-like deficits with literacy skills in their native language, but who showed evidence of succeeding with literacy in English. These results suggested that while the children presented evidence of problems with developing 'advanced' phonological skills, such as phoneme awareness and manipulation skills, which are necessary for the successful acquisition of Swedish literacy, these children could use alternative strategies, such as whole word approaches, when reading English. The consequence was interpreted as such children being more able to keep up with the peer group for English literacy skills than they were for Swedish literacy skills. Everatt *et al.* (2002) also report bilingual children presenting evidence of single-word reading difficulties in a language with a deep orthography (English) without comparable deficits in another language with a much more regular orthography (the Filipino language of

Tagalog). Interestingly, these differential effects were not so apparent in reading compre-hension, suggesting that differential dyslexia may vary depending on the measure of literacy used.

A CROSS-LINGUISTIC FRAMEWORK

The above discussion indicates the need to consider a variety of cognitive factors when determining potential causes of literacy skill deficits. It is also clear that while there has been extensive research in the English language, the cognitive factors leading to literacy difficulties in other languages are far less understood. However, there are a number of commonalities throughout the work presented that may provide the basis for a framework for understanding the relationships between cognitive processing and reading and writing difficulties across languages. Analysis of those factors led Smythe and Everatt (2000) to propose a model that conceptualizes reading and writing difficulties within five modules. These modules were related to the sub-typing perspective of Fletcher *et al.* (1997), although they incorporate an individual differences perspective (described below) rather than a sub-typing viewpoint. The model focuses on five 'key' cognitive areas: (1) phono-logical segmentation and assembly skills; (2) auditory system; (3) visual system; (4) speed of processing; and (5) lexical system. The first two allow a distinction between deficits in phonological manipulation skills and auditory perception/storage. The phonological seg-mentation and assembly skills module is intended to highlight the ability to analyse and synthesize words, as well as manipulate units of sound, separately from storage and retrieval processes. In contrast, the auditory system refers to the perception, storage and comparison of linguistic and non-linguistic sounds rather than the manipulation processes included in the previous module. Equally, the first system is based on linguistic material, whereas the latter is envisaged as including the ability to differentiate between sounds, whether linguistic or non-linguistic. The visual system is the visual analogue of the audi-tory system and refers to the perception and storage of visual stimuli. Despite the focus of English language research on phonological processes, both visual and auditory per-ceptual/storage systems seem vital to an understanding of the deficits presented across different language contexts, particularly when non-alphabetic scripts are considered. The speed of processing module is incorporated to allow consideration of the rapid naming deficits that have been found to be important indicators of literacy difficulties across dif-ferent languages and to allow aspects of fluency to be included in the framework. The lexical system is included because of the evidence that factors related to the processing of semantics and/or morphology have been incorporated in theoretical explanations across several language contexts. Additionally, the storage and retrieval of such semantic/morphology information seem to be dissociable from the storage/retrieval processes involved in the auditory/visual system.

The model also incorporates the perspective of individual differences among children. Each of the five factors proposed in the model has been demonstrated to vary within the population and, hence, may increase the level of explanation of variability in literacy ability. This individual differences perspective may be vital, particularly when considering methods to enhance learning (see Brooks and Weeks, 1999). Simmonds (1992), for example, has criticized the position that all students are assumed to learn from the same method despite acknowledgement that they are all different. Such an individual differences perspective may also provide a way forward for understanding the varied patterns of skills and deficits identified by the approaches discussed in previous sections of this chapter. As Seymour (1986) points out, if the single cause viewpoint were correct, we would expect a relatively homogeneous group of dyslexics, each showing the same cognitive deficits, but possibly with a continuum of ability. If there are a number of discrete underlying causes, one should find a small number of distinctive sub-types each shared by a number of dyslexic individuals. However, if we consider every person as different, then the way dyslexia presents will vary greatly across these individuals due, in part, to typical individual differences found across all humans, but potentially due to variations (both in type and level) in dyslexia-specific factors. Each factor should show variation in functioning within each individual. These dyslexia-specific factors may arise due to certain systems or sub-systems being absent, or due to resources available to those systems/sub-systems differing between individuals, or due to individuals differing in their strategic emphasis on the use of particular processing routes. If this individual differences perspective is used, this would lead to dyslexic individuals showing different profiles of strengths and weaknesses, though with a set of defining characteristics, some or all of which will be presented by each dyslexic.

As the preceding sections of this chapter have argued, the role of the underlying cognitive components in children with reading and writing difficulties varies in accordance with the demands of the different languages, orthographies and scripts they are required to learn. If these three aspects are combined, then one or more of the five factors might be related to variations in performance in literacy in a given language dependent on the individual child's level of functioning in each of the processing areas. Although this produces a complex system that leads to difficulties in precisely predicting the results of investigations of literacy and literacy difficulties, it does mirror the complexity found within the field and provides a basis on which to incorporate cross-language findings. As explained above, the framework is provided as a way of understanding and incorporating the findings that will be reported and discussed in the subsequent chapters, rather than offering a predictive model.

REFERENCES

Adlard, A. and Hazan, V. (1998) Speech perception in children with specific reading difficulties (dyslexia). *Quarterly Journal of Experimental Psychology*, 51, 153–177.

Alegria, J., Pignot, E. and Morais, J. (1982) Phonetic analysis of speech and memory codes in beginning reading. *Memory and Cognition*, 10, 451–456.

Badian, N.A. (1993) Phonemic awareness, naming, visual symbol processing and reading. *Reading and Writing*, 5, 87–100.

Bakker, D.J. (1979) Hemispheric differences in reading strategies: Two dyslexias? *Bulletin of the Orton Society*, 29, 84–100.

Beaton, A., McDougall, S. and Singleton, C. (eds) (1997) Special issues: Dyslexia in literate adults, *Journal of Research in Reading*, 20(1).

Ben-Dror, I., Bentin, S. and Frost, R. (1995) Semantic, phonologic, and morphologic skills in reading-disabled and normal children: Evidence from perception and production of spoken Hebrew. *Reading Research Quarterly*, 30, 876–893.

Ben-Dror, I., Pollatsek, A. and Scarpati, S. (1991) Word identification in isolation and in context by college dyslexic students. *Brain and Language*, 40, 471–490.

Bentin, S., Hammer, R. and Cahan, S. (1991) The effects of aging and first grade schooling on the development of phonological awareness. *Psychological Science*, 2, 271–274.

Biancardi, A. and Milano, G. (1999) *Quando un bambino non sa leggere*. Milan: Rizzoli.

Bishop, D.V.M. (1989) Unstable vergence control and dyslexia: A critique. *British Journal of Ophthalmology*, 73, 223–245.

Boder, E. (1973) Developmental dyslexia: A diagnostic approach based on three atypical reading-spelling patterns. *Developmental Medicine and Child Neurology*, 15, 663–687.

Bogdanowicz, M. (1999) Personal communication.

Bowers, P.G. and Wolf, M. (1993) Theoretical links among naming speed, precise timing mechanisms and orthographic skills in dyslexia. *Reading and Writing: An Interdisciplinary Journal*, 5, 69–85.

Breitmeyer, B.G. (1993) Sustained (P) and transient (M) channels in vision: A review and implications for reading. In D.M. Willows, R.S. Kruk and E. Corcos (eds), *Visual Processes in Reading and Reading Disabilities*. Hillsdale, NJ: Lawrence Erlbaum.

British Psychological Society (1999) *Dyslexia, Literacy and Psychological Assessment*. Report of a Working Party of the Division of Educational and Child Psychology of the British Psychological Society. Leicester: British Psychological Society.

Brooks, P. and Weeks, S. (1999) *Individual Styles in Learning to Spell: Improving Spelling in Children with Literacy Difficulties and All Children in Mainstream Schools*. London: Department for Education and Employment.

Bruck, M. (1990) Word-recognition skills of adults with childhood diagnoses of dyslexia. *Developmental Psychology*, 26, 439–454.

Bruck, M. (1993) Word recognition and component phonological processing skills of adults with childhood diagnosis of dyslexia. *Developmental Review*, 13, 258–268.

Bryant, P. (1998) Sensitivity to Onset and Rhyme does predict young children's reading: A comment on Muter, Hulme, Snowling and Taylor (1997) *Journal of Experimental Child Psychology*, 71, 29–37.

Bryant, P. and Bradley, L. (1985) *Children's Reading Problems*. Oxford: Blackwell.

Bushell, C.M. and Martin, A. (1997) Automatic semantic priming of nouns and verbs in patients with Alzheimer's disease. *Neuropsychologia*, 35, 1059–1067.

Byrne, B. and Fielding-Barnsley, R. (1993) Evaluation of a program to teach phonemic awareness to young children: A 1 year follow up. *Journal of Educational Psychology*, 85, 104–111.

Caravolas, M. (1993) Language-specific influences on phonology and orthography on emergent literacy. In J. Altarriba (ed.), *Cognition and Culture*. Amsterdam: Elsevier Science Publishers.

Cardoso-Martins, C. (1995) Sensitivity to rhymes, syllables and phonemes in literacy acquisition in Portuguese. *Reading Research Quarterly*, 30, 808–828.

Castles, A. and Coltheart, M. (1993) Varieties of developmental dyslexia. *Cognition*, 47, 149–180.

Catts, H.W. (1989) Defining dyslexia as a developmental language disorder. *Annals of Dyslexia*, 39, 50–64.

Cestnick, L. and Jerger, J. (2000) Auditory temporal processing and lexical/nonlexical reading in developmental dyslexics. *Journal of the American Academy of Audiology*, 11, 501–513.

Cipolotti, L. and Warrington, E.K. (1995) Semantic memory and reading abilities: A case report. *Journal of the International Neuropsychology Society*, 1, 104–110.

Critchley, M. and Critchley, E. (1978) *Dyslexia Defined*. London: William Heinemann Medical Books Ltd.

Cronin, V. and Carver, P. (1998) Phonological sensitivity, rapid naming, and beginning reading. *Applied Psycholinguistics*, 19, 447–461.

Crosson, B. (1999) Subcortical mechanisms in language: Lexical-semantic mechanisms and the thalamus. *Brain and Cognition*, 40, 414–438.

Cunningham, A.E. (1990) Explicit versus implicit instruction in phonemic awareness. *Journal of Experimental and Child Psychology*, 50, 429–444.

Daneman, M. (1991) Working memory as a predictor of verbal fluency. *Journal of Psycholinguistic Research*, 20, 445–464.

Daneman, M. and Carpenter, P.A. (1980) Individual differences in working memory and reading. *Journal of Verbal Learning and Verbal Behavior*, 19, 450–466.

DeJong, P.F. and van der Leij, A. (1999) Specific contributions of phonological abilities to early reading acquisition: Results from a Dutch latent variable longitudinal study. *Journal of Educational Psychology*, 91, 450–476.

Denckla, M.B. and Rudel, R.G. (1976) Rapid Automatized Naming (RAN): Dyslexia differentiated from other learning disabilities. *Neuropsychologia*, 14, 471–479.

Elbro, C., Nielsen, I. and Petersen, D.K. (1994) Dyslexia in adults: Evidence for deficits in non-word reading and in the phonological representation of lexical items. *Annals of Dyslexia*, 44, 205–226.

Elbro, C., Rasmussen, I. and Spelling, B. (1996) Teaching reading to disabled readers with language disorders: A controlled evaluation of synthetic speech feedback. *Scandinavian Journal of Psychology*, 37, 140–155.

Ellis, A.W. (1984) *Reading, Writing and Dyslexia: A Cognitive Analysis*. London: Lawrence Erlbaum Associates.

Ellis, A.W., McDougall, S.J.P. and Monk, A.F. (1996) Are dyslexics different? *Dyslexia*, 2, 31–58.

Everatt, J. (ed.), (1999) *Reading and Dyslexia: Visual and Attentional Processes*. London: Routledge.

Everatt, J. (2002) Visual processes. In G. Reid and J. Wearmouth (eds), *Dyslexia and Literacy: Theory and Practice*. Chichester: Wiley.

Everatt, J., Bradshaw, M.F. and Hibbard, P.B. (1999) Visual processing and dyslexia. *Perception*, 28, 243–254.

Everatt, J., McNamara, S., Groeger, J.A. and Bradshaw, M.F. (1999) Motor aspects of dyslexia. In J. Everatt (ed.), *Reading and Dyslexia: Visual and Attentional Processes*. London: Routledge.

Everatt, J., Smythe, I., Adams, E. and Ocampo, D. (2000) Dyslexia screening measures and bilingualism. *Dyslexia*, 6, 42–56.

Everatt, J., Smythe, I., Ocampo, D. and Veii, K. (2002) Dyslexia assessment of the bi-scriptal reader. *Topics in Language Disorders*, 22, 32–45.

Fawcett, A.J. and Nicolson, R.I. (1996) *The Dyslexia Screening Test Manual*. London: The Psychological Corporation.

Fawcett, A.J. and Nicolson, R.I. (2001) Dyslexia: The role of the cerebellum. In A. Fawcett (ed.), *Dyslexia: Theory and Good Practice*. London: Whurr.

Felton, R.H., Naylor, C. and Wood, F. (1990) Neuropsychological profile of adult dyslexics. *Brain and Language*, 39, 485–497.

Fletcher, J.M., Morris, R., Reid Lyon, G., Steubing, K.K., Shaywitz, S.E., Shankweiler, D., Katz, L. and Shaywitz, B.A. (1997) Subtypes of dyslexia: An old problem revisited. In B.A. Blachman (ed.), *Foundations of Reading Acquisition and Dyslexia*. Mahwah, NJ: Lawrence Erlbaum Associates.

Fletcher, J.M. and Satz, P. (1985) Cluster analysis and the search for learning disability subtypes. In B.P. Rourke (ed.), *Neuropsychology of Learning Disabilities*. New York: Guilford Press.

Frederickson, N., Frith, U. and Reason, R. (1997) *Phonological Assessment Battery*. Windsor: NFER-Nelson.

Gathercole, S.E. and Baddeley, A.D. (1989) Evaluation of the role of phonological STM in the development of vocabulary in children: A longitudinal study. *Journal of Memory and Language*, 28, 200–213.

Gathercole, S.E. and Baddeley, A.D. (1993) *Working Memory and Language*. Hillsdale, NJ: Lawrence Erlbaum Associates.

Gathercole, S.E., Hitch, G.J., Service, E. and Martin, A.J. (1997) Phonological short-term memory and new word learning in children. *Developmental Psychology*, 33, 966–979.

Gathercole, S.E. and Pickering, S.J. (2001) Working memory deficits in children with special educational needs. *British Journal of Special Education*, 28, 89–97.

Gathercole, S.E.C., Willis, C. and Baddeley, A.D. (1991) Nonword repetition, phonological memory, and vocabulary: A reply to Snowling, Chiat, and Hulme. *Applied Psycholinguistics*, 12, 375–379.

Gathercole, S.E.C., Willis, C.S., Emslie, H. and Baddeley, A.D. (1992) Phonological memory and vocabulary development during the early school years. *Developmental Psychology*, 28, 887–898.

Gersons-Wolfensberger, D.C.M. and Ruijssenaars, W.A.J.J.M. (1997) Definition and treatment of dyslexia: A report by the Committee on Dyslexia of the Health Council of the Netherlands. *Journal of Learning Disabilities*, 30, 209–213.

Goswami, U. (2000) Phonological representations, reading development and dyslexia: Towards a cross-linguistic theoretical framework. *Dyslexia*, 6, 133–151.

Goswami, U. and Bryant, P. (1990) *Phonological Skills and Learning to Read*. Hove: Lawrence Erlbaum Associates.

Goulandris, N., McIntyre, A., Snowling, M., Bethel, J.-M. and Lee, J.P. (1998) A comparison of dyslexic and normal readers using orthoptic assessment procedures. *Dyslexia*, 4, 30–48.

Goulandris, N. and Snowling, M. (1991) Visual memory deficits: A plausible cause of developmental dyslexia. *Cognitive Neuropsychology*, 8, 127–154.

Graham, N.L., Patterson, K. and Hodges, J.R. (2000) The impact of semantic memory impairment on spelling: Evidence from semantic dementia. *Neuropsychologia*, 38, 143–163.

Gupta, A. and Garg, A. (1996) Visuo-perceptual and phonological processing in dyslexic children. *Journal of Personality and Clinical Studies*, 12, 67–73.

Hatcher, P.J., Hulme, C. and Ellis, A.W. (1994) Ameliorating early reading failure by integrating the teaching of reading and phonological skills: The phonological linkage hypothesis. *Child Development*, 65, 41–57.

Heath, S.M., Hogben, J.H. and Clark, C.D. (1999) Auditory temporal processing in disabled readers with and without oral language delay. *Journal of Child Psychology and Psychiatry*, 40, 637–647.

Helenius, P., Uutela, K. and Hari, R. (1999) Auditory stream segregation in dyslexic adults. *Brain*, 122, 907–913.

Ho, C.S.-H. (1994) A cross-cultural study of the precursors of reading. Unpublished DPhil thesis. University of Oxford.

Ho, C.S.-H. and Bryant, P. (1997) Phonological skills are important in learning to read Chinese. *Developmental Psychology*, 33, 946–951.

Hogben, J.H. (1997) How does a visual transient deficit affect reading? In C. Hulme and M. Snowling (eds), *Dyslexia: Biology, Cognition and Intervention*. London: Whurr Publishers.

Howard, D. and Best, W. (1997) Impaired non-word reading with normal word reading: A case study. *Journal of Research in Reading*, 20, 55–65.

Hulme, C. and Mackenzie, S. (1992) *Working Memory and Severe Learning Difficulties*. Hove: Lawrence Erlbaum Associates.

Hulme, C., Muter, V. and Snowling, M. (1998) Segmentation does predict early progress in learning to read better than rhyme: A reply to Bryant. *Journal of Experimental Child Psychology*, 71, 39–44.

Hulme, C. and Roodenrys, S. (1995) Verbal working memory development and its disorders. *Journal of Child Psychology and Psychiatry*, 36, 373–398.

Inshakova, O. and Boldyreva, T. (1997) Dyslexia in Russia. In R. Salter and I. Smythe (eds), *International Book of Dyslexia*. London: WDNF.

Irlen, H. (1991) *Reading by the Colors*. New York: Avery.

Joanisse, M.F., Manis, F.R., Keating, P. and Seidenberg, M.S. (2000) Language deficits in dyslexic children: Speech perception, phonology, and morphology. *Journal of Experimental Child Psychology*, 77, 30–60.

Kline, C. and Lee, N. (1972) A transcultural study of dyslexia: Analysis of language disabilities in 277 Chinese children simultaneously learning to read and write in English and Chinese. *Journal of Special Education*, 6, 9–26.

Korhonen, T.T. (1995) The persistence of rapid naming problems in children with reading disabilities: A 9 year follow-up. *Journal of Learning Disabilities*, 28, 232–239.

Leker, R.R. and Biran, I. (1999) Unidirectional dyslexia in a polyglot. *Journal of Neurology, Neurosurgery and Psychiatry*, 66, 517–519.

Leppänen, P.H., Pihko, E., Eklund, K.M. and Lyytinen, H. (1999) Cortical responses of infants with and without a genetic risk for dyslexia: II. Group effects. *Neuroreport*, 6, 969–973.

Licht, R. and Spyer, G. (eds), (1994) *The Balance Model of Dyslexia*. Amsterdam: Van Gorcum.

Lie, A. (1991) Effects of a training program for stimulation skills in word analysis in first-grade children. *Reading Research Quarterly*, 24, 234–250.

Lorenzi, C., Dumont, A. and Fullgrabe, C. (2000) Use of temporal envelope cues by children with developmental dyslexia. *Journal of Speech, Language and Hearing Research*, 43, 1367–1379.

Lovegrove, W.J. (1996) Dyslexia and a transient/magnocellular pathway deficit: The current situation and future directions. *Australian Journal of Psychology*, 48, 167–171.

Lovett, M.W., Borden, S.L., DeLuca, T., Lacerenza, L., Benson, N.J. and Brackstone, D. (1994) Treating the core deficits of developmental dyslexia: I Evidence of transfer of learning after phonologically and strategy based reading training programs. *Developmental Psychology*, 30, 805–822.

Lovett, M.W., Steinbach, K.A. and Frijters, J.C. (2000) Remediating the core deficits of developmental reading disability: A double-deficit hypothesis. *Journal of Learning Disabilities*, 33, 334–358.

Lundberg, I., Frost, J. and Peterson, O. (1988) Effects of an extensive programme for stimulating phonological awareness in pre-school children. *Reading Research Quarterly*, 23, 263–284.

Lyon, G.R. (1985) Identification and remediation of learning disability subtypes: Preliminary findings. *Learning Disabilities Focus*, 1, 21–35.

Lyon, G.R., Fletcher, J.M., Shaywitz, S.E., Shaywitz, B.A., Torgesen, J.K., Wood, F.B., Schulte, A. and Olson, R. (2001) Rethinking learning disabilities. In C.E. Finn, A.J. Rotherham and C.R. Hokanson (eds), *Rethinking Special Education for a New Century*. The Fordham Foundation. Web publication: http://www.edexcellence.net/library/special_ed/index.html

Manis, F.R., Seidenberg, M.S., Doi, L.M., McBride-Chang, C. and Petersen, A. (1996) On the bases of two subtypes of developmental dyslexia. *Cognition*, 58, 157–195.

Mann, V.A. (1986) Phonological awareness: The role of reading experience. *Cognition*, 24, 65–92.

Mann, V. and Liberman, I.Y. (1984) Phonological awareness and verbal short-term memory: Can they presage early reading success? *Journal of Learning Disabilities*, 17, 592–599.

Marshall, C.M., Snowling, M.J. and Bailey, P.J. (2001) Rapid auditory processing and phonological ability in normal readers and readers with dyslexia. *Journal of Speech, Language and Hearing Research*, 44, 925–940.

Masland, R. (1997) Defining dyslexia. In R. Salter and I. Smythe (eds), *International Book of Dyslexia*. London: WDNF.

Mattis, S. (1981) Dyslexia syndromes in children: Toward the development of syndrome-specific treatment programs. In F.J. Pirozzolo and M.C. Wittrock (eds), *Neuropsychological and Cognitive Processes in Reading*. New York: Academic Press.

McAnally, K.I. and Stein, J.F. (1996) Auditory temporal coding in dyslexia. *Proceedings of the Royal Society, London, Biological Science*, 22(263), 961–965.

McBride-Chang, C. and Ho, C.S.-K. (2000) Naming speed and phonological awareness in Chinese children: Relations to reading skills. *Journal of Psychology in Chinese Society*, 1, 93–108.

McCrory, E., Frith, U., Brunswick, N. and Price, C. (2000) Abnormal functional activation during a simple word repetition task: A PET study of adult dyslexics. *Journal of Cognitive Neuroscience*, 12, 753–762.

McShane, J. (1991) *Cognitive Development*. London: Blackwell.

Meyer, M.S., Wood, F.B., Hart, L.A. and Felton, R.H. (1998) Longitudinal course of rapid naming in disabled and non-disabled readers. *Annals of Dyslexia*, 48, 91–114.

Miles, T.R. (1993) *Dyslexia: The Pattern of Difficulties*, 2nd edition. London: Whurr.

Miles, T.R. and Haslum, M.N. (1986) Dyslexia: Anomaly or normal variation? *Annals of Dyslexia*, 36, 103–117.

Miller-Guron, L. and Lundberg, I. (2000) Dyslexia and second language reading: A second bite at the apple? *Reading and Writing*, 12, 41–61.

Mody, M., Studdert-Kennedy, M. and Brady, S. (1997) Speech perception deficits in poor readers: Auditory processing or phonological coding? *Journal of Experimental Child Psychology*, 64, 199–231.

Muter, V., Hulme, C., Snowling, M. and Taylor, S. (1998) Segmentation, not rhyming predicts early progress in learning to read. *Journal of Experimental Child Psychology*, 71, 3–27.

Nakamura, K., Meguro, K., Yamazaki, H., Ishizaki, J., Saito, H., Saito, N., Shimada, M., Yamguchi, S., Shimada, Y. and Yamadori, A. (1998) Kanji-predominant alexia in advanced Alzheimer's disease. *Acta Neurologica Scandinavica*, 97, 237–243.

Nation, K. and Snowling, M.J. (1998) Individual differences in contextual facilitation: Evidence from dyslexia and poor reading comprehension. *Child Development*, 69, 996–1011.

Nicolson, R.I. and Fawcett, A.J. (1995) Dyslexia is more than a phonological disability. *Dyslexia*, 1, 19–36.

Olofsson, A. and Lundberg, I. (1985) Evaluation of long-term effects of phonemic awareness training in kindergarten: Illustrations of some methodological problems in evaluation research. *Scandinavian Journal of Psychology*, 16, 21–34.

Olson, A. and Caramazza, A. (1994) Representation and connectionist models: The NET spell experience. In G. Brown and N. Ellis (eds), *Handbook of Spelling: Theory, Process and Intervention*. Chichester: Wiley.

Olson, R.K., Wise, B., Connors, F., Rack, J. and Fulker, D. (1989) Specific deficits in component reading and language skills: Genetic and environmental influences. *Journal of Learning Disabilities*, 22, 339–348.

Paulesu, E., McCrory, E., Fazio, F., Menoncello, L., Brunswick, N., Cappa, S.F., Cotelli, M., Cossu, G., Corte, F., Lorusso, M., Pesenti, S., Gallagher, A., Perani, D., Price, C., Frith, C.D. and Frith, U. (2000) A cultural effect on brain function. *Nature Neuroscience*, 3, 91–96.

Pavlidis G.T. (1981) Sequencing, eye movements and the early objective diagnosis of dyslexia. In G.T. Pavlidis and T.R. Miles (eds), *Dyslexia Research and its Applications to Education*. Chichester: Wiley.

Peer, L. (2001) What is dyslexia? In I. Smythe (ed.), *The Dyslexia Handbook 2001*. Reading: British Dyslexia Association.

Perfetti, C.A. and Tan, L.H. (1998) The time course of graphic, phonological, and semantic activation in Chinese character identification. *Journal of Experimental Psychology: Learning Memory and Cognition*, 24, 101–118.

Rack, J.P., Hulme, C. and Snowling, M.J. (1993) Learning to read: A theoretical synthesis. In H.W. Reeses (ed.), *Advances in Child Development and Behaviour*. Vol. 24. New York: Academic Press.

Rack, J.P., Hulme, C., Snowling, M.J. and Wightman, J. (1994) The role of phonology in young children's learning of sight words: The direct learning hypothesis. *Journal of Experimental Child Psychology*, 57, 42–71.

Rack, J.P., Snowling, M.J. and Olson, R.K. (1992) The nonword reading deficit in developmental dyslexia: A review. *Reading Research Quarterly*, 27, 29–53.

Raymer, A.M. and Berndt, R.S. (1996) Reading lexically without semantics: evidence from patients with probable Alzheimer's disease. *Journal of the International Neuropsychology Society*, 2, 340–349.

Rayner, K. and Pollatsek, A. (1989) *The Psychology of Reading*. Hillsdale, NJ: Lawrence Erlbaum Associates.

Robertson, J. (1996) Specific learning difficulties (for example dyslexia), differential diagnosis and intervention. Unpublished PhD thesis. University of Manchester.

Rodgers, B. (1983) The identification and prevalence of specific reading retardation. *British Journal of Educational Psychology*, 53, 369–373.

Rutter, M. (1978) Prevalence and types of dyslexia. In A.L. Benton and D. Pearl (eds), *Dyslexia: An Appraisal of Current Knowledge*. New York: Oxford University Press.

Salter, R. and Smythe, I. (eds) (1997) *International Book of Dyslexia*. London: WDNF.

Satz, P. and Morris, R. (1981) Learning disability subtypes: A review. In F.J. Pirozzolo and M.C. Wittrock (eds), *Neuropsychological and Cognitive Processes in Reading*. New York: Academic Press.

Scarborough, H.S. (1998) Predicting the future achievement of second graders with reading disabilities: Contributions of phonemic awareness, verbal memory, rapid naming, and IQ. *Annals of Dyslexia*, 48, 115–136.

Schneider, W., Küspert, P., Roth, E., Visé, M. and Marx, H. (1997) Short- and long-term effects of training phonological awareness in kindergarten: Evidence from two German studies. *Journal of Experimental Child Psychology*, 66, 311–340.

Serniclaes, W., Sprenger-Charolles, L., Carre, R. and Demonet, J.F. (2001) Perceptual discrimination of speech sounds in developmental dyslexia. *Journal of Speech, Language and Hearing Research*, 44, 384–399.

Seymour, P. (1986) *Cognitive Analysis of Dyslexia*. London: Routledge.

Seymour, P. (1999) Cognitive architecture of early reading. In I. Lunderg, F.E. Tönnessen and I. Austad (eds), *Dyslexia: Advances in Theory and Practice*. Dordrecht: Kluwer Academic Publishers.

Seymour, P.H.K. and MacGregor, C.J. (1984) Developmental dyslexia: A cognitive developmental analysis of phonological, morphemic and visual impairments. *Cognitive Neuropsychology*, 1, 43–82.

Share, D.L. (1996) Word recognition and spelling processes in specific reading disabled and garden-variety poor readers. *Dyslexia*, 2, 167–174.

Shaywitz, S.E., Escobar, M.D., Shaywitz, B.A., Fletcher, J.M. and Makuch, R. (1992) Evidence that dyslexia may represent the lower tail of a normal distribution of reading disability. *New England Journal of Medicine*, 326, 145–151.

Siegel, L.S. (1988) Evidence that IQ scores are irrelevant to the definition and analysis of reading disability. *Canadian Journal of Psychology*, 42, 201–215.

Simmonds, D.C. (1992) Perspectives on dyslexia: Commentary on educational concerns. *Journal of Learning Disabilities*, 25, 66–70.

Skottun, B.C. and Parke, L.A. (1999) The possible relationship between visual deficits and dyslexia: Examination of a critical assumption. *Journal of Learning Disabilities*, 32, 2–5.

Smythe, I. and Everatt, J. (2000) Dyslexia diagnosis in different languages. In L. Peer and G. Reid (eds), *Multilingualism, Literacy and Dyslexia*. London: David Fulton Publishers.

Smythe, I., Everatt, J., Gyarmathy, É., Ho, C.S.-H. and Groeger, J.A. (submitted). Short-term memory and literacy: A cross-language comparison. *Educational and Child Psychology*.

Snowling, M.J. (1981) Phonemic deficits in developmental dyslexia. *Psychological Research*, 43, 219–235.

Snowling, M.J. (2000) *Dyslexia*. 2nd edition. Oxford: Blackwell.

Snowling, M.J. and Nation, K.A. (1997) Language, phonology and learning to read. In C. Hulme and M. Snowling (eds), *Dyslexia: Biology, Cognition and Intervention*. London: Whurr.

Spencer, L. (2000) The role of phonological awarenss in the beginning reading of Welsh and English-speaking children. Unpublished PhD thesis. University of Liverpool.

Spring, C. and Capps, C. (1974) Encoding speed, rehearsal and probed recall of dyslexic boys. *Journal of Educational Psychology*, 66, 780–786.

Stanovich, K.E. (1986) Matthew effects in reading: Some consequences of individual differences in the acquisition of literacy. *Reading Research Quarterly*, 21, 360–407.

Stanovich, K.E. (1988) Explaining the differences between the dyslexic and the garden-variety poor reader: The phonological-core variable-difference model. *Journal of Learning Disabilities*, 21, 590–612.

Stanovich, K.E. (1989) Learning disabilities in broader context. *Journal of Learning Disabilities*, 22, 287–91, 297.

Stanovich, K.E. (1992) Discrepancy definitions of reading disability: Has intelligence led us astray? *Reading Research Quarterly*, 26, 7–29.

Stanovich, K.E. (2000) *Progress in Understanding Reading: Scientific Foundations and New Frontiers*. New York: Guilford Press.

Stanovich, K.E. and Siegel, L.S. (1994) The phenotypic performance profile of reading disabled children: A regression-based test of the phonological-core variable-difference model. *Journal of Educational Psychology*, 86, 24–53.

Stanovich, K.E., Siegel, L.S. and Gottardo, A. (1997) Progress in the search for dyslexia subtypes. In C. Hulme and M. Snowling (eds), *Dyslexia: Biology, Cognition and Intervention*. London: Whurr.

Stein, J. (1993) Visuospatial perception in disabled readers. In D.M. Willows, R.S. Kruk and E. Corcos (eds), *Visual Processes in Reading and Reading Disabilities*. Hillsdale, NJ: Lawrence Erlbaum Associates.

Stein, J.F. (2001) The magnocellular theory of developmental dyslexia. *Dyslexia*, 7, 12–36.

Stein, J.F., Riddell, P. and Fowler, M.S. (1989) Disordered right hemisphere function in developmental dyslexia. In C. von Euler, I. Lundberg and G. Lennerstrand (eds), *Brain and Reading*. New York: Stockton Press.

Sutter, M.L., Petkov, C., Baynes, K. and O'Connor, K.N. (2000) Auditory scene analysis in dyslexics. *Neuroreport*, 11, 1967–1971.

Swan, D. and Goswami, U. (1997) Picture naming deficits in developmental dyslexia: The phonological representations hypothesis. *Brain and Language*, 56, 334–353.

Tallal, P. (1980) Auditory temporal perception, phonics, and reading disabilities in children. *Brain and Language*, 9, 182–198.

Tallal, P. (1984) Temporal or phonetic processing deficits in dyslexia? This is the question. *Applied Psycholinguistics*, 10, 167–169.

Tallal, P. and Katz, W. (1989) Neuropsychological and neuroanatomical studies of developmental language/reading disorders: Recent advances. In C. von Euler, I. Lundberg, and G. Lennerstrand (eds), *Brain and Reading*. New York: Stockton Press.

Tallal, P., Miller, S.L., Jenkins, W.M. and Merzenich, M.M. (1997) The role of temporal processing in developmental language-based learning disorders: Research and clinical implications. In B.A. Blachman (ed.), *Foundations of Reading Acquisition and Dyslexia: Implications for Early Intervention*. Mahwah, NJ: Lawrence Erlbaum Associates.

Tangel, D.M. and Blachman, B.A. (1992) Effect of phoneme awareness instruction on kindergarten children's invented spelling. *Journal of Reading Behavior*, 24, 233–261.

Thomson, M.E. (1990) *Developmental Dyslexia*. 3rd edition. London: Whurr.

Tönnessen, F.E. (1995) On defining 'Dyslexia'. *Scandinavian Journal of Education Research*, 39, 2–10.

Torgesen, J.K. and Davis, C. (1996) Individual difference variables that predict response to training in phonological awareness. *Journal of Experimental Child Psychology*, 63, 1–21.

Torgesen, J.K., Morgan, S. and Davis, C. (1992) The effects of two types of phonological awareness training on word learning in kindergarten children. *Journal of Educational Psychology*, 84, 364–370.

Torgesen, J.K., Wagner, R.K. and Rashotte, C.A. (1997) Approaches to the prevention and remediation of phonologically based reading disabilities. In B.A. Blachman (ed.), *Foundations of Reading Acquisition and Dyslexia: Implications for Early Intervention*. Mahwah, NJ: Lawrence Erlbaum Associates.

Torneus, M. (1984) Phonological awareness and reading: A chicken and egg problem? *Journal of Educational Psychology*, 76, 1346–1358.

Treiman, R. and Cassar, M. (1997) Spelling acquisition in English. In C. Perfetti, L. Rieben and M. Fayol (eds), *Learning to Spell*. Mahwah, NJ: Lawrence Erlbaum Associates.

Vellutino, F.R. (1978) Towards an understanding of dyslexia: Psychological factors in specific reading disability. In A. Benton and D. Pearl (eds), *Dyslexia: An Appraisal of Current Knowledge*. New York: Oxford University Press.

Vellutino, F.R., Scanlon, D.M. and Spearing, D. (1995) Semantic and phonological coding in poor and normal readers. *Journal of Experimental Child Psychology*, 59, 76–123.

Wagner, R.K. and Torgesen, J.K. (1987) The nature of phonological processing and its causal role in the acquisition of reading skills. *Psychological Bulletin*, 101, 192–212.

Wagner, R.K., Torgesen, J.K. and Rashotte, C.A. (1994) Development of reading-related phonological processing abilities: new evidence of bidirectional causality from a latent variable longitudinal study. *Developmental Psychology*, 30, 73–87.

Warrick, N., Rubin, H. and Rowe-Walsh, S. (1993) Phoneme awareness in language-delayed children: Comparative studies and intervention. *Annals of Dyslexia*, 43, 153–173.

Watson, B.U., Goldgar, D.E. and Ryschon, K.L. (1983) Subtypes of reading disability. *Journal of Clinical Neuropsychology*, 5, 377–399.

Weekes, B.S. (2000) Oral reading in Chinese: evidence from patients with dementia of the Alzheimer's type. *International Journal of Language and Communication Disorders*, 35, 543–559.

Weeks, S., Brooks, P. and Everatt, J. (2002) Differences in learning to spell: Relationships between cognitive profiles and learning responses to teaching methods. *Educational and Child Psychology*, 19, 47–62.

Wilkins, A.J., Evans, B.J.W., Brown, J.A., Busby, A.E., Wingfield, A.E., Jeanes, R.J. and Bald, J. (1994) Double-masked placebo-controlled trial of precision spectral filters in children who use coloured overlays. *Ophthalmic and Physiological Optics*, 14, 365–370.

Wimmer, H. (1993) Characteristics of developmental dyslexia in a regular writing system. *Applied Psycholinguistics*, 14, 1–33.

Wimmer, H., Mayringe, H. and Landerl, K. (1998) Poor reading: A deficit in skill automatization or a phonological deficit? *Scientific Studies of Reading*, 2, 321–340.

Wittgenstein, L. (1953) *Philosophical Investigations*. Translated by G.E.M. Anscombe. Oxford: Blackwell.

Wolf, M. (1997) A provisional, integrative account of phonological and naming-speed deficits in dyslexia: Implications for diagnosis and intervention. In B. Blachman (ed.), *Foundations of Reading Acquisition and Dyslexia*. Hillsdale, NJ: Lawrence Erlbaum Associates.

Wolf, M. and Bowers, P.G. (2000) Naming speed processes and developmental reading disabilities: An introduction to the special issue on the double-deficit hypothesis. *Journal of Learning Disabilities*, 33, 322–324.

Wolf, M., Miller, L. and Donnelly, K. (2000) Retrieval automaticity, vocabulary elaboration, orthography (RAVE-O): A comprehensive fluency-based reading intervention programme. *Journal of Learning Disabilities*, 33, 375–386.

Wolf, M. and O'Brien, B. (2001) On issues of time, fluency and intervention. In A. Fawcett (ed.), *Dyslexia: Theory and Good Practice*. London: Whurr.

Wolff, P.H., Michel, G.F. and Ovrut, M. (1990) Rate and timing precision of motor coordination in developmental dyslexia. *Developmental Psychology*, 26, 349–359.

World Health Organisation (1993) *ICD-10 Classification of Mental and Behavioural Disorders: Diagnostic Criteria for Research*. Geneva: World Health Organisation.

Wydell, T.N. and Butterworth, B. (1999) An English-Japanese bilingual with monolingual dyslexia. *Cognition*, 70, 273–305.

Yule, W.M., Rutter, M., Berger, M. and Thompson, J. (1974) Over- and under-achievement in reading: Distribution in the general population. *British Journal of Educational Psychology*, 44, 1–12.

Zabell, C. and Everatt, J. (2002) Surface and phonological subtypes of adult developmental dyslexia. *Dyslexia*, 8, 160–177.

2

DYSLEXIA IN ARABIC

Salim Abu-Rabia

INTRODUCTION

Although dyslexia in Arabic has not been widely studied, the reading processes of Arabic have been investigated. This work may not only inform issues related to dyslexia in Arabic but also the existing characteristics of dyslexic readers of English and the other related orthographies. In order to understand Arabic dyslexia one needs to understand some basic information about Arabic orthography and the nature of Arabic.

THE NATURE OF ARABIC

Diglossia

In their homes and neighbourhoods Arab children speak 'spoken Arabic', a language totally different from 'literary Arabic'. This linguistic phenomenon is called diglossia (Ferguson, 1959). Educated Arabs use literary Arabic for reading, writing and speaking on all official occasions. However, both educated and uneducated native Arabic speakers use the spoken language on a daily basis for everyday communication: family dialogues, shopping, cultural conversation and entertainment. Literary Arabic differs in vocabulary, phonology, grammar, morphology and syntax from the accepted spoken language, in which there is a diversity of dialects (Abu-Rabia, 2000a; Ayari, 1996). Most Arabic-speaking countries use different dialects, and sometimes even within the same country different dialects are used in different regions.

Arabic morphology

The morphology of Arabic is based on the 'root and pattern' principle that characterizes Semitic languages. Roots are composed of three or four consonants, although some roots

International Book of Dyslexia: A Cross-Language Comparison and Practice Guide. Edited by Ian Smythe, John Everatt and Robin Salter. ISBN 0471498416 © 2004 John Wiley & Sons, Ltd.

consist of five or two consonants (Abu-Rabia, 2001, 2002). The root represents the basic sense of the word, and every pattern is composed of vowels and additional consonantal letters that impart specific lexical meaning and also grammatical and syntactic information. In addition, patterns produce nouns with number and gender and define the final word-form (Madkor, 1987). Like other Semitic languages, such as Hebrew, Arabic is characterized by a rich derivational and inflectional morphology. The former produces words consisting of the basic root letters. The latter refers to such words with the addition of affixes and the short vowels. Inflectional morphology enables the reader to pronounce the word accurately and to realize the grammatical function of the word in the sentence by taking into account the short vowels, especially the vowelization of the word's final letter (Abu-Rabia, 2001).

The role of morphology in reading Arabic has not been studied (Abu-Rabia, 1995, 2001); this omission is especially noteworthy in the study of dyslexic as compared with normal readers. I predict a significant role for morphology because Arabic is a Semitic language and morphological knowledge has been shown to be an important factor in Hebrew reading (Ben-Dror *et al.*, 1995; Share and Levin, 1999).

Arabic orthography

Literary Arabic is written in an alphabetical system with 28 basic letters. It is a system of consonants, and it is read and written from right to left. In literary Arabic there is a predictable sound–symbol correspondence between the letters and their sounds if the text is vowelized. However, there are certain irregularities that require the mature reader to bring to the text considerable knowledge of literary Arabic – grammar, syntax, vocabulary and contextual interpretations – in order to derive meaning from print, especially if the text is written without vowels, namely, it is orthographically 'deep'. Texts are typically written in vowelized so-called shallow orthography for beginning readers and in unvowelized deep orthography for more advanced readers. As stated above, verbs, nouns and adjectives are a combination of root letters and short vowels. Additions of certain short vowels (diacritics) to the root provide specific meanings and specific pronunciations. Further, vowelizing the end of words in texts indicates their grammatical function in the sentence. If texts are not vowelized, these short vowels must be deduced by the reader, which is a cognitively demanding task. In most modern written and printed literary Arabic texts, no short vowel signs are given, so the reader must deduce them by relying on context or prior linguistic knowledge: grammar, syntax and exposure to print (Abu-Rabia, 1998, 2001, 2002). Reading Arabic script without short vowels can be a difficult task for poor and/or beginning readers because of word and letter similarities and homographs. Certain letters are distinguished from each other only by a single stroke, or may be phonologically indistinct in the colloquial dialect of Arabic spoken by the individual.

In Arabic script the form of a particular letter varies depending on its position in the word. Some letters have three different forms: one at the beginning, one in the middle, and one at the end of a word. Further, different rules are used for the writing of each form.

Recognizing the nature of these letters and their diverse writing rules in different positions, and recognizing the different short vowels under, in, and above the letters, are critical for readers' word pronunciation, which may demand considerable cognitive attention. Furthermore, short-vowel diacritics are located above, and/or in, and/or below the letters for letter-sound pronunciation. Thus, reading a fully vowelled text is likely to be cognitively demanding for a beginning reader, who simultaneously must process many rules in order to extract meaning from print or read out loud accurately. A minor error can lead to a mistaken decoding through confusion of letters of the same shape (Abu-Rabia, 1998).

Literary Arabic is taught to children at school almost as a second language. Because there is almost no research on Arabic reading disabilities, which is the topic of this article, a brief discussion of the literature is presented with special focus on Arabic reading disability.

WORD RECOGNITION PROCESSES

Phonological decoding

Phonological decoding ability is essential in the process of reading acquisition (Abu-Rabia, 1995, 2001, 2002; Jorm, 1979; Perfetti, 1985; Share, 1995). It is well established in the literature that measuring the pseudoword reading is the benchmark test of children's phonological decoding skill (Abu-Rabia, 1995; Vellutino and Scanlon, 1987). Many studies have been conducted using pseudowords as their phonological decoding measure among normal readers and reading-disabled (RD) children (Bruck, 1988, 1990; Castles and Coltheart, 1993; Ehri and Wilce, 1983; Jorm and Share, 1983; Perfetti, 1985; Siegel, 1989; Siegel and Ryan, 1988; Stanovich and Siegel, 1994). The difficulty experienced by these RD children in reading pseudowords seems to be the result of deficiencies in their basic phonological processing.

Consistently the dyslexic readers of Arabic showed poor phonological decoding abilities on the pseudowords and phonological choice test as compared with their chronological age readers and with their reading level readers (Abu-Rabia, Share and Mansour, 2003). Further, these dyslexic children also showed poor phonological awareness results when they were tested on the two phoneme deletion tests: on the first, participants were asked to delete the first phoneme of the first ten words without the short vowel words and sound out the rest of the word. In the other ten words the participants had to delete the first phoneme with the first short vowel.

The nature of Arabic orthography demands high phonological decoding ability. Arabic beginning and poor readers have to process words with short vowels. A series of studies by Abu-Rabia (1997, 1998, 2001, 2002) indicated that short vowels (phonology) have a significant effect on reading accuracy and reading comprehension, regardless of reading level and type of reader and writing style. Even highly skilled Arabic readers were significantly affected by the short vowels. Arabic is a highly phonetic language, and mastering its phonology (short vowels) is cognitively very demanding and correct pronunciation of words is context and/or syntax dependent (Abu Rabia, 2001, 2002). Thus, decoding Arabic words could be a hard task for dyslexic readers.

The results with Arabic dyslexics were similar to those of reading-disabled subjects reported in other studies (Ben-Dror *et al.*, 1995; Siegel and Ryan, 1988). The phonological lag may be related to lack of exposure to literary Arabic at home, for most families believe that reading literary Arabic to children is not helpful because it is almost a second language (Abu-Rabia, 2000a). Lack of exposure may be added to the reasons for the poor results in phonological processing.

Orthographic processing

Studies have demonstrated the important contribution of the orthographic component to reading over and above phonological decoding (Cunningham and Stanovich, 1990; Stanovich and West, 1989). In spite of the different orthographic testing measures, specific orthographic knowledge and orthographic combinations, however, the results for disabled readers are similar in many studies. On orthographic measures participants on one text had to choose the word spelled correctly and, on the second, they had to choose the acceptable letter combination in Arabic. Arabic RD children performed as well as or even better than their normal counterparts matched by reading-level age (Abu-Rabia et al., 2003; Siegel, 1986). However, their performance was poorer than that of their chronological age counterparts. One may conclude that Arabic RD children are relatively better at visual-orthographic processing than phonological processing (Abu-Rabia et al., 2003).

BASIC COGNITIVE PROCESSES

Syntax

Studies measuring syntactic ability in normal and RD students have all resulted in superior performance by the former (Abu-Rabia, 1995; Bentin et al., 1990; Deutsch and Bentin, 1996; Fowler, 1988; Menyuk, 1981; Siegel and Ryan, 1988; Stanovich and Siegel, 1994; Vellutino, 1979; Vogel, 1974; Willows and Ryan, 1981), although the interpretation of these findings has been controversial (Bryant et al., 1990). Among Arabic dyslexics this ability was measured by an oral cloze test in which a word was missing and the listener had to fill it in orally. Participants then had to repeat the completed sentence. Further, a sentence correction test was also given in which participants had to read and correct the sentences. In the study by Abu-Rabia, Share and Mansour (in press), the syntactic measure results were ambivalent: the RD children performed as well as the younger normal readers on the oral cloze test, but poorer than both groups of normal readers on the grammatical judgement test. The oral cloze results perhaps highlight the importance of oral skills in Arab society. Oral skills have long been and still are considered essential in transmitting culture from one generation to another. Still, the percentage of illiterate people in the Arab world is very high. It seems possible that this cultural oral skill may have positively affected the RD children's ability on this specific measure, unlike their results for the written syntax measure. The results of the written syntax measure accord with previous Hebrew and English findings (Bentin et al., 1990; Deutsch and Bentin, 1996; Fowler, 1988).

Morphology

Studies indicate the difficulty that RD people have in dealing with morphology (Leong, 1989). Their reading process is dependent upon their ability to apply the morphological rules of the language (Vogel, 1975, 1983).

Ben-Dror et al. (1995) tested morphology, phonology and semantics of Hebrew in 60 students who were divided into three sub-groups: (1) a group of RD children in grade 5;

(2) a control group of normal readers matched by chronological age; and (3) a younger control group matched by reading level. The RD children performed worse than the chronological-age control group and were also slower than the younger control group. The most significant differences were found in the morphological tasks. Arabic is a Semitic language like Hebrew and similar results were expected. Morphology was also found to be an important discriminator of normal and dyslexic readers (Abu-Rabia et al., 2003). The morphology of the Arabic language is considered root-based. The root of a word functions as an autonomous semantic unit that supports initial lexical access (Abu-Rabia, 2000b, 2001, 2002). Usually skilled readers read without short vowels, i.e. in text with many homographs. Reading these homographs demands from the reader considerable morphological, phonological, syntactical, grammatical and semantic knowledge. Skilled readers usually identify roots of words, which are sufficient for initial lexical access, and later the phonology is retrieved to convey the exact contextually appropriate meaning. Thus, morphology is a key variable in reading Arabic, and other Semitic languages (for a more detailed discussion, see Abu-Rabia, 2001, 2002). In this study the RD children performed very poorly on the morphological measures. Similar findings have also been presented in Hebrew (Ben-Dror et al., 1995) and in English (Leong, 1989; Vogel, 1975, 1983).

Working memory

This ability involves executive control of processing cognitive ability, which helps to control all operations performed in tasks such as reading (Baddeley and Hitch, 1974). Many studies investigating working memory among RD children have found impaired working memory performance as compared with normal readers (Abu-Rabia, 1995; Brady et al., 1987; Cermak, 1983; Daneman et al., 1982; Holligan and Johnston, 1988; Johnston et al., 1987; Jorm and Share, 1983). As for working memory, Arabic dyslexic readers performed significantly worse than the normal readers (Abu-Rabia et al., 2003). These findings accord with previous results (Abu-Rabia, 1995; Brady et al., 1987; Cermak, 1983; Daneman et al., 1982).

Visual processing

Although not consistently replicated, some studies have provided evidence of deficiencies in basic visual processing in RD children (Crammond, 1992; Fletcher, 1985; Lovegrove, 1993; Meyler, 1993; Wright and Groner, 1993). In a longitudinal study in Hebrew, Meyler and Breznitz (1998) tested the development of visual and verbal memory in children followed from kindergarten to Grade 2. They found positive significant predictive correlations between both visual and verbal ability and reading. An important difference between English and Hebrew is worth noting: pointed Hebrew writing may require unique visuo-spatial processing due to the visual complexity of vowel diacritics (Share and Levin, 1999).

Regarding the visual processing results of the study (Abu-Rabia et al., 2003), basic visual memory appears to be clearly an important process in acquiring Arabic reading, as is evident in Hebrew (Meyler, 1993; Meyler and Breznitz, 1998) but not in English (Ellis and Large, 1987, 1988). The findings in Arabic are similar to the Hebrew results, which is not surprising because the two languages have many commonalities (see Share and Levin, 1999). The differences between Semitic and English orthography may explain the different findings. Both Arabic and Hebrew scripts appear to make heavy demands on the visuo-spatial processing of letters, roots, affixes and short vowels posted on and/or under the letters, and of letter similarities (Abu-Rabia, 2001; Share and Levin, 1999).

In sum, the RD population in Arabic generally showed similar characteristics to those reported in the literature: poor phonological processing, poor working memory skills and poor syntactic skills. However, they tended to show strong visual-orthographic patterns of reading from an early age. Phonology seems to be extremely powerful, followed by morphology and visual memory. Syntax and working memory are also important, although they show less consistency (Abu-Rabia, 1995; Abu-Rabia *et al.*, 2003).

REFERENCES

Abu-Rabia, S. (1995) Learning to read in Arabic: Reading, syntactic, orthographic and working memory skills in normally achieving and poor Arabic readers. *Reading Psychology: An International Quarterly*, 16, 351–394.

Abu-Rabia, S. (1997) Reading in Arabic orthography: The effect of vowels and context on reading accuracy of poor and skilled native Arabic readers. *Reading and Writing: An Interdisciplinary Journal*, 9, 65–78.

Abu-Rabia, S. (1998) Reading Arabic texts: Effects of text type, reader type, and vowelization. *Reading and Writing: An Interdisciplinary Journal*, 10, 106–119.

Abu-Rabia, S. (2000a) Effects of exposure to literary Arabic on reading comprehension in a diglossic situation. *Reading and Writing: An Interdisciplinary Journal*, 13, 147–157.

Abu-Rabia, S. (2000b) *Dyslexia*. Nazareth: Alnahda Publications (in Arabic).

Abu-Rabia, S. (2001) The role of vowels in reading Semitic scripts: Data from Arabic and Hebrew. *Reading and Writing: An Interdisciplinary Journal*, 14, 39–59.

Abu-Rabia, S. (2002) Reading in a root-based morphology: The case of Arabic. *Journal of Research in Reading*, 25, 320–330.

Abu-Rabia, S., Share, D. and Mansour, M. (2003) Word recognition and basic cognitive processes among reading-disabled and normal readers in Arabic. *Reading and Writing: An Interdisciplinary Journal*, 16, 423–442.

Ayari, S. (1996) Diglossia and illiteracy in the Arab world. *Language, Culture and Curriculum*, 9, 243–253.

Baddeley, A. and Hitch, G. (1974) Working memory. In G.A. Bower (ed.), *The Psychology of Learning and Motivation*. New York: Academic Press.

Ben-Dror, I., Bentin, S. and Frost, R. (1995) Semantic, phonologic, and morphologic skills in reading-disabled and normal children: Evidence from perception and production of spoken Hebrew. *Reading Research Quarterly*, 30, 876–893.

Bentin, S., Deutsch, A. and Liberman, I. (1990) Syntactic competence and reading ability in children. *Journal of Experimental Child Psychology*, 48, 147–172.

Brady, S., Mann, V. and Schmidt, R. (1987) Errors in short-term memory for good and poor readers. *Memory and Cognition*, 15, 444–453.

Bruck, M. (1988) The word recognition and spelling of dyslexic children. *Reading Research Quarterly*, 23, 51–69.

Bruck, M. (1990) Word-recognition skills of adults with childhood diagnoses of dyslexia. *Developmental Psychology*, 26, 439–454.

Bryant, P.E., Maclean, M. and Bradley, L. (1990) Rhyme, language, and children's reading. *Applied Psycholinguistics*, 11, 237–252.

Castles, A. and Coltheart, M. (1993) Varieties of developmental dyslexia. *Cognition*, 47, 149–180.

Cermak, L.S. (1983) Information processing deficits in children with learning disabilities, *Journal of Learning Disabilities*, 16, 599–605.

Crammond, J. (1992) Analyzing the basic cognitive developmental processes of children with specific types of learning disability. In R. Case (ed.), *The Mind's Staircase*. Hillsdale, NJ: Erlbaum.

Cunningham, A.E. and Stanovich, K.E. (1990) Assessing print exposure and orthographic processing skill in children: A quick measure of reading experience. *Journal of Educational Psychology*, 82, 733–740.

Daneman, M., Carpenter, P.A. and Just, M.A. (1982) Cognitive processes and reading skills. *Advances in Reading Language Research*, 1, 83–124.

Deutsch, A. and Bentin, S. (1996) Attention factors mediating syntactic deficiency in reading-disabled children. *Journal of Experimental Child Psychology*, 63, 386–415.

Ehri, L.C. and Wilce, L.S. (1983) Development of word identification speed in skilled and less skilled beginning readers. *Journal of Educational Psychology*, 75, 3–18.

Ellis, N. and Large, B. (1987) The development of reading: As you seek so shall you find. *British Journal of Psychology*, 78, 1–28.

Ellis, N. and Large, B. (1988) The early stages of reading: Longitudinal study. *Applied Cognitive Psychology*, 2, 47–76.

Ferguson, C.H. (1959) Diglossia. *Word*, 15, 325–340.

Fletcher, J.M. (1985) Memory for verbal and nonverbal stimuli in learning disability subgroups: Analysis by selective reminding. *Journal of Experimental Child Psychology*, 40, 244–259.

Fowler, A.E. (1988) Grammaticality judgement and reading skills in grade 2. *Annals of Dyslexia*. 38, 73–94.

Holligan, C. and Johnston, R.S. (1988) The use of phonological information by good and poor readers in memory and reading tasks. *Memory and Cognition*, 16, 522–523.

Johnston, R.S., Rugg, M.D. and Scott, T. (1987) Phonological similarity effects, memory span and developmental reading disorders: The nature of the relationship. *British Journal of Psychology*, 78, 205–211.

Jorm, A.F. (1979) The nature of reading in developmental dyslexia: A reply to Ellis. *Cognition*, 1, 421–433.

Jorm, A.F. and Share, D.L. (1983) Phonological recoding and reading acquisition. *Applied Psycholinguistics*, 4, 103–147.

Leong, C.K. (1989) Productive knowledge of derivational rules in poor readers. *Annals of Dyslexia*, 39, 94–115.

Lovegrove, W. (1993) Do dyslexics have a visual deficit? In S.F. Wright and R. Groner (eds), *Facets of Dyslexia and its Remediation* (pp. 33–49). North-Holland: Elsevier Science Publishers.

Madkor, A. (1987) *Language and Current Folklore*. Cairo: Dar-Altha Kafa Publications (in Arabic).

Menyuk, P. (1981) Syntactic competence and reading. In *Proceedings of Interdisciplinary Conference on Language Learning and Reading Disabilities*. New York: Queens College Press.

Meyler, A. (1993) Developmental associations between verbal and visual short-term memory and the acquisition of reading. Unpublished MA dissertation, University of Haifa.

Meyler, A. and Breznitz, Z. (1998) Developmental associations between verbal and visual short-term memory and the acquisition of decoding skill. *Reading and Writing: An Interdisciplinary Journal*, 10, 519–540.

Perfetti, C.A. (1985) *Reading Ability*. New York: Oxford University Press.

Share, D.L. (1995) Phonological recoding and self-teaching. *Cognition*, 55, 151–218.

Share, D. and Levin, I. (1999) Learning to read and write in Hebrew. In M. Harris and G. Hatano (eds), *A Cross-Linguistic Perspective on Learning to Read* (pp. 89–111). Cambridge: Cambridge University Press.

Siegel, L.S. (1986) Phonological deficits in children with a reading disability. *Canadian Journal of Special Education*, 2, 45–54.

Siegel, L.S. (1989) IQ is irrelevant to the definition of learning disabilities. *Canadian Journal of Psychology*, 42, 201–215.

Siegel, L.S. and Ryan, E.B. (1988) Development of grammatical sensitivity, phonological, and short-term memory skills in normally achieving and learning children. *Developmental Psychology*, 24, 28–37.

Stanovich, K.E. and Siegel, L.S. (1994) The phenotypic performance profile of reading-disabled children: A regression-based test of the phonological-core variable-difference model. *Journal of Educational Psychology*, 86, 24–53.

Stanovich, K. and West, R. (1989) Exposure to print and orthographic processing. *Reading and Research Quarterly*, 24, 402–429.

Vellutino, F.R. (1979) *Dyslexia: Theory and Research*. Cambridge, MA: MIT Press.

Vellutino, F.R. and Scanlon, D.M. (1987) Phonological coding, phonological awareness, and reading ability: Evidence from a longitudinal and experimental study. *Merrill-Palmer Quarterly*, 33, 321–363.

Vogel, S.A. (1974) Syntactic abilities in normal and dyslexic children. *Journal of Learning Disabilities*, 7, 103–109.

Vogel, S. (1975) *Syntactic Abilities in Normal and Dyslexic Children*. Baltimore, MD: University Park.

Vogel, S. (1983) A qualitative analysis of morphologic development in learning disabled and achieving children. *Journal of Learning Disabilities*, 6, 457–465.

Willows, D.M. and Ryan, E.B. (1981) Differential utilization of syntactic and semantic information by skilled and less skilled readers in the intermediate grades. *Journal of Educational Psychology*, 73, 607–615.

Wright, S.F. and Groner, R. (1993) *Facets of Dyslexia and its Remediation*, North-Holland: Elsevier.

3

DYSLEXIA IN CHINESE

Wengang Yin and Brendan Weekes

INTRODUCTION

Relatively little is known about disorders of written language processing among Chinese speakers. This is not surprising when we consider that differences exist both within and between Chinese languages such as Cantonese, Min and Mandarin (Putonghua) and the more familiar Indo-European languages within which most of our knowledge about dyslexia has developed. Given that Chinese languages differ, it is important to distinguish carefully between reports of dyslexia in different Chinese-speaking environments. The aim of this chapter is to review research on dyslexia in Chinese children from different language environments, specifically Hong Kong, Singapore, Taiwan and mainland China with some emphasis on dyslexia in mainland China. The chapter is divided into two parts. First, we will explain the essential features of the Chinese language necessary to understand dyslexia in Chinese. Two important points to note here are that, first, the scripts that are used in Chinese languages typically (though not always) share the same printed characters and, second, literacy in Putonghua Chinese-speaking environments usually requires mastery of modern (simplified) Chinese characters. Then, we will consider the question of whether or not dyslexia exists in Chinese at all by reviewing research on dyslexia with an emphasis on our own work in mainland China (Beijing). Throughout the chapter we will focus on those issues that, in our view, are most likely to be critical to understanding dyslexia in Chinese. Our overall aim is to offer a framework to guide research on causes and remediation of dyslexia in Chinese.

CHINESE LANGUAGES

Chinese words

All Chinese languages contain a relatively small number of syllables that can be used in isolation or in combination to represent a single morpheme or multi-morphemic word. For

International Book of Dyslexia: A Cross-Language Comparison and Practice Guide. Edited by Ian Smythe, John Everatt and Robin Salter.   ISBN 0471498416   © 2004 John Wiley & Sons, Ltd.

example, there are approximately 1,200 syllables in spoken Putonghua. The onset of each syllable is invariant but the rime (which is defined as the vowel plus the final consonant combination) can be pronounced in many different ways thus allowing for polysemy among Chinese syllables (e.g. *zhu* which can mean 'red', 'dwarf' and 'pearl'). Chinese syllables are typically made up of an onset that is a single consonant followed by a short or a long vowel that is followed by a coda, comprising at least one consonant (however, some syllables, e.g. *ai*, have no consonantal onset). One unique feature of Chinese languages is that there are no consonantal blends or clusters before or after the nuclear vowel. There are 22 onsets and 37 rimes in the Chinese syllabary and only two consonants ever follow the vowel in the rime of a syllable (these are velar and alveolar nasal). This feature of Chinese means that homophony is more prevalent than in most Indo-European languages. Homophonic syllables in Chinese are distinguished by supra-segmental changes in tone and these occur at the level of the vowel. Tone changes thus give each syllable a different meaning, i.e. tones change the morphemic content of each syllable. In Putonghua there are four tones and in Cantonese there are at least eight. This feature of morphemes in Chinese makes the task of *phonological* awareness at the level of the onset and the rime a potentially critical part of learning new words in Chinese. However, *phoneme* awareness may be relatively weak given that phonemes are not made explicit in speech or in print. In fact, we know that the phoneme awareness of Chinese speakers depends on whether or not they are exposed to an alphabetic script during first exposure to print (Huang and Hanley, 1994).

The Chinese script

All Chinese languages have a non-alphabetic script characterized by strokes formed into components written together into a square shape to form a printed *character*. All characters represent an individual morpheme. This makes Chinese a *morphographic* script which means that the smallest pronounceable unit in a character is associated with a syllable. Each morpheme is represented in the script by a character and these can be called *heterographic homophones*. Heterographic homophones are distinguished by tones. The Chinese script contains over 40,000 characters, although the modern reader needs to learn only the most common 3,000 characters to be literate.

One common myth about the Chinese script is that it represents the meaning of words in a completely transparent manner. It is true that mappings between orthography and meaning are often systematic in non-alphabetic scripts, whereas in alphabetic scripts these mappings between orthography and meaning are almost always arbitrary. Many traditional Chinese characters were *pictographic*, meaning that the written character portrayed the basic form of the object it represented. A small number of these characters are still in use today. For example, the character for horse, 马 'ma' has been defined as a pictograph (e.g. Wang, 1973). To some Chinese readers this character suggests an abstract figure galloping across the page. The modern Chinese writing system uses simplified characters that are usually considered to be *logographic* (Henderson, 1982). This means that the basic unit in writing (the character) is associated with a unit of meaning (morpheme) in the spoken language, unlike the letters in an alphabet that do not ordinarily represent meaning (an exception is *I*).

The notion that modern written Chinese is a logography has been challenged, however. De Francis (1989) argued that there are four different types of simple character in modern use: (1) *pictographic* characters which represent a specific object (e.g. 日 'ri' meaning 'sun'); (2) *indicative* characters which represent abstract meanings that cannot be easily sketched (e.g. 本 'ben' which means 'base' and is derived from 木 'mu' meaning 'tree'); (3) *associative* characters which combine existing characters to produce a new meaning (e.g. 尘 'chen' which means 'dust' and is derived from 小 'xiao' meaning 'small' and 土 'tu' meaning 'earth'*)*; and (4) *phonetic-compound* characters which are constructed from a meaning component called the *semantic radical* and a pronunciation component called the *phonetic radical* (e.g. 狐 'hu' meaning 'fox' which contains the semantic radical for animal on the left and the phonetic component pronounced 'hu' on the right).

Approximately 80 to 90 per cent of the characters in modern use are compounds. An important point to note is that the phonetic component is itself a character (and thus represents a syllable) and it provides information about the pronunciation of the whole compound. The semantic component hints at the semantic category that the compound comes from (e.g. an animal) though this radical is often unreliable (Chen, 1996; Tzeng and Wang, 1983).

Oral reading in Chinese

Even though the majority of characters contain a phonetic radical, the information contained in the phonetic radical is usually an unreliable guide to its pronunciation. Yin (1991) estimated that no more than 38 per cent of characters contain a phonetic radical that is a consistent guide to the correct oral reading of characters in Putonghua. Furthermore, it is not always possible to read aloud a character correctly by decoding component parts, unlike alphabetic scripts where it is possible to read aloud many words by decoding their constituent letters. This can be seen by considering two facts about orthography in Chinese. First, phonetic radicals can be positioned to the left or to the right (or the top or the bottom) of a character. For example, the phonetic radical 'qi' 其 is on the right for the character 棋 and means 'Chinese chess', but it is on the left for the character 期 which means 'a period of time'. Second, character components can act as both the phonetic radical and the semantic radical in different words. For example, the character 木 which means 'wood' is a semantic radical in over 1,500 Chinese characters, including 棋 'qi', however, it is also the phonetic radical in the character 沐 'mu' which means 'wash'. Therefore, knowing which component in a character is the phonetic and which is the semantic cannot be determined from orthographic information alone. To read aloud a Chinese character correctly, the reader must know the pronunciation of the character as a whole. This means that oral reading in Chinese is always a lexical event. We have argued (Yin and Butterworth, 1992; Weekes *et al.*, 1997a, 1997b) that oral reading can proceed via two pathways: a *lexical semantic pathway* allowing reading for meaning and a *direct lexical pathway* linking orthography to phonological components.

Many psycholinguists distinguish between regular and irregular Chinese characters. A regular character contains a phonetic radical that is congruent with the pronunciation of the character as a whole. However, the majority of compound characters (at least 60 per cent) can be considered irregular in pronunciation because there is an unpredictable correspondence between their components and the pronunciation of the whole character. In order to read aloud an irregular character correctly, a Chinese reader must know the correct pronunciation of the character and inhibit the legitimate (though incorrect) alternative pronunciations of components. Ho and Bryant (1997b) classified compound characters as high regularity if they contained a phonetic component that was homophonic with the compound itself; medium regularity if they contained a phonetic component that shared the same onset and rime with the compound but was pronounced in a different tone; and low regularity if they had a phonetic component with a different onset, rime and tone. The latter are examples of pure irregular compound characters. An important point is that irregular characters can be read legitimately (though incorrectly) in more than one way. This leads to a tendency for beginning readers, inexperienced readers and some acquired dyslexic patients to read irregular characters according to legitimate alternative readings. This type of error is called a Legitimate Alternative Reading of Components or LARC. Weekes and Chen (1999) called this type of reading 'surface dyslexia' in Chinese.

The Pinyin script

Pinyin is another type of script that is now widely used in mainland China. Pinyin is made up of the Roman alphabet together with inflectional symbols (marked stress) that are used to represent the different pronunciations of Chinese syllables. Pinyin was introduced in the 1970s in mainland China to enhance the teaching of literacy among beginning readers and is now compulsory in all elementary schools. Pinyin words are learned during the first stages of literacy and these words are later paired with characters to link orthographic units (strokes, radicals, characters) with phonology (syllables, onsets, rimes and tones). Recent surveys in China suggest that Pinyin is now used extensively for writing. This is because most literate speakers write characters using an electronic format by typing syllables into an alphabetic keyboard that can then be mapped on to a choice of characters presented on-screen for writing. Pinyin is not compulsory in Hong Kong nor is it used in Taiwan where a different phonetic script called Zhu Yin Fu Hao is used to learn traditional characters.

DYSLEXIA IN CHINESE?

Prevalence of dyslexia in Chinese

We know little about the prevalence of dyslexia in China and even less about the cognitive and biological mechanisms that might cause dyslexia in Chinese. Some researchers have expressed doubts over the existence of dyslexia in Chinese. This debate over the definition and the nature of dyslexia in Chinese stems from differences over where (Canada, mainland China, Hong Kong and Taiwan) and how research has been carried out. For example, Kline and Lee (1972) reported a cross-cultural study on reading disability comparing the reading of English words and Chinese characters among Canadian bilingual speakers (n = 277 students all simultaneously learning English and Chinese). These bilingual children had a lower incidence of reading difficulties with characters than with words. Kuo (1978) conducted a study of 11,557 pupils from elementary schools in Taiwan and argued that, even though dyslexia was present, the incidence of dyslexia was relatively low (2.9 per cent). By contrast, Stevenson *et al.* (1982) reported similar levels of dyslexia in Chinese- and English-speaking children.

Studies of monolingual Chinese-speaking children with dyslexia are rare. However, there is no doubt that a proportion of Chinese-speaking children with an average IQ (or above) struggle to attain literacy in Chinese. Reports suggest that these children make a variety of reading and writing errors including stroke confusions and omissions, LARC errors, semantic errors, homophone substitutions and writing of non-existent characters revealing the application of phonetic principles in the transference of sound to print (Moser, 1994).

In order to determine the characteristics of dyslexia in mainland China we are carrying out an ongoing survey with elementary school pupils in Beijing. The study is designed to detect the common symptoms of dyslexia in Chinese speakers. The main diagnostic criterion for a diagnosis of dyslexia is a discrepancy between intelligence (measured via Ravens Coloured Progressive Matrices) and reading achievement for a given grade, i.e. average intelligence with delayed reading. So far we have collected data from over 8,000 students. The prevalence of dyslexia is relatively low (1.92 per cent) which is consistent with the lower ratio of dyslexia reported in Taiwan (Kuo, 1978). Despite this, the study found similarities between dyslexia in Chinese and Indo-European languages. For example, there are differences in prevalence between sex and handedness. More boys (2.63 per cent) have dyslexia than girls (1.17 per cent) and the prevalence of dyslexia is higher in left-handed (5.53 per cent) than right-handed students (1.83 per cent). Another finding is that, as grade increases, the prevalence of dyslexia decreases (ranging from 2.56 per cent in Grade 2 to 1.54 per cent in Grade 6). This suggests to us that early reading problems might be the result of a delay in development that can be overcome with further tuition or exposure to print in Chinese. All pupils show a mixed variety of reading problems ranging from difficulties with the visual configuration of characters to semantic and LARC errors. One interesting finding from our survey is that even though the prevalence of delayed reading with Chinese characters is relatively low, the percentages of beginning readers who have problems reading Pinyin are higher and comparable to estimates of dyslexia in alphabetic scripts. Moreover, the errors of pupils who manifest problems reading Pinyin share many common characteristics such as a tendency to confuse the letters 'b', 'd', 'p' and 'q'.

Chinese scripts and dyslexia

One unique feature of Chinese characters is their visual complexity. The visual and graphomotor problems that are sometimes reported for dyslexics may have an impact on learning to read and write in Chinese because here literacy requires making fine visual distinctions between heterographic homophones. Surprisingly, however, research data are not consistent with this hypothesis. Although there are only a few studies that have looked at this question, reports of visual problems in Chinese dyslexia are rare (Tzeng *et al.*, 1995). Woo and Hoosain (1984) found that dyslexics made more visual errors in character recognition than controls, indicating the importance of visual processing in skilled reading of characters. However, dyslexic children made relatively more errors when processing the phonetic and semantic radical components in the character, suggesting that visual deficits are not an exclusive problem in Chinese dyslexia. Indeed, given that many dyslexic children have unimpaired visual memory (though poor phonological awareness), the task of learning to read in Chinese may actually be *easier* for dyslexic children. The classic study by Rozin *et al.* (1971) demonstrated this when they taught American dyslexic pupils to read words printed as Chinese characters and found that they were more successful at reading English words presented as Chinese characters. This suggests to us that the unique properties of a script will determine the phenotype of dyslexia in different language environments and that, critically, many of these properties may diminish the tendency for phonological processing impairments to have an effect on reading and writing in Chinese.

That is not to say that phonological processing problems are not a key feature of dyslexia in Chinese. We know from studies of children in Hong Kong that problems with phonological awareness are a characteristic feature of dyslexia in Chinese. Ho and Lai (1999) examined the rapid naming-speed of dyslexic children on tasks of naming digits, colours, pictures and Chinese characters as well as phonological memory tasks such as digit repetition, word repetition and non-word repetition. Their results showed that naming-speed was slower for dyslexics and that performance on phonological memory tasks was worse for dyslexics than controls, suggesting these are core deficits in Chinese dyslexia. Ho et al. (2000) also found that dyslexic children performed significantly worse than controls on a variety of other phonological processing tasks. Taken together, these data suggest Chinese dyslexic children have naming speed and phonological memory deficits that are similar to their peers from Indo-European language environments (see also Chan and Siegel, 2001; Ho and Bryant, 1997a; Siok and Fletcher, 2001).

How is dyslexia diagnosed in China?

There are very few diagnostic tests for dyslexia available in Chinese. In elementary and secondary schools Chinese language is a major course of instruction and there are tests used to examine character reading ability. Pupils are required to master specific characters throughout the whole of elementary school and by the time they graduate from elementary school they are expected to know 2,500 Chinese characters. The middle and final Chinese examinations are important language tests and they are given in all schools. There are items where oral reading ability is measured in these examinations and this provides information about reading level achievement. As dyslexia is not a concern for families or teachers, there are few remedial facilities. If a child has suspected dyslexia, a parent would be referred to a general hospital. Consultants may come from Neurology or Psychiatry or, more rarely in the larger cities, from Psychology departments. Children may be referred to local psychiatric hospitals. In local teaching training universities or in advanced schools, psychologists or an education specialist would provide consultation. A recent trend in the larger cities of China is for schools to establish psychological education and consultation. However, as dyslexia is not treated as a serious disorder, many doctors and psychologists have little knowledge of aetiology and treatment. However, in recent years, clinical psychology services are becoming more available in the larger cities (Beijing, Shanghai and Guangzhou).

There is no organization specializing in the assessment or remediation of dyslexia in mainland China. The Learning Disabilities Research Association of China (LDRAC) is a national, non-profit, volunteer organization with a membership that includes professionals and education administrative personnel from a variety of educational settings. The mission of LDRAC is to advance the education and general welfare of elementary and secondary school pupils who have perceptual, conceptual, or coordinative disabilities. There are three major research and educational settings for dyslexia: (1) the Institute of Psychology, Chinese Academy of Sciences, Beijing; (2) the Special Education Department, Beijing Normal University, Beijing; and (3) the Institute of Education Research,

Beijing. Two websites relevant to dyslexia in China are www.brainweb.com.cn which is dedicated to brain research, cognitive neuroscience and neuropsychology. Dyslexia is one focus of the website and this includes discussion and consultation forums for dyslexics and families. The other website is www.eastudy.org which is linked to the LDRAC.

REFERENCES

Chan, C.K.K. and Siegel, L.S. (2001) Phonological processing in reading Chinese among normally achieving and poor readers. *Journal of Experimental Child Psychology*, 80(1), 23–43.

Chen, M.J. (1996) An overview of the characteristics of the Chinese writing system. *Asia Pacific Journal of Speech, Language and Hearing*, 1, 43–54.

De Francis, J. (1989) *Visible Speech: The Diverse Oneness of Writing Systems*. Honolulu: University of Hawaii Press.

Henderson, L. (1982) *Orthography and Word Recognition in Reading*. London: Academic Press.

Ho, C.S.H. and Bryant, P. (1997a) Phonological skills are important in learning to read Chinese. *Developmental Psychology*, 33(6), 946–951.

Ho, C.S.H. and Bryant, P. (1997b) Learning to read Chinese beyond the logographic phase. *Reading Research Quarterly*, 32(3), 276–289.

Ho, C.S.H. and Lai, D.N.C. (1999) Naming-speed deficits and phonological memory deficits in Chinese developmental dyslexia. *Learning and Individual Differences*, 11(2), 173–186.

Ho, C.S.H., Law, T.P.S. and Ng, P.M. (2000) The phonological deficit hypothesis in Chinese developmental dyslexia. *Reading and Writing*, 13(1–2), 57–79.

Huang, H.S. and Hanley, J.R. (1994) Phonological awareness and visual skills in learning to read Chinese and English. *Cognition*, 54, 73–98.

Kline, C.L. and Lee, N. (1972) A trans-cultural study of dyslexia: Analysis of language disabilities in 277 Chinese children simultaneously learning to read and write in English and in Chinese. *Journal of Special Education*, 6(1), 19–72.

Kuo, W.F. (1978) A preliminary study of reading disability in the Republic of China. *Collected Papers*, 20, 57–78. Taiwan: National Taiwan Normal University.

Moser, D. (1994) Phonetic processes in writing Chinese: Evidence from written errors. In Qicheng Jing, Houcan Zhang and Danling Peng (eds), *Information Processing of Chinese Language*. Beijing: Normal University Publishing Company.

Rozin, P., Poritsky, S. and Sotsky, R. (1971) American children with reading problems can easily learn to read English represented in Chinese characters. *Science*, 171, 1264–1267.

Siok, W.T. and Fletcher, P. (2001) The role of phonological awareness and visual-orthographic skills in Chinese reading acquisition. *Developmental Psychology*, 37(6), 886–899.

Stevenson, H.W., Stigler, J.W., Lucker, G.W. and Lee, S.Y. (1982) Reading disabilities: The case of Chinese, Japanese and English. *Child Development*, 53, 1164–1182.

Tzeng, O.J.L. and Wang W.S.-Y. (1983) The first two r's. *American Scientist*, 71(3), 238–243.

Tzeng, O.J.L, Zhong, H.L., Hung, D.L. and Lee, W.L. (1995) Learning to be a conspirator: A tale of becoming a good Chinese reader. In B. de Gelder and J. Morais (eds), *Speech and Reading*. London: Erlbaum (UK).

Wang W.S.-Y. (1973) The Chinese language. *Scientific American*, 228, 50–60.

Weekes, B.S. and Chen, H.-Q. (1999) Surface dyslexia in Chinese. *Neurocase*, 5(2), 161–172.

Weekes, B.S., Chen, M.J. and Yin, W.G. (1997a) Anomia without dyslexia in Chinese. *Neurocase*, 3, 51–60.

Weekes, B.S., Chen, M.J. and Yin, W.G. (1997b) Anomia without surface dyslexia in Chinese. *Brain and Language*, 60(1), 140–143.

Yin, W.G. (1991) On reading Chinese characters: An experimental and neuropsychological study. PhD thesis, University College London.

Yin, W.G. and Butterworth, B. (1992) Deep and surface dyslexia in Chinese. In H.C. Chen and O.J.L. Tzeng (eds), *Language Processing in Chinese*. Amsterdam: Elsevier Science Publishers.

4

RESEARCH ON DYSLEXIA IN DANISH

Dorthe Haven and Birgit Dilling Jandorf

INTRODUCTION

This chapter will focus on what we believe to be the results of a fruitful approach concerning research on dyslexia in Denmark that has gained increasing popularity in the past few decades. This approach is based on an operational definition of dyslexia and on evidence from several studies carried out on a Danish orthography. First, we provide a brief historical overview of dyslexia in Denmark.

AN HISTORICAL OVERVIEW

Throughout history many researchers have attempted to define dyslexia in ways that reflected a particular view of the causes of dyslexia. As in many other countries, it was among physicians that Danish research in the dyslexia field began. Professor Henning Skydsgaard, who was an opthalmologist, published the first thesis *Den konstitutionelle dyslexi* (Constitutional Dyslexia) in 1942. It is said to be the world's first on this subject (Norrie, 1960). He defined dyslexia as hereditary, with a predominant tendency of left-handedness and mainly affecting males. He also defined dyslexia as being independent of intelligence and stated that dyslexics have a normal speech function and no sensory dysfunctions such as vision and hearing problems. Skydsgaard also adds that dyslexics' reading development is slow and may never reach an age-matched reading level. Professor Skydsgaard concluded that dyslexia is a language problem (Skydsgaard, 1942). In 1955 came the next thesis on dyslexia *Om medfødt ordblindhed* (On Congenital Dyslexia) by Professor Knud Hermann, who was a neurologist. Professor Hermann stressed the hereditary component in word blindness and also the fact that a definition can only be descriptive, as the specific underlying causes have not yet been found. However, Professor Hermann found the directional function to be a common underlying factor in

International Book of Dyslexia: A Cross-Language Comparison and Practice Guide. Edited by Ian Smythe, John Everatt and Robin Salter.   ISBN 0471498416   © 2004 John Wiley & Sons, Ltd.

congenital word blindness. These directional difficulties were also found to cause persistent reversals in spelling and speech difficulties such as transposition of syllables (Hermann, 1955). Though these definitions are from the beginnings of dyslexia research, and therefore are not the most up-to-date ones, we wonder how much of them we would still include in our present definition of dyslexia.

THE LATEST DANISH DESCRIPTION AND DEFINITION OF DYSLEXIA

Professor Carsten Elbro formulated a definition of dyslexia that has now been published in the national encyclopaedia:

> Dyslexia: severe difficulties in learning to read and write caused by a slow and inaccurate coding of letters and letter patterns into speech sounds and sound patterns. Dyslexics are particularly disabled with written words they have not seen before. Their misreadings and misspellings are often inconsistent with common letter-sound relations, e.g. tale read as 'table', or her written as 'his'. In 1990 7 per cent of Danish adults called themselves dyslexic, while 3 per cent were found to read everyday texts very poorly. Dyslexia is not caused by low intelligence, visual problems, or difficulties in telling left from right. Most dyslexics are poor at segmentation of coherent speech into single speech sounds (phonemes) which correspond to letters, the basic units of written language. Thus, dyslexia often occurs in connection with other language problems (dysphasia). Symmetry between left and right upper parts of the temporal cortex of the brain has been found in cases of severe dyslexia, where left asymmetry is the normal pattern. A predisposition to dyslexia is hereditary. This is the case for difficulties with letter-sound conversion that are characteristic of dyslexia as well as for the difficulties in phonemic segmentation. Most dyslexics are able to acquire some reading and spelling skills. Early, systematic language and reading instruction has proven particularly effective.
>
> (Elbro, 1999)

This definition is comparable to the research-based definition put forward by Reid Lyon and the International Dyslexia Association (Lyon, 1995). Both stress that the core deficit in dyslexia is the phoneme-grapheme correspondence. All of the above mentioned descriptions or definitions include the hereditary component in dyslexia. But this latest Danish definition correlates with the theory put forward by Hermann, that a neurological deficit (direction function) underlies dyslexia. Left–right disorientation cannot be the cause of dyslexia.

RESEARCH INTO THE CORE PROBLEM OF DYSLEXIA

From a number of studies in Denmark it is now well known that many problems in reading can be traced back to fundamental difficulties in making use of the alphabetic principle (Elbro, 1990). The phonemic principle is the one that constitutes all alphabetic writing systems. According to this principle, single letters represent spoken sounds at approximately the phoneme level. Few languages have a one-to-one correspondence between letters and sounds but in any case letters in principle represent speech sounds at a level roughly corresponding to what is called phonemes in linguistics.

These difficulties are seen in a variety of ways, but one of the clearest and best documented is a difficulty in non-word reading. Deficits in such phonological recoding have been found in poor readers across a wide range of general cognitive abilities, and are characteristic of adults with a school history of difficulties in learning to read. This failure is long-lasting and in many cases clearly detectable well into childhood (Elbro *et al.*, 1994).

SUB-TYPES OF DYSLEXIA

Teachers frequently observe that dyslexics use somewhat different strategies in reading. The most commonly observed difference is that between a more word-by-word oriented strategy and that of a painstaking letter-by-letter recoding strategy. Elbro (1990) found that some severely dyslexic teenagers (1 per cent of the most severely affected) displayed a more pronounced word-by-word strategy than any of the reading-level matched normal controls (from the 2nd and 3rd grades). This finding may not be so surprising given that dyslexics have such great difficulties with phonological processing in reading. After years of struggling with letter-sound correspondence, some dyslexics may give up and try to rely on a whole-word recognition strategy.

Dyslexics, who continue to use a letter-by-letter reading strategy, would seem to be the ones who use a strategy ill-suited to their abilities. In fact, Elbro showed in a (1993) study that this slow spelling strategy can be viewed as an effort to retrieve the word to be read, and that dyslexics exhibiting this strategy tended to be relatively slow in picture naming. Some researchers have suggested that dyslexics with a pronounced letter-by-letter decoding strategy may have problems with visual form memory. However, this visual hypothesis has never received empirical support in Denmark. The cause is more likely to be verbal. The reportedly very slow development of dyslexics with a continued tendency to use a letter-by-letter recoding strategy fits in well with the view that they may have a 'double deficit'. This hypothesis is based upon the finding that some dyslexics are slow in rapid automatized naming, i.e. naming of a series of colours, figures, digits, and letters. They may have an additional problem on top of their primary problem with phonological recoding in reading, and they are among the most severely affected dyslexics and have a poor prognosis in so far as they continue to be slow readers (Wolf, 1997).

UNDERLYING LINGUISTIC CAUSES

Dyslexia research took a major leap when in 1988 Lundberg, Frost and Petersen conducted the first study of phonological awareness on the eastern Danish island of Bornholm. The training programme aimed at directing the attention of the children towards the form of the spoken language rather than its content. It proceeds in a highly structured format from listening games and activities with whole words and with rhymes to activities that direct the attention of the pre-school children towards individual phonemes. The results of this study showed that the programme had a considerable positive impact not only on the phoneme awareness of the children, but also on their subsequent reading and spelling development. Furthermore, the study showed that this kind of training was especially beneficial for children with weak phonological awareness skills at the beginning of pre-school (Lundberg *et al.*, 1988).

Elbro, Nielsen and Petersen found in 1994 that dyslexics are not only behind their peers in reading and closely related skills, such as spelling and rapid naming of letters. They are also behind in most language abilities, including receptive and production vocabulary, verbal short-term memory, and awareness of phonemes, rhymes and morphemes, and syntax. But the problem with correlational studies is that it is impossible to distinguish between causes and the consequences of reading difficulties.

Elbro and his group of researchers conducted the Copenhagen Dyslexia Study from 1994 to 1997 which was a combined prediction and intervention study. The study focused on early indicators of dyslexia in children at risk, namely, in the children of dyslexic parents. Approximately 80 children of dyslexic parents and approximately 80 children of parents with normal reading were followed from the beginning of pre-school class until the beginning of 3rd grade.

The results of this study showed that three measures seemed to be the main precursors: (1) knowledge of letter names; (2) phonemic awareness; and (3) quality of phonological representations of spoken words (Elbro et al., 1998). Four out of five children who later developed reading difficulties could be identified before entering pre-school class.

The training part of the Copenhagen Dyslexia Study showed that phoneme awareness training also has a preventive effect in groups of at-risk children (Borstrøm and Elbro, 1997). In this training study 36 at-risk children attending 27 different classes received intensive and extensive instruction in phonemic awareness. The children received highly structured phonological awareness training for 17 weeks. When their development was compared with that of 52 other at-risk children at the beginning of 2nd grade, a significant reduction in the incidence of possible dyslexia was observed – from 40 per cent in the control group to 17 per cent in the experimental group.

SOCIAL CONSEQUENCES

Difficulty with phonological processing in reading is also a powerful predictor of the choice of education after school. In a longitudinal study, the reading comprehension spelling and decoding skills of a group of Danish teenagers were studied just before they left school (Elbro et al., 1997). One year later they were contacted and interviewed again. The poorest readers were compared with a group of average readers, and significant differences were found in the choice of further education and associated social indicators. Among the poor readers, not a single participant was enrolled in upper secondary school, whereas more than half of the average readers were. The single best predictor of choice of education was phonological recoding in reading (pseudo-homophone detection) at grade 9 – not reading comprehension.

These differences were not explained by differences in the socio-economic backgrounds of the teenagers, that is, the educational level, job, and status of their parents. In fact, the strongest correlation was found between the choice of education among teenagers and the reading ability of their parents – in terms of presence or absence of reading difficulties. Even after two years, only 2 per cent of the poor readers had entered upper secondary school (Haven, 1998).

Social consequences of reading difficulties were also found in an earlier literacy study (Elbro, 1991), that showed that adult poor readers in general have less training (if any) than good readers, and they are considerably more often out of the labour market than good readers are.

COMPENSATORY STRATEGIES

There has been an increased focus on the role of morpheme recognition as a compensatory strategy for dyslexics. A study conducted by Elbro and Arnbak (1996) showed that the use of morpheme recognition was partly dependent upon awareness of morphemes in the spoken language. A second study – a pilot training study – focused on morpheme awareness. These results may indicate that morpheme recognition may be a true compensatory strategy for dyslexics (Arnbak and Elbro 2001).

COMPUTER-AIDED READING

In a series of studies at the Centre of Reading Research in Denmark, research on the effects of PC-based systems, that give dyslexics the opportunity to hear difficult words read aloud (by synthetic speech) and segmented into letters, syllables or morphemes, is being conducted. In the first programme called 'Syntekst', the dyslexics could both read and write with speech-feedback. The other programme, called 'Synord', is a combined reading and spelling programme, where the pupils work with morphemes and syllables. The Centre hopes that they will be able to include speech recognition in a third programme called 'Computerlæs', so dyslexics can have instant feedback and support to ensure whether they have read correctly or not (Elbro, 1991).

FUTURE RESEARCH

Most reading difficulties can be prevented, but this is a large and extensive task, which demands full utilization of the knowledge available. Still many questions remain unanswered in relation to reading development and dyslexia. But scientists are working continuously and gaining more knowledge about the reading process and how teachers and others can help children with dyslexia. The Centre of Reading Research, Copenhagen University, is participating together with 16 other countries to uncover the relevance of variations in alphabetic orthographies for the occurrence of dyslexia, character and language correlates.

An obvious target for dyslexia research in the future is still the prevention of reading difficulties and hopefully preventive programmes will be a part of everyday school practices. But the development and implementation of such programmes will depend on reliable knowledge and teacher resources. We think that research will concentrate on ability differences among dyslexics rather than looking at a whole range of abilities.

Future research will also be concerned with reading demands within a number of the daily activities in our information society. The system of education will in the future make clear what kind of reading demands are expected in different training and education environments. New screening materials and assessments will be developed, which adapt the relation between the reading level of the participants and the reading demands in training or education. Probably we will see more systematic evaluations of special education for children, adolescents and adults. We hope that more efforts will be made to emphasize how important it is to be able to read and write, and the information will be given in such a way that the recipients feel that they are personally concerned. Guidance, linguistic accessibility and breadth will be the keywords.

REFERENCES

Arnbak, E. and Elbro, C. (2001) The effects of morphological awareness training on the reading and spelling skills of young dyslexics. *Scandinavian Journal of Educational Research*, 44(3), 229–251.

Borstrøm, I. and Elbro, C. (1997) Prevention of dyslexia in kindergarten: Effects of phoneme awareness training with children of dyslexic parents. In C. Hulme and M. Snowling (eds), *Dyslexia: Biology, Cognition and Intervention*. London: Whurr.

Elbro, C. (1990) *Differences in Dyslexia: A Study of Reading Strategies and Deficits in a Linguistic Perspective*. Copenhagen: Munksgaard.

Elbro, C. (1991) Computer-based techniques in remediation of dyslexia. In I. Lundberg and T. Høien (eds), *Literacy in a World of Change: Perspectives on Reading and Reading Disability*. Stavanger: Center for Reading Research.

Elbro, C. (1993) Dyslexic reading strategies and lexical access: A comparison and validation of reading strategy distributions in dyslexic adolescents and younger, normal readers. In R.M. Joshi and C.K. Leong (eds), *Reading Disabilities and Component Processes*. Dordrecht: Kluwer.

Elbro, C. (1996) Early linguistic abilities and reading development: A review and a hypothesis. *Reading and Writing: An Interdisciplinary Journal*, 8, 453–485.

Elbro, C. (1999) *Ordlindhed: Den store danske encyklopædi*, Vol. 14. Gyldendal.

Elbro, C. and Arnbak, E. (1996) The role of morpheme recognition and morphological awareness in dyslexia. *Annals of Dyslexia*, 46, 209–240.

Elbro, C., Borstrøm, I and Petersen, D.K. (1998) Predicting dyslexia from kindergarten. The importance of distinctness of phonological representations of lexical items. *Reading Research Quarterly*, 33(1), 36–60.

Elbro, C., Haven, D. and Jandorf, B.D. (1997) Gode og dårlige læsere efter 9. klasse. Første del af en efterundersøgelse. *Psykologisk Pædagogisk Rådgivning*, 34(1), 19–42.

Elbro, C., Møller, S. and Nielsen, E.M. (1991) *Danskernes læsefærdigheder*. Copenhagen: Undervisningsministeriet og projekt læsning.

Elbro, C., Nielsen, I. and Petersen, D.K. (1994) Dyslexia in adults: Evidence for deficits in non-word reading and in the phonological representation of lexical items. *Annals of Dyslexia*, 44, 205–226.

Haven, D. (1998) Gode og dårlige læsere efter 9. klasse: Anden del af en efterundersøgelse. *Psykologisk Pædagogisk Rådgivning*, 35(5–6), 454–472.

Hermann, K. (1955) *Om medfødt ordblindhed*. Copenhagen: Munksgaard.

Lundberg, I., Frost, J. and Petersen, O.-P. (1988) Effects of an extensive program for stimulating phonological awareness in preschool children. *Reading Research Quarterly*, 23, 263–284.

Lyon, R.G. (1995) Toward a definition of dyslexia. *Annals of Dyslexia*, 45, 3–27.

Norrie, E. (1960) *Ordblindeundervisning med fonetisk sættekasse*. Copenhagen: Nyt Nordisk Forlag – Arnold Busck.

Skydsgaard, H.B. (1942) *Den konstitutionelle dyslexi*. Copenhagen: Nyt Nordisk Forlag – Arnold Busck.

Wolf, M. (1997) A provisional, integrative account of phonological and naming-speed deficits in dyslexia: Implications for diagnosis and intervention. In B. Blachman (ed.), *Foundations of Reading Acquisition and Dyslexia*. Hillsdale, NJ: Lawrence Erlbaum Associates.

5

DEVELOPMENTAL DYSLEXIA IN THE DUTCH LANGUAGE

Pieter Reitsma

INTRODUCTION

Recent research on developmental dyslexia in the Dutch language is summarized in this chapter. First, an overview of the rules of the Dutch orthography is provided. Dutch orthography appears to be rather transparent when compared to other languages. Some general principles of teaching to read and write are then described. A balanced approach with a strong focus on decoding is most common in the Netherlands. The characteristics of dyslexics in Dutch are listed and a summary of research shows that most are common to dyslexics in other alphabetic languages too. Finally, a brief review of some current treatment approaches is given. It is concluded that there are still many unresolved issues before adequate treatment can be provided to dyslexic individuals in the Netherlands.

DUTCH ORTHOGRAPHY

Dutch spelling can be considered a relatively shallow orthography (Reitsma and Verhoeven, 1990; Nunn, 1998). The relationship between the phonemes in the spoken language and the graphemes in the written forms is rather transparent. In fact, the first and major rule in spelling is that the graphemes are intended to represent the individual phonemes of words. Using the regular grapheme-to-phoneme correspondences, the spoken word can often be reconstructed. As in all other alphabetic orthographies, however, in spelling one has to abstract from assimilation and coarticulation effects, and from individual or dialect variations in pronunciation. For example, the insertion of the schwa in coda clusters is never represented in spelling.

One of the problems in Dutch orthography is the lack of a sufficient number of letters for vowel sounds. Only five letters (a, e, i, o, u) are available to represent the thirteen

International Book of Dyslexia: A Cross-Language Comparison and Practice Guide. Edited by Ian Smythe, John Everatt and Robin Salter. ISBN 0471498416 © 2004 John Wiley & Sons, Ltd.

Dutch vowels (diphthongs not included). The solution is to geminate or combine letters in digraphs: a, aa, e (both for /ɛ/ and the schwa), ee, eu, i, ie, o, oo, oe, u, uu. The three diphthongs of Dutch /ɛi/, /ɑu/, and /œy/ are spelled as digraphs too, but etymology plays a role in the spelling. The diphthong /ɛi/ is spelled as ei or as ij, the latter when the word historically had a long i in its pronunciation. Similar etymological factors determine the choice between the digraphs au or ou for /ɑu/, and sometimes the letter w is added to represent the off-glide in spelling (as in gauw, 'soon'). The /œy/ is spelled as ui, eui (in loan words, 'fauteuil'), or eu.

The single vowel symbols a, e, u, o, i in initial or medial positions of monosyllabic words serve to represent the short vowels. When the letters a, o, or u are positioned at the end of the word, however, they represent long vowels. The i in word-final position is only used in foreign words (e.g. in 'ski'), while ie is used in native words (e.g. in drie – 'three') to represent a long i. The vowel symbols i and u as the last elements of a trigraph vowel stand for the consonant phonemes /j/ and /w/, respectively, as in taai ('tough') and eeuw ('century'). The word-final single e usually represents the neutral 'schwa' vowel (as in 'father'; e.g., de – 'the').

A similar change in pronunciation of a, o, e or u compared to their pronunciation in monosyllabic words appears when these vowel symbols occur in open syllable words (i.e. polysyllabic words with a syllable ending in a vowel). For example, while the long vowel /o/ is represented as a geminated form in a closed syllable in the singular word boom ('tree'), in the plural the same vowel occurs in an open syllable (bomen – 'trees') and is represented by a single symbol. To indicate a short vowel phoneme in this situation, the following consonant letter needs to be written twice (bommen – 'bombs', which is the plural form of bom). Thus the doubling or gemination of the consonant following a single vowel grapheme determines whether this vowel should be pronounced short or long (checked or free), comparable with English (matting – 'mating').

The spelling of the consonants is relatively straightforward. Most consonants meet the requirement of one-to-one correspondence, except four consonants (c, q, x and y) that are predominantly used in words of Latin origin. The c corresponds either to /s/ as in cijfer ('number') or /k/ as in cadeau ('present'), and can also occur in the digraph ch. The q and x are pronounced as /k/ and /ks/ as in English, and the y corresponds to /i/ as in cyclus ('cycle') to /I/ as in 'dyslexia', as /j/ in 'yoghurt', and as /ɛi/ when used in 'mathematics'.

The stop consonants b, d are exceptions in that they normally represent voiced stops, but in word-final position they represent the corresponding voiceless stops /p/ and /t/. Also, the letter g indicates the voiced velar fricative, except in word-final position where it represents the corresponding voiceless sound. In practice, the distinction is often neutralized, however, and nowadays the unvoiced form is frequently pronounced throughout, especially in urban dialects. Other exceptions to a straightforward conversion of consonant letters to phonemes include the digraphs ch for the voiceless velar fricative and both ng, occurring only in final position, and n before k as used to indicate a velar nasal (as in jong – 'young' and bank – 'bank').

In order to assign the correct pronunciation to polysyllabic words, it is often necessary to recognize the affixes and to segment the string of letters into appropriate morphemic units. The correct reading of polysyllabic words and the appropriate assignment of stress certainly require a substantial knowledge of morphology. The rule of congruence or uniformity prescribes that a word (or morpheme) must be spelled in the same way as it appears in a derivation or in a composition. The effect of writing grammatical morphemes congruently is that for each lexical item a constant orthographic representation is provided.

For example, while only one is pronounced, two d's are written in handdoek ('towel'), because the word is a compound of the two words hand ('hand') and doek ('cloth'). Also, while the singular form, hand, of the plural noun handen ('hands') is pronounced with a final voiceless obstruent /t/, it is spelled with a d on account of congruence with the plural form. Final f and s are exceptions to the rule of writing the voiced alternant for the voiceless obstruent in final positions, e.g. huis – huizen ('houses').

Also, the rule of analogy serves to clarify the crucial morphological relationship between words and syntactic function. An example is the spelling of verb forms, which is a regular trial to Dutch schoolchildren (and to many adults as well). The phonologically superfluous final t in hij wordt ('he becomes') is retained in analogy to, for example, hij spreekt ('he speaks') to indicate the third person singular present tense indicative (for other examples of peculiarities of the spelling of Dutch verbs, see Assink, 1985). Another example is the spelling of the noun grootte ('size') in analogy to hoogte ('height'), while grootte has exactly the same pronunciation as the adjective grote (een grote boom – 'a tall tree').

To sum up, the correspondence between graphemes and phonemes is highly regular in Dutch orthography, although there is not a perfect one-to-one relationship. Nondistinctive variation in pronunciation due to sociolects or ideolects is ignored. Departures from a consistent phonemic mapping in the orthography are further motivated by morphological or etymological considerations. Although the spelling is generally rather transparent – 95 per cent of native Dutch words can be considered to be morpho-phonologically regular (Nunn, 1998) – many forms including loan words have to be memorized when the orthographic form is not predictable from the phonological form.

TEACHING TO READ AND WRITE

Normally Dutch children enter elementary school at the age of 4. Although during the first two kindergarten years some preparational education is given, formal reading education at school starts after the summer holidays in the third year. Following international conventions we will refer to this year as Grade 1. By that time most children are 6 years old with a mean age of about 6 and 5 months.

Approaches to initial reading instruction generally incorporate a great amount of explicit phonics instruction right from the very beginning (Reitsma et al., 1981; Reitsma, 1998). The major principle of the method for beginning reading is that children should learn the basic structure of the written language. In order to arrive at an understanding of what the orthography is all about, the instructional strategies (through the teacher's manual) and exercises (through workbooks and skill sheets) are focused on discerning the structural elements of spoken and written words and learning about the correspondences between these two. Most methods are intrinsically word-based in that words are provided that serve as concrete exemplars to illustrate the letter–sound relationships within words. The structure of the word is focused on in different modalities: auditory, visual, articulatory aspects are treated separately and in combination. Learning the structure also implies acquiring the ability to analyse a word into different parts and to synthesize the elements into one whole.

Although varying amounts of time may be spent in the beginning reading books, these books and related instructions are generally completed within four or five months of teaching. Because the basics of decoding the Dutch orthography have been completely covered by then, one can safely conclude that halfway through the first year of formal reading instruction most (not necessarily all) children are able to decode simple, and regularly written, Dutch words.

Since the grapheme–phoneme correspondences in Dutch orthography permit a valid prediction of the pronunciation of a word, the beginning reader is encouraged to identify written words by recoding graphemes into phonemes. The words which are presented in the reading lessons during the first few months are therefore selected on regularity or 'decodability', i.e. all words comprise consistent and unambiguous one-to-one grapheme–phoneme correspondences. Gradually, word length is increased and irregularities or specific context-sensitive conversion rules for letters to sounds are introduced. For example, the principle of pronouncing the single vowel letter as a long phoneme (in open syllables) is generally not dealt with until the second half of the school year. Other difficulties for reading are also attended to, such as reading words in which the final voiced symbol should be pronounced as a voiceless sound (hond – 'dog', /t/ for d), and so on (see the previous section for peculiarities of Dutch orthography).

By and large, reading instruction in the first year is focused on attempts to foster decoding skills. However, it is commonly acknowledged that reading is not a matter of learning to recognize words and then learning to comprehend. Rather, it is matter of learning to recognize words in order to comprehend. Also, reading is not considered an algorithmic process in which straightforward application of a set of rules or procedures will invariably yield comprehension of a text. Although the programmes for early reading include stories to be read, so that reading comprehension is already an integral part, instructional activities specifically oriented toward development of reading comprehension and the establishment of study strategies are predominantly focused upon in higher grades.

INDIVIDUAL DIFFERENCES IN DUTCH BEGINNING READERS

It is evident that not all children become proficient readers. For most children, reading development starts at school with formal education in Grade 1. However, the development of skills necessary to acquire reading skills starts well before the beginning of formal instruction in reading. Even before they start school, differences among children exist as a result of innate competencies and the quality and intensity of parental care invested in them. Taking initial differences between individuals as a starting point, an important question is whether these differences remain stable or whether individuals converge or diverge in level of performance with further instruction in reading.

The Matthew effect model of Stanovich (1986) provides a theoretical framework in which the development of individual differences in reading ability can be described and explained. The Matthew effect refers to the phenomenon that, over time, better readers get even better, and poorer readers become relatively poorer.

Reciprocal relationships between reading and other factors seem to cause these increasing differences. A longitudinal study of three years (Bast and Reitsma, 1998a) clearly indicated increasing individual differences for word recognition skills. An auto-regressive growth model could adequately describe the development of individual differences in word recognition. The absolute difference in word recognition skills increased with time, but the rank ordering of individuals remained stable. Poor readers remain poor readers during the first three grades and the performance gap relative to good readers became larger over the course of development. Differences in phonological skills determine a considerable part of the individual variation in word recognition skill, and vice versa, word recognition skill affects differences in phonological skills.

For reading comprehension, differences in Grade 2 are due to differences in word recognition and vocabulary. The effect of vocabulary increases compared to the effect of word recognition, and is the only significant predictor of reading comprehension at the end of Grade 3. Also, some evidence of interactive relationships between reading and other cognitive skills, behaviour and motivational factors, hypothesized to cause increasing differences between readers, was found. The results indicate that good readers tend to read more frequently in their leisure time than poor readers. The level of word recognition skill is also associated with attitude towards reading. Good readers express more positive attitudes towards reading than poor readers do. Furthermore, children with positive attitudes tend to read more frequently in their leisure time.

Another longitudinal study (De Jong and Van der Leij, 1999) also found an important role for phonological abilities in initial reading acquisition, and they also found that the effects diminished as reading skill further developed. A study by Wesseling and Reitsma (1998, 2001) showed that during kindergarten years only a small increase in phonological skills can be observed, but as soon as reading instruction starts in Grade 1, a sensational increase in phonological abilities is found. It is therefore suggested that instruction which is basically very phonics oriented makes all the difference and almost overrules all previous individual differences.

CHARACTERISTICS OF DIAGNOSED DYSLEXICS

Not all children learn to read within one year and, of course, after the basic skills are acquired, a great deal of practice is needed to attain proficiency. It is evident that not all children become proficient readers (Reitsma and Verhoeven, 1998). At the lower end of the continuum of reading skills are dyslexic children. These children progress only very slowly in their reading development, sometimes without obvious reasons. Although no large-scale data are available in the Netherlands, my estimate is that about 1 or 2 per cent of the children can be diagnosed as pure dyslexics, but often there is comorbidity of other learning problems, or of problems in attention, conduct, or specific speech or general language disorders.

Discussion about the appropriate diagnosis seems inevitable, in the Netherlands too. The common approach in the past has been a diagnosis by exclusion, i.e. dyslexia as an unexpected impairment of reading and spelling development which cannot be attributed to obvious causes, such as lack of opportunities, emotional disturbances, neurological damage, sensory handicaps, or low intelligence. A related approach emphasizes the discrepancy between intelligence and reading attainment, i.e. to determine whether the reading score deviates significantly from the predicted score on the basis of IQ. But there are serious limitations to this approach, one is that it is incorrectly assumed that intelligence is an independent variable that 'explains' variation in reading skill (Van den Bos, 1998), and another that it uses an unwarranted arbitrary cut-off point to define dyslexia (Rispens, 1991). Still another approach is to view dyslexia as a syndrome, which is marked by various signs, such as difficulties in sequencing, and reversals in left–right orientation.

One such an approach in particular research has been published: dyslexics may differ in the extent to which they rely on the left and right brain hemisphere in the learning-to-read process and may therefore differ in various related behavioural signs (Bakker, 1990). The difficulty of the syndrome approach is that it is not clear what does or does not constitute a definitive sign, and whether they are causally linked to reading difficulty or function merely as markers.

In 1995 a committee of the Health Council of the Netherlands prepared a report on the definition and treatment of dyslexia (see Gersons-Wolfensberger and Ruijssenaars, 1997). The following 'working' definition was agreed upon: 'Dyslexia is present when the automatization of word identification (reading) and/or word spelling does not develop or does so very incompletely or with great difficulty.' Automatization refers to the fact that reading should be relatively automatic, and does not require a lot of resources and attention (Yap and van der Leij, 1993). The definition is generally accepted, but discussion continues. From a research perspective, it is clear that in the current definition the orthographic module is considered to be central and distinct from other aspects of intelligence and language. It also leaves open that the reading disorder may take different forms, depending on the subcomponents of the orthographic module.

One of the possibilities is that impairment of the orthographic module is caused by a prior or accompanying impairment in the phonological module. There is some evidence for involvement of phonological deficits in Dutch dyslexics (cf. van den Bos, 1998). For example, van Bon and van der Pijl (1997) found that dyslexics had significantly lower pseudoword repetition scores than reading-ability matched younger normal readers. De Jong (1998) suggested that working memory deficits, i.e. deficits in the capacity to process and store verbal information might be basic to phonological problems of dyslexics. Evidence has been found that there is also a relationship between phonological awareness and the acquisition of new words. For example, De Jong et al. (2000) reported that phonological awareness of 5-year-old kindergartners was related to the paired associate learning of phonologically unfamiliar words. Thus, there is certain evidence that the phonological module may be involved in dyslexia in Dutch, but it is uncertain which phonological level is important and to what extent (explicit) phonological development is dependent on literacy development rather than vice versa (Wesseling and Reitsma, 1998, 2001).

Although the development of the orthographic module may intrinsically be related to phonological awareness, in various studies it has been shown that the acquisition of word-specific orthographic forms is a separate dimension. Research has demonstrated significant individual variations and also that dyslexics are much slower to acquire and store such orthographic information than normally developing readers (Reitsma, 1983a, 1983b, 1989, 1990, 1997). The availability of stored knowledge on word-specific letter patterns may contribute to improved and faster word identification, i.e. recognition of letter clusters instead of letter by letter or cluster decoding. In transparent orthographies like Dutch, a common description of poor readers is that they are 'spellers'. They laboriously translate each letter or letter cluster into its corresponding sound and then synthesize these sounds into a word sound (Wesseling and Reitsma, 2000). Other disabled readers seem to partly recognize some of the words, and attempt to read more fluently, but at the cost of more errors. They seem to guess at words (Hendriks and Kolk, 1997).

The neuropsychologically motivated distinction in L and P types (Bakker, 1990) greatly resembles this popular distinction between spellers and guessers, i.e. dyslexics who are accurate but slow versus dyslexics who are fast but inaccurate. Recent research showed that guessers seem to have a greater level of impairment regarding inappropriate responses.

On tasks such as the Logan stop-signal task, Stroop, or the Tower of London, they also exhibit control inefficiencies which suggests that some comorbidity with attention problems may be present (van der Schoot *et al.*, 2000).

To conclude, the Dutch operational definition of dyslexia allows the possibility that manifestations of serious reading problems can take different forms, depending on which component of the process of learning to read is most strongly affected. This may also have implications for treatment.

TREATMENT OF DYSLEXIA

It is unfortunate that relative little research in the Netherlands has been devoted to the systematic evaluation of treatment approaches; however, this is the situation in many other countries also. A few studies, however, have been reported. For example, Kappers (1997) reported an in-depth study of treatment effects with 80 dyslexics. Although inspired by the neuropsychological theory of Bakker (1990), the treatment was individually tailored, depending on the style of reading, the phase of the learning-to-read process, and the intermediate results of the treatment. Effects on reading performance measured after pre-clinical (home training), clinical, and post-clinical intervention periods, were analysed through multiple time-series and multilevel analyses. Treatment appeared to have robust effects. As to differential results, it was found by comparing the group with the largest rate of gain to the group with the lowest rate of gain that there was no relation between intelligence and the rate of gain in the training. The groups did not differ on the duration of the treatment. The only difference found was that relatively older children with initially higher absolute levels of reading skill benefited most from the treatment programme. Although this research generally presented positive results, replication studies carried out along similar theoretical lines (Dryer *et al.*, 1999) or in the same clinic (van Daal and Reitsma, 1999) were much less positive.

Effective factors probably included the fact that explicit, highly structured exercises were provided to improve the basic skills of decoding and efficiently link the spoken to the written language. A similar treatment approach to attack specific components in impaired decoding seems to have positive effects too. For example, systematic training in phonemic awareness by using a computer program appeared to be successful (Reitsma and Wesseling, 1998). Providing dyslexics with feedback on the sounds of the words during single word decoding exercises also appeared to be beneficial (Spaai *et al.*, 1991; van Daal and Reitsma, 1990, 1993, 2000). Similarly, experiments with dyslexics who repeatedly read words with limited exposure duration showed positive effects (van den Bosch, *et al.*, 1995). Thus, effective procedures for basic skills seem available, also using recent computer-assisted exercises.

But another issue is how to treat dyslexics who seem to have mastered all the basic requirements for decoding, but are unable to attain fluency. Repeated reading is a commonly selected approach, sometimes altered into a 'reading while listening' training. Van Bon *et al.* (1991) compared the effects of repeated reading while listening with those of non-repetitive reading while listening and with non-repetitive error detection. Various practice effects were found, but no transfer to the reading of new texts of single words was obtained. The fact that researchers always are focused on transfer effects, however, should not discredit positive effects for specific materials for dyslexics who are often quite resistant to treatment anyway.

It is generally recognized that a substantial number of poor readers are deficient in decoding skills but have adequate comprehension skills (Bast and Reitsma, 1998b). But there are also children who can decode fairly well but cannot comprehend what they have read. It would be logical to focus remedial instruction on improving the comprehension skills of these children. Research has shown that teaching these children directly and explicitly comprehension strategies and metacognitive knowledge may be quite successful (Walraven and Reitsma, 1993; Reitsma, 1994).

To conclude, although in this chapter some interesting and promising results have been reviewed, overall too little is known about remedial instruction and treatment. Additional research is badly needed, but there is no evidence yet that dyslexia in alphabetic languages should be treated differentially according to the respective languages. Therefore, the international research community should intensify and co-ordinate the efforts to look in more detail at the effective treatment options for dyslexia.

REFERENCES

Assink, E.M.H. (1985) Assessing spelling strategies for the orthography of Dutch verbs. *British Journal of Psychology*, 76, 35–363.

Bakker, D.J. (1990) *Neuropsychological Treatment of Dyslexia*. London: Oxford University Press.

Bast, J.W. and Reitsma, P. (1998a) Analysing the development of individual differences in terms of Matthew effects in reading: Results from a Dutch longitudinal study. *Developmental Psychology*, 34, 1373–1399.

Bast, J.W. and Reitsma, P. (1998b) The simple view of reading: A developmental perspective. In P. Reitsma and L. Verhoeven (eds), *Problems and Interventions in Literacy Development*. Dordrecht, The Netherlands: Kluwer Academic Publishers.

De Jong, P.F. (1998) Working memory deficits of reading disabled children. *Journal of Experimental Child Psychology*, 70, 75–96.

De Jong, P.F., Seveke, M.J. and van Veen, M. (2000) Phonological sensitivity and the acquisition of new words in children. *Journal of Experimental Child Psychology*, 76, 275–301.

De Jong, P.F. and van der Leij, A. (1999) Specific contributions of phonological abilities to early reading acquisition: Results from a Dutch latent variable longitudinal study. *Journal of Educational Psychology*, 91, 450–476.

Dryer, R., Beale, I.L. and Lambert, A.J. (1999) The balance model of dyslexia and remedial training: An evaluative study. *Journal of Learning Disabilities*, 32, 174–186.

Gersons-Wolfensberger, D.C.M. and Ruijssenaars, A.J.J.M. (1997) Definition and treatment of dyslexia: A report by the Committee on Dyslexia of the Health Council of the Netherlands. *Journal of Learning Disabilities*, 30, 209–213.

Hendriks, A.W. and Kolk, H.H.J. (1997) Strategic control in developmental dyslexia. *Cognitive Neuropsychology*, 14, 321–366.

Kappers, E.J. (1997) Outpatient treatment of dyslexia through stimulation of the cerebral hemispheres. *Journal of Learning Disabilities*, 30, 100–125.

Nunn, A.M. (1998) *Dutch Orthography: A Systematic Investigation of the Spelling of Dutch Words*. Den Haag: Holland Academic Graphics.

Reitsma, P. (1983a) Word–specific knowledge in beginning reading. *Journal of Research in Reading*, 6, 41–56.

Reitsma, P. (1983b) Printed word learning in beginning readers. *Journal of Experimental Child Psychology*, 36, 321–339.

Reitsma, P. (1989) Orthographic memory and learning to read. In P.G. Aaron and R. Malatesha Joshi (eds), *Reading and Writing Disorders in Different Orthographic Systems*. Dordrecht: Kluwer.

Reitsma, P. (1990) The acquisition of orthographic knowledge. In P. Reitsma and L. Verhoeven (eds), *Acquisition of Reading in Dutch*. Dordrecht: Foris Publications.

Reitsma, P. (1994) Instructional approaches to problems in reading comprehension of dyslexics. In K.P. van den Bos, L.S. Siegel, D.J. Bakker and D.L. Share (eds), *Current Directions in Dyslexia Research*. Lisse: Swets and Zeitlinger.

Reitsma, P. (1997) How to get friends in beginning reading. In C.K. Leong and R.M. Joshi (eds), *Cross-Language Studies of Learning to Read and Spell: Phonologic and Orthographic Processing*. Dordrecht: Kluwer.

Reitsma, P. (1998) Literacy teaching in the Low Countries. In V. Edwards and D. Corson (eds), *Encyclopedia of Language and Education*, Vol. 2, *Literacy*. Dordrecht: Kluwer.

Reitsma, P., Komen, N. and Kapinga, T. (1981) Methoden voor aanvankelijk lezen: vergelijk van leesresultaten na een jaar. [Methods for beginning reading: a comparison of effects after one year]. *Pedagogische Studiën*, 58, 174–189.

Reitsma, P. and Verhoeven, L. (1990) Introduction. In P. Reitsma and L. Verhoeven (eds), *Acquisition of Reading in Dutch*. Dordrecht: Foris Publications.

Reitsma, P. and Verhoeven, L. (1998) Problems in literacy acquisition and interventions. In P. Reitsma and L. Verhoeven (eds), *Problems and Interventions in Literacy Development*. Dordrecht: Kluwer Academic Publishers.

Reitsma, P. and Wesseling, R. (1998) Effect of computer-assisted training of blending skills in kindergartens. *Scientific Studies of Reading*, 2, 301–320.

Rispens, J. (1991) The irrelevance of IQ to the definition of learning disabilities: Some empirical evidence. *Journal of Learning Disabilities*, 24, 434–438.

Spaai, G.W.G., Reitsma, P. and Ellermann, H.H. (1991) Effect of segmented and whole-word sound feedback on learning to read single words. *Journal of Educational Research*, 84, 204–213.

Stanovich, K.E. (1986) Matthew effects in reading: some consequences of individual differences in the acquisition of literacy. *Reading Research Quarterly*, 21, 360–407.

Van Bon, W.H.J., Bokseveld, L.M., Font Freide, T.A.M. and Van Hurk, A.J.M. (1991) A comparison of three methods of reading-while-listening. *Journal of Learning Disabilities*, 24, 471–476.

Van Bon, W.H.J. and van der Pijl, J. (1997) Effects of word length and wordlikeness on pseudoword repetition by poor and normal readers. *Applied Psycholinguistics*, 18, 101–114.

Van Daal, V.H.P. and Reitsma, P. (1990) Effects of independent word practice with segmented and whole-word sound feedback in disabled readers. *Journal of Research in Reading*, 13, 133–148.

Van Daal, V.H.P. and Reitsma, P. (1993) The use of speech feedback by normal and disabled readers in computer-based reading practice. *Reading and Writing*, 5, 243–259.

Van Daal, V.H.P. and Reitsma, P. (1999) Effects of outpatient treatment of dyslexia. *Journal of Learning Disabilities*, 32, 447–456.

Van Daal, V.H.P. and Reitsma, P. (2000) Computer-assisted learning to read and spell: Results from two pilot studies. *Journal of Research in Reading*, 23(2), 181–193.

Van den Bos, K.P. (1998) IQ, phonological awareness, and continuous-naming speed related to decoding in poor Dutch readers. *Dyslexia*, 4, 73–89.

Van den Bosch, K., van Bon, H.H.J. and Schreuder, R. (1995) Poor reader's decoding skills: Effects of training with limited exposure duration. *Reading Research Quarterly*, 30, 110–125.

Van der Schoot, M., Licht, R., Horsley, T.M. and Sergeant, J.A. (2000) Inhibitory deficits in reading disability depend on subtype: Guessers but not spellers. *Child Neuropsychology*, 6, 297–312.

Walraven, A.M.A. and Reitsma, P. (1993) The effect of teaching strategies for reading comprehension to poor readers and the surplus effect of activating prior knowledge. In D.J. Leu and C.K. Kinzer (eds), *Examining Central Issues in Literacy: Research, Theory, and Practice*. Chicago: NRC.

Wesseling, R. and Reitsma, P. (1998) Phonemically aware: Just a hop, skip and a jump. In P. Reitsma and L. Verhoeven (eds), *Problems and Interventions in Literacy Development*. Dordrecht: Kluwer Academic Publishers.

Wesseling, R. and Reitsma, P. (2000) The transient role of explicit phonological recoding for reading acquisition. *Reading and Writing*, 13, 313–336.

Wesseling, R. and Reitsma, P. (2001) Preschool phonological representations and development of reading skills. *Annals of Dyslexia*, 52, 203–229.

Yap, R.L. and Van der Leij, A. (1993) Word processing in dyslexics: An automatic decoding deficit? *Reading and Writing: An Interdisciplinary Journal*, 5, 261–279.

6

DEVELOPMENTAL DYSLEXIA IN ENGLISH

Usha Goswami

INTRODUCTION

The usual definition of developmental dyslexia states that affected children have specific problems with reading and spelling in the absence of any apparent environmental or neurological cause. In English, these problems with both reading and spelling are quite marked. The irregular orthography of English causes accuracy as well as speed deficits in reading, and makes the achievement of accurate spelling extremely difficult.

The most widely accepted hypothesis of the cause of developmental dyslexia in English is the 'phonological representations' hypothesis (e.g., Goswami, 2000; Snowling, 2000). This hypothesis is well supported by recent studies in developmental psychology and brain imaging, as described below. The 'phonological representations' hypothesis argues that the central deficit in developmental dyslexia is a linguistic one. It is thought that the literacy difficulties experienced by dyslexics are most likely due to pre-existing difficulties in the accurate specification and neural representation of the sequential sounds of speech. In order to understand the possible basis for these representational difficulties, it is therefore important to understand the normal development of lexical representation.

THE NORMAL DEVELOPMENT OF LEXICAL REPRESENTATION

Children with developmental dyslexia often appear to have good spoken language skills and extensive vocabularies. However, dyslexic children appear to have difficulties in the accurate specification of phonology when storing lexical representations of speech. A schematic view of a lexical representation is shown in Figure 6.1. Researchers in

International Book of Dyslexia: A Cross-Language Comparison and Practice Guide. Edited by Ian Smythe, John Everatt and Robin Salter.   ISBN 0471498416   © 2004 John Wiley & Sons, Ltd.

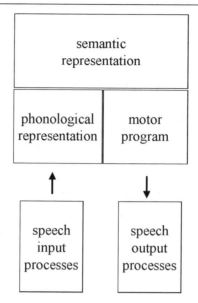

FIGURE 6.1 Schematic depiction of a lexical representation

child phonology have shown that, in the normal course of development, the phonological aspects of children's lexical representations become increasingly segmental and distinctly specified in terms of phonetic features. When vocabulary size is small, there is no need to represent words in a systematic or detailed manner, and so early word representations are thought to encode fairly global phonological characteristics (e.g., Jusczyk, 1993). As vocabulary grows, these holistic representations are gradually 'restructured', so that smaller segments of sound are represented (Metsala and Walley, 1998: Lexical Restructuring Theory).

Developmentally, children appear to first represent syllables (a word like *wigwam* has two syllables), then onsets and rimes (the onset in a syllable corresponds to the sound/s before the vowel, the rime corresponds to the vowel and any subsequent sounds, e.g., *p – it*; *scr – ew*), and ultimately, phonemes (phonemes are the smallest units of sound that change word meaning, e.g., *pit* differs from *sit*, *pot* and *pin* by the initial, medial and final phonemes respectively). Most children have represented syllables, onsets and rimes prior to being taught to read. The degree to which segmental representation has taken place is in turn thought to determine how easily the child will become phonologically 'aware' and will learn to read and write.

According to Metsala and Walley (1998), lexical restructuring is relatively word-specific, depending on factors such as overall vocabulary size/rate of expansion, word frequency/familiarity, and the number of similar-sounding words in the lexicon (phonological 'neighbourhood density'). For example, words with many similar-sounding neighbours (words in 'dense' neighbourhoods) should experience more pressure for phoneme-level restructuring than words with few similar-sounding neighbours (words in 'sparse' neighbourhoods). There is already evidence that neighbourhood density affects the emergence of phonemic awareness (e.g., Metsala, 1999). However, as full segmental representation of phonemes is largely dependent on reading tuition (Goswami and Bryant, 1990), full

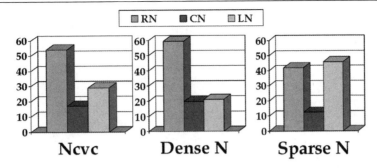

FIGURE 6.2 Phonological neighbourhoods in English, showing (left panel) overall neighbourhood statistics, and (central and right panels) statistics for dense (+1 s.d.) versus
sparse (–1 s.d.) neighbourhoods of the phonological lexicon
Note: Database = 4,086 English monosyllabic words
Source: See De Cara and Goswami (2002)

lexical restructuring at the phoneme level cannot be an emergent property of vocabulary
growth *per se*. Rather, prior to literacy, the development of segmental representation might
depend critically on the *nature* of the words that constitute densely versus sparsely popu-
lated phonological neighbourhoods in different languages.

It is clear from connectionism that brains learn the statistical structure of any input (e.g.,
Harm and Seidenberg, 1999). For English phonology, this statistical structure seems to
emphasize the rime (Kessler and Treiman, 1997). If phonological awareness emerges partly
because of implicit processing of inter-item phonological similarity relations as vocabulary
grows, then the characteristics of the phonological lexicon might in themselves contribute
to the psychological salience of onsets and rimes in English pre-readers. In other words, lots
of phonological neighbours in the English child's lexicon might be rhyming words.

This is in fact the case. We recently analysed all the monosyllabic words in English in
terms of their phonological similarity to other words (see Goswami and De Cara, 2000;
De Cara and Goswami, 2002). We looked at three kinds of neighbours, *rime* neighbours
(e.g., *cot–pot*), onset-vowel neighbours (e.g., *cot–cop*), and consonant neighbours (e.g.,
cot–cat). All of these phonological neighbours differ from the target word *cot* by a single
phoneme. However, words that differ by more than one phoneme can also rhyme (e.g.,
cot – spot, blot, trot), and words that differ by more than one phoneme can also share
onset-vowel units (e.g., *cot – cost*). We therefore defined phonological neighbourhoods in
terms of all words that differed from the target by one onset, vowel or coda. The results
of these statistical analyses are shown in Figure 6.2. Comparable analyses defining phonological neighbourhoods in terms of adding, substituting or deleting a single phoneme produced very similar results (De Cara and Goswami, 2002).

Figure 6.2 (left panel) shows that rime neighbours predominate in English phonology.
Furthermore, rime neighbours are particularly prevalent in dense neighbourhoods (Figure
6.2, central and right panels). In English, 59 per cent of neighbours in dense phonological
neighbourhoods are rime neighbours (e.g., *cot – pot, hot, dot*). In contrast, only 42 per cent
of neighbours in sparse phonological neighbourhoods are rime neighbours (e.g., *mud – bud,
thud*). If these statistical patterns in English phonology actually affect the development of
phonological representation, then children should find it easier to decide that 'cot' and 'pot'
rhyme in a phonological awareness task than to decide that 'thud' and 'mud' rhyme.

Given that words like 'cot' and 'mud' are highly familiar and early-acquired, it may seem counter-intuitive to propose that children will show better phonological awareness of the rime in one word compared to another. However, if such an effect could be demonstrated, it would help us to understand the basis of phonological representation. In essence, phonological representation must be a consequence of how the brain processes language. If implicit comparisons between similar-sounding words are an important part of the development of phonological representation, as suggested by Metsala and Walley's (1998) Lexical Restructuring Theory, then effects of neighbourhood density should emerge in phonological awareness tasks, even when the child is recognizing a salient phonological unit in very familiar words.

In ongoing work, we have found that normally developing 5- and 6-year-old children do show neighbourhood density effects in phonological awareness tasks. For example, they are more accurate in the rime oddity task (Which is the odd word out? pit, hit, got) when the words are from a dense phonological neighbourhood (e.g., 'hot, lot, wait'), than from a sparse phonological neighbourhood (e.g., 'mud, thud, good', Goswami and De Cara, 2000). In our work with dyslexic children, we have also found neighbourhood density effects. Dyslexic children aged 8 to 9 years take significantly longer to process words in dense phonological neighbourhoods than to process words in sparse phonological neighbourhoods, as do control children (Goswami and Giraudo, work in progress). The demonstration that dyslexic children show phonological neighbourhood density effects suggests that their brains are responding to the same developmental factors as the brains of normally-reading children in terms of developing phonological awareness. However, the dyslexic brain is carrying out phonological processing considerably less efficiently. In our study, the dyslexic children took three times longer than normally-reading controls matched for reading level to make rime oddity judgements. This lack of phonological processing efficiency can also be demonstrated in the difficulties that dyslexic children show in a wide variety of phonological awareness tasks in English.

EXAMPLES OF DYSLEXIC DIFFICULTIES IN TASKS TAPPING LEXICAL REPRESENTATION

Evidence from a whole range of 'phonological awareness' tasks demonstrates specific difficulties in the representation of segmental phonology for English dyslexic children. As already shown, they find it difficult to make judgements about shared phonology (e.g., they show deficits in the *rime oddity* task, performing significantly less accurately than reading level controls, e.g. Bradley and Bryant, 1978). They also find it difficult to manipulate phonology, as in the *Spoonerism* task, in which the child is asked to substitute the initial phonemes in words (so that Bob Dylan becomes Dob Bylan, e.g. Landerl *et al.*, 1997). The use of a reading level match design in these example studies is methodologically important. In this research design, dyslexic children's performance is being compared to that of *younger* children who are reading and spelling at the same level as them (the design holds reading level constant rather than chronological age, and thus gives a *mental* age advantage to the dyslexic children).

Developmental dyslexics also have poor phonological memory skills. They find it difficult to remember verbal sequences, and they show poor performance on standardized tests of phonological memory, such as the non-word repetition test designed by Gathercole and Baddeley (e.g., Gathercole and Baddeley, 1989; Stone and Brady, 1995). In the non-word repetition task, the child has to repeat nonsense words like *ballop* and *thickery* which are played on a tape recorder. Repeating nonsense (novel) word forms requires the child to set up new phonological representations, and this is very difficult for dyslexic children. English-speaking developmental dyslexics are also slower to recognize familiar words on the basis of acoustic input. For example, they require more acoustic-phonetic information than age-matched controls to recognize familiar words in speech gating tasks, in which incremental segments of speech from word-onset are presented through headphones (Metsala, 1997). On the output side, developmental dyslexics show deficits in rapid 'automatized' speeded naming tasks (e.g., Denckla and Rudel, 1976). Such tasks require the child to name familiar items presented in lists (such as digits) as quickly as possible, thereby accessing and outputting what should be well-practised and thus well-specified phonological forms ('nine, two, five, . . .'). They also show deficits in confrontation naming tasks (in which simple pictures must be named on demand), even though they may be very familiar with the items in the pictures (e.g., Swan and Goswami, 1997a).

Swan and Goswami (1997a) then attempted to link the deficits in confrontation naming and in phonological representation more closely, by examining confrontation naming performance for words that would theoretically be expected to differ in their degree of lexical restructuring. They demonstrated that dyslexic problems were particularly marked when naming familiar names that were long and of low frequency. These names correspond to phonological forms that have presumably been encountered less frequently during language acquisition and that also require the accurate specification of more phonological segments. Swan and Goswami further showed that when dyslexic children were given phonological awareness tasks based on words that they could name without difficulty, then the phonological deficit usually found in syllable or onset-rime level tasks disappeared (Swan and Goswami, 1997b). However, even when the dyslexic children had no difficulty in naming the words being used in the phonological awareness tasks, a phonemic deficit remained. This suggests that even words with fairly well-specified lexical representations had not been adequately restructured to the phonemic level. Given that attainment of the phonemic level of phonological representation depends critically on literacy, this is perhaps not surprising.

This analysis of lexical representation suggests that the problem for developmental dyslexics is not restricted to phonemes *per se*. Rather, there is a general problem with the accurate specification of lexical forms prior to becoming literate. As a basic linguistic processing problem reduces the efficiency of the accurate neural specification of phonological segments, literacy acquisition is itself made more difficult. This in turn leads to difficulties in attaining the phonemic level of lexical representation that characterizes the mental lexicons of normally-reading children.

POTENTIAL AUDITORY PROCESSING PROBLEMS UNDERLYING THE REPRESENTATIONAL DEFICIT IN DYSLEXIA

A number of researchers have attempted to find the basic auditory processing deficits that are expected to explain dyslexic children's difficulty in representing phonological forms in memory. In English, these studies have so far produced mixed results. Typically, a basic auditory processing task will show dramatic impairments for some English dyslexic children, and no apparent impairment for others, despite extremely careful subject selection. For example, some dyslexic children have great difficulty with 'minimal pairs' tasks that require the discrimination of similar-sounding words (e.g., *smack–snack*), yet others do not (Adlard and Hazan, 1998). Some dyslexic children find phoneme categorization and repetition tasks very difficult (e.g., discriminating between or repeating /b/ and /d/), and others do not (e.g., Joanisse *et al.*, 2000; Manis *et al.*, 1997). Some dyslexic children find temporal order judgements very difficult. Such tasks require them to decide whether a high tone preceded a low tone or vice versa. Dyslexic children seem to have particular difficulties when the tones are close together in time. Accordingly, it has been proposed that dyslexia is caused by temporal processing deficits (e.g., Tallal, 1980). This view is quite controversial, however, as most of Tallal's participants have also suffered from overt linguistic problems. For example, Mody *et al.* (1997) have shown that dyslexic children who find it difficult to discriminate phonemes like ba/da show no deficit with a non-speech analogue task that makes the same temporal processing demands (based on sine wave speech). Thus far, however, one area of convergence between different studies is that most auditory processing deficits that have been found appear to be specific to linguistic stimuli.

Nevertheless, the lack of uniformity across participants in these studies is puzzling. One possibility is that the primary basic processing deficit that is causing the difficulties with phonological representation has not yet been discovered. A second is that the most basic problem lies not in perception *per se*, but in *representing* the segments that can be detected in the input. This is difficult to investigate, as the processes whereby the brain represents the information that it detects in the environment are not well understood. However, it is logically possible that the dyslexic brain can detect the same elements in speech input as the brain that develops normal reading, but cannot *represent* these elements in the same way. A third possibility is that sensory deficits in basic auditory processing and phonological deficits are not causally related, but arise from the dysfunction of a neural system common to both (Eden and Zeffiro, 1998). Finally, it is logically possible that there may be a variety of causes of dyslexia, with some children's primary problems lying outside the auditory realm.

BRAIN IMAGING STUDIES OF PHONOLOGICAL PROCESSING DEFICITS IN DYSLEXIA

Evidence from brain imaging work is consistent with the view that the key difficulty in dyslexia is a weakness in the *representation* of phonological information. The phonological processing system spans a number of cortical and subcortical regions in the brain, including frontal, temporal and parietal cortex. Studies of aphasia long ago revealed the importance of Broca's area (frontal cortex) and Wernicke's area (posterior superior temporal gyrus) for the motor production and receptive aspects of speech respectively, and the lateralization of language-related processes to the left hemisphere is equally well documented.

Interpretation of functional neuroimaging studies of dyslexia is complicated by the fact that only adult developmental dyslexics can be scanned, which means that the brain's compensatory responses to any initial disorder may account for some of the patterns of task-related activity that are found. Nevertheless, despite seemingly inconsistent results in early studies, localization of phonological mechanisms in the temporoparietal junction and abnormalities in activation surrounding this junction in adult developmental dyslexics during phonological processing tasks have been documented by a number of research groups (see Eden and Zeffiro, 1998, for review). When performing tasks like rhyme judgement, rhyme detection, and word and nonsense word reading, dyslexic subjects show reduced activation in temporal and parietal regions, particularly within the left hemisphere. Such studies have been interpreted to support the 'phonological deficit' framework for understanding dyslexia, with the most recent studies suggesting a specific disruption in left hemisphere functional connectivity only when phonological assembly is required, as in word and nonsense word reading (Pugh et al., 2000).

ARE THERE SUB-TYPES OF DEVELOPMENTAL DYSLEXIA?

Some researchers have argued strongly for two sub-types of developmental dyslexia in English, 'surface' dyslexia and 'phonological' dyslexia (but see Oliver et al., 2000). *Phonological* dyslexics are thought to have problems in assembling sub-lexical phonology (reading using abstract spelling-to-sound 'rules'). *Surface* dyslexics are thought to have problems in using stored lexical knowledge to pronounce words (they seem to have difficulty in directly addressing orthographic representations). This 'double dissociation' model of developmental dyslexia has been drawn from patterns of adult pathology (the 'acquired' dyslexias).

The sub-typing argument has depended critically on the use of regression procedures, in which performance relationships between the use of lexical and sublexical phonology characteristic of normal children are used to derive confidence limits for assessing the same performance relationships in dyslexic populations. These regression procedures typically depend on the use of *chronological* age-matched normal readers. As processing trade-offs between the reliance on lexical and sublexical phonology may depend on the overall level of word recognition that the child has attained, *reading level* matched controls are more appropriate. Stanovich et al. (1997) demonstrate clearly that when reading level matched controls are used to define processing trade-offs, then almost no 'surface dyslexic' children are found, even in the original samples of English-speaking children used to support the notion of sub-types of developmental dyslexia. They conclude that the 'surface' dyslexic profile arises from a milder form of phonological deficit accompanied by exceptionally inadequate reading experience.

TOWARDS A PHENOTYPE OF DYSLEXIA

Neuro-developmental disorders such as developmental dyslexia are not discrete syndromes, but most typically have a graded character. They are also seldom highly specific, and rarely involve a single deficit. Although a difficulty in representing segmental phonology appears to be the core symptom of developmental dyslexia in English, many researchers have noted a number of associated deficits that more or less frequently accompany the phonological deficit. For example, dyslexic children can be clumsy, they can have attentional problems, they may display mild cerebellar signs such as slow motor tapping, and they may have subtle abnormalities in visual processing such as poor motion processing when visual stimuli are of low contrast and low luminance (e.g., Fawcett *et al.*, 1996; Talcott *et al.*, 1999). At present, the most widely accepted phenotype of developmental dyslexia depends on deficits in performance on a battery of cognitive tasks that tap the integrity of the child's phonological representations of speech. This battery most typically includes phonological awareness tasks, single word and nonsense word reading tasks, and rapid 'automatized' naming tasks. Developmental dyslexia is thus currently best conceived as a subtle linguistic deficit that involves an impairment in the representation of the phonological segments of speech in the brain.

However, this phenotype may manifest differently in different languages. As noted earlier, the degree to which the segmental representation of phonology has taken place is thought to determine how easily the child will become phonologically 'aware' and will learn to read and write. Pre-readers in all languages so far studied appear to represent words in terms of the phonological segments of syllable, onset and rime (Goswami, 1997). Attainment of 'phonemic' awareness is dependent on literacy, and for the dyslexic child who is learning English, phonemic awareness may never be fully realized. If learning to read itself affects the representation of segmental phonology, then the orthographic consistency of the language being learned would be expected to have an impact on representation at the phonemic level.

For example, for English, the variability of grapheme–phoneme correspondence may in itself compound the literacy acquisition problems faced by dyslexic children. Accordingly, the difficulties in representing phonemes faced by developmental dyslexics in more transparent languages (e.g., Spanish, Greek, German) may be reduced. This is because of the almost 1 : 1 consistency of mappings between graphemes and phonemes in such languages. For example, dyslexic children who are learning to read and spell transparent orthographies like German do not show accuracy deficits in nonsense word reading tasks, although they do show marked speed deficits (e.g., Wimmer, 1993). When nonsense words are carefully matched across languages, German dyslexic children are much better at reading nonsense words than English dyslexic children (Landerl *et al.*, 1997). This presumably reflects the consistency of grapheme–phoneme relations in German compared to English. The German child, even the child with a linguistic difficulty, is learning a less variable orthographic code. Variations in orthographic consistency may therefore in themselves lead to apparent variations in the dyslexic phenotype across languages (Goswami, 2000). Nevertheless, for dyslexic children who are learning to read English, the most noticeable problems in terms of functional literacy concern the accuracy and speed of reading and spelling.

REFERENCES

Adlard, A. and Hazan, V. (1998) Speech perception in children with specific reading difficulties (dyslexia). *Quarterly Journal of Experimental Psychology*, 51A, 153–177.

Bradley, L. and Bryant, P.E. (1978) Difficulties in auditory organisation as a possible cause of reading backwardness. *Nature*, 271, 746–747.

De Cara, B. and Goswami, U. (2002) Statistical analysis of similarity relations among spoken words: Evidence for the special status of rimes in English. *Behavioural Research Methods and Instrumentation*, 34(3), 416–423.

Denckla, M.B. and Rudel, R.G. (1976) Naming of object-drawings by dyslexic and other learning disabled children, *Brain and Language*, 3, 1–15.

Eden, G.F. and Zeffiro, T.A. (1998) Neural systems affected in developmental dyslexia revealed by functional neuroimaging. *Neuron*, 21, 279–282.

Fawcett, A.J., Nicholson, R.I. and Dean, P. (1996) Impaired performance of children with dyslexia on a range of cerebellar tasks. *Annals of Dyslexia*, 46, 259–283.

Gathercole, S.E. and Baddeley, A. (1989) Evaluation of the role of phonological STM in the development of vocabulary in children: A longitudinal study. *Journal of Memory and Language*, 28, 200–213.

Goswami, U. (1997) Learning to read in different orthographies: Phonological skills, orthographic representations and dyslexia. In M. Snowling and C. Hulme (eds), *Dyslexia: Biology, Identification and Intervention*. London: Whurr Publishers.

Goswami, U. (2000) Phonological representations, reading development and dyslexia: Towards a cross-linguistic theoretical framework. *Dyslexia*, 6, 133–151.

Goswami, U. and Bryant, P.E. (1990) *Phonological Skills and Learning to Read*. Hillsdale, NJ: Lawrence Erlbaum Associates.

Goswami, U. and De Cara, B. (2000) Lexical representations and development: The emergence of rime processing. In A. Cutler, J. McQueen and R. Zondervan (eds), *Proceedings of the Workshop on Spoken Word Access Processes*, Nijmegen, NL: Max-Planck Institute of Psycholinguistics.

Harm, M.W. and Seidenberg, M.S. (1999) Phonology, reading acquisition and dyslexia: Insights from connectionist models. *Psychological Review*, 106, 491–528.

Joanisse, M.F., Manis, F.R., Keating, P. and Seidenberg, M.S. (2000) Language deficits in dyslexic children: Speech perception, phonology and morphology. *Journal of Experimental Child Psychology*, 77, 30–60.

Jusczyk, P.W. (1993) From general to language-specific capacities: The WRAPSA model of how speech perception develops. *Journal of Phonetics*, 21, 3–28.

Kessler, B. and Treiman, R. (1997) Syllable structure and the distribution of phonemes in English syllables. *Journal of Memory and Language*, 37, 295–311.

Landerl, K., Wimmer, H. and Frith, U. (1997) The impact of orthographic consistency on dyslexia: A German-English comparison. *Cognition*, 63, 315–334.

Manis, F.R., McBride-Chang, C., Seidenberg, M.S., Keating, P., Doi, L.M., Munsun, B. and Petersen, A. (1997) Are speech perception deficits associated with developmental dyslexia? *Journal of Experimental Child Psychology*, 66, 211–235.

Metsala, J.L. (1997) Spoken word recognition in reading disabled children. *Journal of Educational Psychology*, 89, 159–169.

Metsala, J.L. (1999) Young children's phonological awareness and nonword repetition as a function of vocabulary development. *Journal of Educational Psychology*, 91, 3–19.

Metsala, J.L. and Walley, A.C. (1998) Spoken vocabulary growth and the segmental restructuring of lexical representations: Precursors to phonemic awareness and early reading ability. In J.L. Metsala and L.C. Ehri (eds), *Word Recognition in Beginning Literacy*. Hillsdale, NJ: Lawrence Erlbaum Associates.

Mody, M., Studdert-Kennedy, M. and Brady, S. (1997) Speech perception deficits in poor readers: Auditory processing or phonological coding? *Journal of Experimental Child Psychology*, 64, 199–231.

Oliver, A., Johnson, M.H., Karmiloff-Smith, A. and Pennington, B. (2000) Deviations in the emergence of representations: A neuro-constructivist framework for analysing developmental disorders. *Developmental Science*, 3, 1–25.

Pugh, K.R., Mencl, W.E., Shaywitz, B.A., Shaywitz, S.E., Fulbright, R.K., Constable, R.T., Skudlarski, P., Marchione, K.E., Jenner, A.R., Fletcher, J.M., Liberman, A.M., Shankweiler, D.P., Katz, L., Lacadie, C. and Gore, J.C. (2000) The angular gyrus in developmental dyslexia: Task specific differences in functional connectivity within posterior cortex. *Psychological Science*, 11, 51–56.

Snowling, M.J. (2000) *Dyslexia*. 2nd edition. Oxford: Blackwell.

Stanovich, K.E., Siegel, L.S. and Gottardo, A. (1997) Converging evidence for phonological and surface subtypes of reading disability. *Journal of Educational Psychology*, 89, 114–127.

Stone, B. and Brady, S.A. (1995) Evidence for deficits in basic phonological processes in less-skilled readers. *Annals of Dyslexia*, 45, 51–78.

Swan, D. and Goswami, U. (1997a) Picture naming deficits in developmental dyslexia: The phonological representations hypothesis. *Brain and Language*, 56, 334–353.

Swan, D. and Goswami, U. (1997b) Phonological awareness deficits in developmental dyslexia and the phonological representations hypothesis. *Journal of Experimental Child Psychology*, 66, 18–41.

Talcott, J.B., Witton, C., Green, G.G.R, Stein, J.F. *et al.* (1999) Can sensitivity to auditory frequency modulation predict children's phonological and reading skills? *Neuroreport*, 10, 2045–2050.

Tallal, P. (1980) Auditory temporal perception, phonics and reading disabilities in children. *Brain and Language*, 9, 182–198.

Walley, A. (1993) The role of vocabulary development in children's spoken word recognition and segmentation ability. *Developmental Review*, 13, 286–350.

Wimmer, H. (1993) Characteristics of developmental dyslexia in a regular writing system. *Applied Psycholinguistics*, 14, 1–33.

7

DYSLEXIA IN FARSI

Kaveh Farrokh

INTRODUCTION

Dyslexia research in Farsi word reading is presently defined by three distinct areas of research: (1) Farsi word reading processes of children (Arab-Moghaddam and Senechal, 2001; Gholamain and Geva, 1999); (2) reaction time studies of Farsi word reading among adults (Baluch, 1993, 1996; Baluch and Besner, 1991; Baluch and Shahidi, 1991); and (3) the Farsi word reading processes of adults (Farrokh, 2001). Before discussing these areas of research, we will first discuss the nature of Farsi script as well as reading-related cognitive processes.

FARSI ORTHOGRAPHY

Farsi (a dialect of Persian) is a member of the Iranian branch of the Indo-European language family (Mallory, 1989) and is not related to Arabic (Khanlari, 1979). Written Farsi is based on a modified version of the Arabic alphabet (Jahani, 1989; Lentz, 1937; Oranskij, 1975, 1977). The shape of Arabic-based letters (Farsi script) changes according to their position in the beginning, middle or end of the word (Khanlari, 1979). Writing goes from right to left in Farsi (Jahani, 1989). Farsi script contains three long vowels, while diacritics can be added to indicate short vowels (Baluch and Besner, 1991). In written Farsi, spelling (grapheme) to sound (phoneme) correspondences are always consistent, however, only some of the words include vowels as a fixed part of their spelling. These are transparent Farsi words (Baluch and Shahidi, 1991). Transparent Farsi words resemble highly regular orthographies such as Finnish (see Chapter 8) or Dutch (see Chapter 5).

In other Farsi words, vowels are not specified in the spelling. These are opaque Farsi words (Baluch and Besner, 1991). Vowels are represented by slashes (diacritics) for beginning readers only. Diacritics are eliminated from words in regular text. As a result, only

International Book of Dyslexia: A Cross-Language Comparison and Practice Guide. Edited by Ian Smythe, John Everatt and Robin Salter. ISBN 0471498416 © 2004 John Wiley & Sons, Ltd.

consonants appear in opaque Farsi words. Opaque Farsi words resemble Hebrew orthography since vowels are not represented in regular Hebrew text (see Chapter 11).

READING-RELATED COGNITIVE PROCESSES

Researchers in reading have begun to conceptualize the word reading process in terms of interacting cognitive processes (August and Hakuta, 1997; Carlo and Sylvester, 1996; Siegel, 1993). These processes consist of syntactic awareness, phonological awareness, phonological recoding, orthographic awareness and memory processes. These are briefly defined below:

1 Syntactic awareness refers to students' grammatical sensitivity or the ability to comprehend the basic syntactic aspects of language (Da Fontoura and Siegel, 1995; Willows and Ryan, 1986). In addition, syntactic awareness allows individuals to make use of context in reading by facilitating their sensitivity to the predictability of text (Carr *et al.*, 1990). Syntactic awareness is important for the fluent and efficient reading of text that requires making predictions about the words that come next in a sentence (Siegel, 1993). Better readers may be more sensitive to syntactic information in text than less skilled readers (Bialystok and Ryan, 1985).

2 Phonological awareness is the metalinguistic awareness of the sound structure of language (Rohl and Pratt, 1995; Wagner and Torgesen, 1987) and refers to sensitivity or awareness of phonemes, syllables, and the phonological rules that operate them (Mann, 1998). A large amount of variance in word reading in English can be attributed to phonological awareness (Rohl and Pratt, 1995; Wagner *et al.*, 1993). Poor readers may have a core phonological deficit (Stanovich, 1988).

3 Phonological recoding involves the decoding of written symbols or graphemes into a sound-based representational system or phonemes (Fox and Routh, 1976; Olson *et al.*, 1997).

4 Orthographic awareness involves knowledge of the spelling conventions of words, recognition of word properties, as well as the sequences and typical positions of letters in words (Olson *et al.*, 1994; Siegel *et al.*, 1995). There may be a relationship between poor orthographic skills and syntactic processing in reading (Smith *et al.*, 1989). In addition, there may be a strong genetic influence on deficits in orthographic processes (Olson *et al.*, 1997).

5 Memory processes in reading refer to the recoding of written symbols into their sound based representations and holding them efficiently in working memory (Torgesen *et al.*, 1994; Wagner and Torgesen, 1987). Working memory is important to reading because the reader must recognize words while remembering what has been read and retrieving information (i.e. grapheme–phoneme conversion rules) (Siegel, 1993). Carr *et al.* (1990) and Siegel and Ryan (1989) note that disabled readers have significant difficulties with respect to working memory. In addition, Mann (1998) notes that poor readers do not perform as well as good readers on a wide variety of phonological short-term memory tasks. Specifically, 'poor readers are less able to use phonetic structure as a means of holding material in short-term memory' (ibid., p. 178).

A number of studies have investigated the reading processes of bilingual children and adults using the above model of word reading (in terms of interacting components). For example, in a study of Portuguese Canadian children, Da Fontoura and Siegel (1995) found significant relationships (in Portuguese and English) between reading and processes such as syntactic awareness, phonological coding, and working memory. Similar findings have been found with Arab Canadian children (Abu-Rabia and Siegel, 1997). Geva (see Chapter 20 on assessment of reading disability in second language children) has noted that word reading development across different languages is generally parallel. Examples cited by Geva include Farsi-English, Cantonese-English, French-English and Turkish-Dutch.

With the exception of Farrokh (2001), no research studies have investigated the relationship among adult Farsi speakers of all the aforementioned cognitive processes proposed to be involved in Farsi word reading. However, a number of studies with Farsi-speaking children (e.g. Gholamain and Geva, 1999), as well as reaction time studies with Farsi word reading (e.g. Baluch and Besner, 1991), have been conducted. The findings of these studies are discussed below.

FARSI WORD READING PROCESSES OF CHILDREN

Gholamain and Geva (1999) investigated the relationships between Farsi word reading, phonological recoding, working memory, and letter naming speed. Significant relationships were found between Farsi word reading and all of the measures (ibid.). However, the strongest relationship was between Farsi word reading and phonological recoding (ibid.). Gholamain and Geva conclude that 'the structure of regular orthographies such as Persian favors the grapheme-phoneme "phonological" route to lexical retrieval in beginning readers' (ibid., p. 211). In a similar study, Arab-Moghaddam and Senechal (2001) examined the relationships between Farsi word reading, phonological recoding and orthographic processing skills among bilingual Farsi-speaking children. Both phonological and orthographic skills were found to be significantly related to word reading. The findings of the Farsi word reading studies with children are consistent with those reported in various other languages such as Arabic (see Chapter 2 on Arabic), English (see Chapter 6). Portuguese (see Chapter 16), or Spanish (see Chapter 18).

It must be noted that the results of the Farsi word reading studies with children (Arab-Moghaddam and Senechal, 2001; Gholamain and Geva, 1999) may be limited in their generalizability to adult Farsi speakers because children and adults are different with respect to cognitive development and background literacy (Brown and Haynes, 1985).

REACTION TIME STUDIES OF FARSI WORD READING AMONG ADULTS

Baluch (1993), Baluch and Besner (1991) and Baluch and Shahidi (1991) have investigated the processes of Farsi word reading among adults. The majority of these studies (e.g., Baluch and Besner, 1991) used the technique of measuring the speed and accuracy of Farsi word and pseudoword naming. The words appeared in the centre of a computer screen. The recording devices measured the time elapsed between the moment the word or pseudoword appeared and the moment it was named. The results of the Farsi word reading studies (e.g., Baluch, 1993) indicate that for higher frequency words, the reaction times were as fast for both opaque and transparent Farsi words. However, reaction times to lower frequency transparent words were faster than matched opaque words. Baluch (1993) states that this difference in reaction times is an indication that Farsi word reading is achieved entirely by orthographic recognition, without the implication of any phono-logical processes. Baluch (2000) claims that Farsi word reading is achieved primarily by orthographic processes since 'transparency of a [Farsi] word's spelling is not crucial in a lexical decision task' (Baluch, 1993, p. 26). In addition, Baluch and Shahidi (1991) note that 'skilled adult reading is dominated by the use of the orthographic route, regardless of the consistency of a word's spelling-sound correspondences' (Baluch and Shahidi, 1991, p. 1329). Specifically, Baluch has claimed that 'readers of scripts (e.g. Farsi) use visual orthographic rather than phonological codes for access' (1993, p. 21). Phonological processes are said to be mainly confined to beginning readers (i.e. Baluch, 1993; Baluch and Shahidi, 1991). This is consistent with the aforementioned findings of Gholamain and Geva (1999) as well as Arab-Moghaddam and Senechal who found strong relationships between word reading and phonological processes in Farsi among Farsi-speaking children.

The conclusions of the Farsi reaction time studies (e.g., Baluch and Shahidi, 1991), however, may be questioned since the delay in reaction times between low frequency trans-parent and opaque words may have as much to do with phonological decoding processes as they do with orthographic matching. In addition, none of the cited studies made com-parisons between good and poor Farsi reading adults. The studies with Farsi-speaking children (Arab-Moghaddam and Senechal, 2001; Gholamain and Geva, 1999) did not make specific comparisons with respect to reading ability. Instead of reading ability, Arab-Moghaddam and Senechal used reading experience or the indication by parents of 'how frequently during a typical week they observed their child read Persian books' (2001, p. 144). Gholamain and Geva devised the factor of Persian oral proficiency in which 'Teachers . . . were asked to rate the oral proficiency of students in Persian on a 7-point scale' (1999, pp. 194–195).

FARSI WORD READING PROCESSES OF ADULTS

Farrokh (2001) investigated Farsi word reading by using the cognitive processes paradigm (August and Hakuta, 1997; Siegel, 1993) described earlier. Specially, the relationship of Farsi word reading to syntactic awareness, phonological processes, orthographic aware-ness, working memory and long-term memory was investigated. Farsi reading was found to be significantly related to all processes except long-term memory (Farrokh, 2001). In contrast to Baluch (1993), Farrokh (2001) found phonological processes to have strong relationships to Farsi word reading. However, as predicted by Baluch and Besner (1991), the relationship between orthographic awareness and word reading was also strong in Farsi. These findings are consistent with Henderson (1983) who found that Arab univer-sity students use both phonological and orthographic processes in Arabic word reading. Arabic and Farsi use similar scripts.

Farrokh (2001) also made comparisons between good and poor Farsi readers. Good readers performed better than poor readers on Farsi syntactic awareness, auditory analysis, pseudoword reading, orthographic awareness, and working memory tasks. Similarly, Abu-Rabia (see Chapter 2) reports that good readers of Arabic do better than poor readers in the domains of phonological processing, working memory skills, and syn-tactic skills.

The results of the Farrokh study (2001) question the notion that good Farsi readers rely exclusively on orthographic processes (Baluch, 1993) and that less skilled readers rely on phonological processes (Baluch and Shahidi, 1991). In fact, phonological processes appear to be very important to the reading processes of both good and poor adult Farsi readers. These results are similar to findings reported for Spanish (see Chapter 18). Giménez de la Peña notes that both lexical and phonological routes are used in Spanish reading, and that normal and poor readers differ in their use of these routes. Specifically, normal readers are able to utilize both routes with efficiency, while poor readers exhibit inefficient phonological processing.

The above results concur with Henderson (1983) who compared adult good and poor readers of Arabic. Her data indicated that 'more effective readers use a phonological coding strategy' (ibid. p. 118). Abu-Rabia (see Chapter 2) also reports phonological processes as having a crucial role in Arabic word reading. In the Farrokh study (2001), the use of phonological coding was also associated with superior word reading performance.

SUMMARY OF RESEARCH FINDINGS

Reading ability differences among Farsi speakers (children or adults) are explained by differences in reading-related cognitive processes. Phonological and orthographic processes are important to Farsi word reading in children (Arab-Moghaddam and Senechal, 2001) and adults (Farrokh, 2001). Note that previous studies (e.g. Baluch, 1993) indicated only orthographic processes as being significantly related to Farsi word reading among adults. Examination of the findings of the Farrokh study (2001) suggests that good adult Farsi readers appear to perform significantly better than their poor reading counterparts on all reading-related cognitive processes such as syntactic awareness, phonological awareness, phonological recoding, orthographic awareness, and working memory. The performance of Farsi-speaking children also varies significantly with respect to cognitive measures such as phonological recoding (Arab-Moghaddam and Senechal, 2001; Gholamain and Geva, 1999), orthographic processes (Arab-Moghaddam and Senechal, 2001), and working memory (Gholamain and Geva, 1999). The general pattern of the results of the Farsi studies are consistent with studies in other languages (Arabic: Abu-Rabia, Chapter 2; Henderson, 1983; Portuguese: Da Fantoura and Siegel, 1995; Giménez de la Peña, Chapter 18) indicating that differences in reading ability are significantly related to (reading-related) cognitive processes.

REFERENCES

Abu-Rabia, S. and Siegel, L.S. (1997) Reading, syntactic, orthographic and working memory skills of bilingual Arabic-English-speaking children. Unpublished manuscript.

Arab-Moghaddam, N. and Senechal, M. (2001) Orthographic and phonological processing skills in reading and spelling in Persian/English bilinguals. *International Journal of Behavioral Development*, 25(2), 140–147.

August, D. and Hakuta, K. (1997) *Improving Schooling for Language Minority Children*. Washington, DC: National Academy Press.

Baluch, B. (1993) Lexical decisions in Persian: A test of the orthographic depth hypothesis. *International Journal of Psychology*, 28(11), 19–29.

Baluch, B. (1996) Word frequency effects in naming for experienced and previously experienced adult readers of Persian. *Reading and Writing: An Interdisciplinary Journal*, 8, 433–441.

Baluch, B. (2000) Basic processes in reading: Semantics affects speeded naming of high frequency words in an alphabetic script. Unpublished manuscript.

Baluch, B. and Besner, D. (1991) Visual word recognition: Evidence for strategic control of lexical and nonlexical routines in oral reading. *Journal of Experimental Psychology: Learning, Memory, and Cognition*, 17(4), 644–652.

Baluch, B. and Shahidi, D. (1991) Visual word recognition in beginning readers of Persian. *Perceptual and Motor Skills*, 72, 1327–1331.

Bialystok, E. and Ryan, E.B. (1985) Towards a definition of metalinguistic skill. *Merrill-Palmer Quarterly*, 31, 229–251.

Brown, T.L. and Haynes, M. (1985) In T.H. Carr (ed.), *The Development of Reading Skills*. San Francisco: Jossey-Bass.

Carr, T.H., Brown, T.L., Vavrus, L.G. and Evans, M.A. (1990) Cognitive skill maps and cognitive skill profiles: Componential analysis of individual differences in children's reading efficiency. In T.H. Carr and B.A. Levy (eds), *Reading and its Development: Component Skills Approaches*. New York: Academic Press.

Da Fontoura, H.A. and Siegel, L.S. (1995) Reading, syntactic, and working memory skills of bilingual Portuguese-English Canadian children. *Reading and Writing: An Interdisciplinary Journal*, 7, 139–153.

Farrokh, K. (2001) The relationships among cognitive processes, language experience and errors in Farsi-speaking ESL adults. Unpublished doctoral dissertation, University of British Columbia, Vancouver, British Columbia.

Gholamain, M. and Geva, E. (1999) Orthographic and cognitive factors in the concurrent development of basic reading skills in English and Persian. *Language Learning*, 49(2), 183–217.

Henderson, R.T. (1983) Basic perceptual and cognitive processes employed by Arabic-speaking students in the development of reading skills in English as a second language. Unpublished doctoral dissertation, University of Pittsburgh, PA.

Jahani, C. (1989) Standardization and orthography in the Balochi language. *Acta Universitatis Upsaliensis: Studia Iranic Upsaliensia*, 1, 1–268.

Khanlari, P.N. (1979) *The History of the Persian Language*. Vol. 1. New Delhi: New Delhi Press.

Lentz, W. (1937) *Ein Lateinalphabet für das Paschto*. [A Latin alphabet for Pashto.] Berlin: Deutsche Schrift.

Mallory, J.P. (1989) *In Search of the Indo-Europeans: Language, Archeology and Myth*. London: Thames & Hudson.

Mann, V. (1998) Language problems: A key to early reading problems. In B.Y.L. Wong (ed.), *Learning about Learning Disabilities*. San Diego: Academic Press.

Olson, R., Forsberg, H. and Wise, B. (1994) Genes, environment, and the development of orthographic skills. In V.W. Berninger (ed.), *The Varieties of Orthographic Knowledge I: Theoretical and Development Issues*. Dordrecht: Kluwer Academic Publishers.

Olson, R.K., Wise, B., Johnson, M. and Ring, J. (1997) The etiology and remediation of phonologically based word recognition and spelling disabilities: Are phonological deficits the 'hole' story? In B. Blachman (ed.), *Foundations of Reading Acquisition*. Mahwah, NJ: Lawrence Erlbaum Associates.

Oranskij, I.M. (1975) Die neu-Iranischen Sprachen der Sowjetunion. [The new Iranian languages of the Soviet Union.] *Janua Linguarum: Series Critica*, 12, I–II.

Oranskij, I.M. (1977) *Les Langues Iraniennes*. [The Iranian languages.] Paris: Documents et Ouvrages de Reférence.

Rohl, M. and Pratt, C. (1995) Phonological awareness, verbal working memory and the acquisition of literacy. *Reading and Writing*, 7, 327–360.

Siegel, L.S. (1993) The development of reading. *Advances in Child Development and Behavior*, 24, 63–97.

Siegel, L.S. and Ryan, E.B. (1989) The development of working memory in normally achieving and subtypes of learning disabled children. *Child Development*, 60, 973–980.

Siegel, L.S., Share, D. and Geva, E. (1995) Evidence for superior orthographic skills in dyslexics. *Psychological Science*, 6(4), 250–254.

Smith, S.T., Macaruso, P., Shankweiler, D. and Crain, S. (1989) Syntactic comprehension in young poor readers. *Applied Psycholinguistics*, 10, 429–454.

Stanovich, K.E. (1988) Explaining the differences between the dyslexic and the garden-variety poor reader: The phonological-core variable-difference deficit model. *Journal of Learning Disabilities*, 21(10), 590–612.

Torgesen, J.K., Wagner, R.K. and Rashotte, C.A. (1994) Longitudinal studies of phonological processing and reading. *Journal of Reading Disabilities*, 27(5), 276–286.

Wagner, R.K. and Torgesen, J.K. (1987) The nature of phonological processing and its causal role in the acquisition of reading skills. *Psychological Bulletin*, 101, 192–212.

Wagner, R.K., Torgesen, J.K., Laughon, P., Simmons, K. and Rashotte, C. (1993) The development of young readers' phonological processing abilities. *Journal of Educational Psychology*, 85, 83–103.

Willows, D.M. and Ryan, E.B. (1986) The development of grammatical sensitivity and its relation to early reading achievement. *Reading Research Quarterly*, 21, 253–266.

8

DYSLEXIA IN HIGHLY ORTHOGRAPHICALLY REGULAR FINNISH

Heikki Lyytinen, Mikko Aro and Leena Holopainen

INTRODUCTION

The first part of this chapter illustrates the features of the Finnish language as an example of a highly orthographically regular language and its implications for reading acquisition and dyslexia. The second part summarizes recent Finnish research on dyslexia.

FEATURES OF THE FINNISH ORTHOGRAPHY AND LEARNING TO READ

Until recently, the cross-linguistic comparative aspect of reading development and dyslexia has largely been neglected in the research. The vast majority of published studies deal with English-speaking participants and thus the English language has become the 'prototypic' linguistic context for reading research. There has been at least an implicit underlying assumption that findings concerning the development of literacy skills, as well as the features and underlying problems of developmental dyslexia are universal, and that such findings in English can be generalized to other languages. Somewhat contradictory, the research findings in other languages are usually published with explicit remarks regarding the non-English language context, thus indirectly implying that the findings are less universal. However, a number of studies posit that the development of reading skills and the features of reading problems are dependent on the language context, and that English differs from more regular orthographies (e.g. Aro and Wimmer, in press; Landerl *et al.*, 1997; Seymour *et al.* 2003; Thorstad, 1991; Wimmer and Goswami, 1994). The aim of

International Book of Dyslexia: A Cross-Language Comparison and Practice Guide. Edited by Ian Smythe, John Everatt and Robin Salter. ISBN 0471498416 © 2004 John Wiley & Sons, Ltd.

this section is to present a brief summary of those characteristics of the Finnish orthography (for more details, see Karlsson, 1999) that differ from other orthographies, especially English, and which, in turn, may affect the development of reading skills and possibly the phenotype of developmental dyslexia in Finnish.

HOW DO ALPHABETIC ORTHOGRAPHIES DIFFER?

The minimum requirement for phonological recoding, i.e. the ability to independently read (or spell) unfamiliar words, is knowledge of the grapheme–phoneme (G–P) correspondences combined with phonemic awareness and synthetic (and segmental) phonological manipulation skills. From the perspective of beginning reading, the most relevant differences between languages relate to this G–P correspondence system. In regular orthographies, graphemes map consistently onto their respective phonemes (and vice versa). In irregular orthographies, the correspondence rules vary for a number of reasons including contextual rules (e.g. 'chord', 'chore'), and morphophonology (e.g. 'nation–nationality'). There are also lexical items with completely exceptional pronunciations that cannot be attempted through recourse even to infrequent G–P conversion rules ('yacht', 'two').

Orthographic regularity can be viewed as a continuum, whereby different orthographies are located relative to each other, albeit there are no current methods to directly quantify these differences. An example of a highly regular orthography is Finnish with extremely consistent grapheme–phoneme mappings, even at the level of single letters. English is considered to be an irregular orthography, where grapheme–phoneme mappings are inconsistent and often unpredictable for the novice reader. In some orthographies, the correspondence between spoken and written language is asymmetrical, with more regular correspondences in the direction of written to spoken language (reading) than from spoken to written (writing). For example in German, the pronunciation of a written word is usually fairly unambiguous whereas the spelling for a given pronunciation requires word-specific knowledge (*/fuks/* → fuchs / vux / phuks).

In regular (also referred to as transparent or shallow) orthographies, a beginning reader (or speller) can successfully decode unfamiliar words with a relatively small set of explicitly learned G–P correspondence rules. In more irregular (opaque, deep) orthographies, one needs to master a larger and more complicated set of rules from the outset, and this set of rules has to be fine-tuned in a more implicit manner during increasing reading experience to cover all possible contextual effects and exceptions.

Languages also differ with respect to other linguistic features such as syllabic structure and their morphological system. The number of phonemes, the complexity of the phonemic structures or the length of the words can also vary a lot between languages. From the perspective of phonological recoding skills, these differences can be considered secondary as they do not affect the principles of phonological assembly as such, but rather the quantitative demands of the phonological recoding process.

GRAPHEME–PHONEME CORRESPONDENCES IN THE FINNISH ORTHOGRAPHY

Finnish has extremely regular G–P correspondences. In standard Finnish there are only 21 phonemes (8 vowels: *a, e, i, o, u, y, ä, ö*; 13 consonants: *d, h, j, k, l, m, n, p, r, s, t, v,* ŋ).

In addition, there are three consonant sounds (*b, g* and *f*) that exist only in loan words. All of these phonemes are consistently marked with a corresponding single letter grapheme, with the exception of ŋ, that is marked with *n* when short (preceding *k*) and *ng* when long. All of these G–P correspondences are regular in both directions.[1] The letters *c, q, w, x, z,* and *å* are used in citation loans only.

There are two phonemic lengths (quantities), long and short. Lengthening of quantity (i.e. long phoneme) is possible for all Finnish phonemes[2] except *d, h, j* and *v*. This leads to a very common feature of Finnish for the differentiation of words. Thus e.g. words like *tuli, tulli* and *tuuli* i.e. 'fire', 'customs' and 'wind' have different meanings although their only difference is in the quantity variation associated with a phoneme in the word. Long phoneme quantity is consistently marked by doubling of the grapheme.[3]

SYLLABLES IN THE FINNISH ORTHOGRAPHY

In spoken Finnish, stress is placed on the first, third, fifth, etc. syllables of words but the final syllable is always unstressed. Because of this stress pattern, the syllable can be considered a natural unit of spoken language. Altogether, there are ten possible types of syllables:[4] CV, CVC, CVV, CVVC, VC, V, VV, CVCC, VVC and VCC. The number of distinct syllables in Finnish is estimated to be between 3,000 and 3,300. Open syllables are more frequent than closed syllables. A syllable (and consequently, a word) never begins with a consonant cluster.[5] Consonant clusters can appear at the end of the syllables, but never at the end of the word.[6] The maximum length of a syllable is four phonemes.

Syllabic segmentation of spoken words closely matches the syllabification of written words. In long quantities, the syllable segments split the double consonants. This produces syllables with a separate consonant sound in each syllable. However, in the case of stop consonants, these orthographic syllables do not perfectly match the phonological syllable segments of the spoken language.

Explicit segmentation of syllables forms a central part of the early reading instruction and syllables are usually explicitly delineated in the reading materials for beginning readers. Finnish words are often quite long and working memory capacity is easily exceeded at the level of the phonemes. The standard instruction methods guide the child to use the syllable as a sub-stage of assembly, thus reducing the memory demands during recoding.

WORDS IN THE FINNISH ORTHOGRAPHY

The vast majority of Finnish words are multi-syllabic (there are only around 50 mono-syllabic words, and most of these are interjections). Because of highly productive compounding, a derivational system, as well as synthetic and agglutinative morphology, the average length of the words depending on the texts can be close to ten letters.

The morphological system is synthetic and agglutinative which results in words containing multiple semantic information, as can be seen in the following examples:

taloissani (in my houses)

root	number	case	possessive
talo	+i	+ssa	+ni

or past participle construction:

näytettyämmehän (indeed, after we have shown)

root	derivative	participle	case	possessive	clitic
näy	+te	+tty	+ä	+mme	+hän

A Finnish noun can have over 2,000 distinct orthographic forms with different combinations of case (15), number (2), possessive (6) and a variety of clitics. The number is even higher for verbs. When one takes into account derivation and compounding, the same root can exist in a large number of orthographic contexts. In some word items the morphology is not purely agglutinative but also fusional, which means that the root is changed in some inflected forms (e.g. *lammas* 'sheep', *lampaan* 'sheep + gen.'; *käsi* 'hand', *kättä* 'hand + partit.').

RECODING IN FINNISH

The English-based models of reading acquisition typically describe separate processes of phonological recoding and direct word recognition. Because of the synthetic and agglutinative nature of Finnish, the use of a direct strategy for word recognition in beginning reading would be inefficient. The nouns and verbs are inflected which means that the number of possible word forms for any given item is vast. In the case of fusional structures, even the root is changed with inflections. Hence the ability to recognize the uninflected root does not help. This means that phonological recoding is the only efficient route to word recognition. For this reason, reading instruction methods in Finland are almost uniformly based on phonics approaches.

From the point of view of phonological recoding, the simple Finnish G–P correspondence system has very clear advantages. The orthography is purely phonemic, the number of phonemes is relatively small and G–P conversion rules are perfectly regular. Because there are only single letter graphemes (with one exception), the written word also makes the otherwise abstract phonemic structure explicit for the reader. Consequently, phonological assembly is a fairly simple serial process of putting the single letter sounds together.[7] As long as a beginning reader is able to perform phonemic synthesis after mastering the basic letter–sound correspondences, he or she has the tools for recoding any given word, including unfamiliar words. This simplicity is in marked contrast to phonological recoding in an irregular orthography such as English, where one first has to be able to make orthographic segmentation of multi-letter graphemes (*thick* → /th/ /i/ /ck/) and where the knowledge of basic letter sounds is not nearly helpful enough to be able to use the G–P correspondences. In English, serial phonological recoding is also complicated by the need to take contextual effects into consideration and in the fact that some irregular words cannot be read by phonemic assembly at all.

Compared to more irregular orthographies, it seems plausible to conclude that the features of the Finnish orthography make it relatively easy to master and systematically apply phonological recoding in the early stage of reading development. This conclusion is also supported by the empirical findings reviewed later in this chapter. In comparison to their English-speaking counterparts, it seems that even Finnish dyslexic children are able to master phonological recoding and attain relatively good accuracy in their reading skills. The Finnish dyslexic problems seem to manifest more in poor fluency and problems in dealing with the quantity aspect of the written language. Whereas Lieberman *et al.* (1980, p. 139) refer to English as a 'language that assumes a reader, who has achieved phonological maturity', Finnish is a language that treats a phonologically immature reader in a lenient manner.

FINNISH RESEARCH ON DYSLEXIA

The recent research into dyslexia in Finland has focused on early precursors, brain and cognitive predictors and correlates of dyslexia, intervention, as well as social and motivational factors associated with learning disorders, especially dyslexia. A number of results from these studies have general interest, independent of the language context within which the participants are reading. The issue of cognitive correlates earns a special mention due to the possible consequences of the extreme orthographic regularity of Finnish.

Development of Children at Familial Risk for Dyslexia

The Jyväskylä Longitudinal study of Dyslexia (JLD; Lyytinen *et al.*, 1994; Lyytinen *et al.*, 1995; Lyytinen, 1997) attempts to identify early precursors and developmental paths associated with dyslexia. Approximately 200 children, half with and half without familial risk for dyslexia, were intensively assessed during their development from birth. At the beginning of 2002, all these children had reached the age of six and the oldest was nine years old. According to earlier results concerning familial transmission of dyslexia (for summary, see van der Leij *et al.*, 2001), a substantial portion of children born to parent(s) with dyslexia can be expected to face reading problems. In the JLD, children had in addition to parent(s) with diagnosed dyslexia, at least one close relative with reported reading problems. The results thus far reveal that the groups already differ at birth in brain event-related potentials to speech sounds (Guttorm *et al.*, 2001) and also at the age of six months, both in the categorical perception of speech, and brain responses to speech stimuli (see Lyytinen *et al.*, 2003), for a summary of the psychophysiological studies of the JLD completed thus far. The most recent general summary of the results of the JLD (Lyytinen *et al.*, 2001) reveals that language-related developmental paths do not show any substantial differences during the second year but begin to diverge from this point. Differences have emerged between groups in the production of language in measures such as maximum sentence length at two years, and pronunciation of diphthongs and long words at the age of 2½ years. At age 3½ years, the most explicit differences between the groups include Boston Naming, Emerging Phonological Awareness measures and Inflectional Morphology. In addition, at the age of 5 years, Digit Span, vocabulary, and letter naming, for example, show reliably higher scores among non-risk children, even after controlling for non-verbal IQ. One of the first conclusions which in practice seems important, is as follows: a child who is at familial risk for dyslexia may be in need of preventative measures concerning language development if he/she is a late talker at age of 2½. Our prediction data show convincingly that a substantially higher proportion of the late talkers within the at-risk group than within the control group are also later delayed in speech (Lyytinen *et al.*, 2001b). This difference has been now validated up to five years of age in our follow-up covering the whole group.

Psychophysiology of dyslexia

Recent Finnish research has focused on the brain functions associated with dyslexia. A number of relevant studies are based on brain electro-magnetic responses, more specifically, event-related responses (ERP). One very interesting ERP in this context is termed mismatch negativity (MMN) identified by Risto Näätänen and his co-workers more than 20 years ago. It reflects the sound discrimination process in the brain and thus provides a potential measure of sound/speech perception, which is believed to be affected in dyslexia. Kujala and Näätänen (2001) have recently reviewed MMN findings associated with dyslexia. There are indications that at least a substantial proportion of individuals with dyslexia (e.g. Kujala *et al.*, 2000) and even infants at risk for dyslexia (Leppänen *et al.*, 2003), show atypical MMN. With the aid of a programme developed by Karma (1989) to train sound perception skills, a recent report (Kujala *et al.*, 2001) refers to the possibility that the brain process reflected by differential MMN can be affected among individuals with dyslexia.

Two groups of researchers in the Cold Temperature Laboratory at Helsinki University of Technology have reported interesting findings concerning differences between adults with and without dyslexia. Päivi Helenius and Riitta Salmelin and their colleagues have published a number of interesting studies based on ERPs (assessed using magnetoencephalography, MEG). For example, they have identified locations in the temporal and posterior brain auditory and speech-related areas which show atypical activation among adults with dyslexia in reading-related tasks (e.g. Salmelin *et al.*, 1996; Helenius *et al.*, 1999b). The group, led by Riitta Hari, has shown that not only do adults with dyslexia differ from normal readers on tasks requiring temporal perception of sound (Hari and Kiesilä, 1996; Helenius *et al.*, 1999), but they also differ on comparable visual tasks (Hari *et al.*, 1999, 2001). These authors propose that 'sluggish attentional shifting' can account for the impaired processing of rapid stimulus sequences in dyslexia (Hari and Renvall, 2001).

A group led by Veijo Virsu in Helsinki University has examined the sensory input processing of individuals with dyslexia. They report substantial (IQ independent) correlations between different measures of temporal input processing and reading (Laasonen *et al.*, 2002). In another study, children with developmental dyslexia were shown to require a longer SOA than controls in order to judge whether two spatially separate trains of brief stimuli, presented at various stimulus onset asynchronies (SOA), were synchronous or not. Surprisingly, this was observed to be the case independent of the modality – in auditory, visual and tactual modalities as well as in polysensory tasks (Laasonen *et al.*, 2000).

COGNITIVE AND MOTIVATIONAL PREDICTORS AND CORRELATES OF DYSLEXIA

Researchers at the Centre for Learning Research (CLR) at the University of Turku have examined the motivational correlates of learning disorders including dyslexia (e.g. Lehtinen *et al.*, 1995). They have also evaluated the effects of intervention on early reading (e.g. Poskiparta *et al.*, 1998; Poskiparta *et al.*, 1999), as well as the cognitive correlates of reading skills (Dufva *et al.*, 2001).

They have also tried to explain the resistance to treatment associated with dyslexia (Niemi *et al.*, 1999) as well as poor decoders' compensatory use of listening comprehension skills while reading for meaning (Kinnunen *et al.*, 1998). Studies in another Finnish research centre for learning disorders, the Niilo Mäki Institute (NMI in Jyväskylä), have examined the cognitive correlates of dyslexia (e.g. Lyytinen *et al.*, 1994; Holopainen *et al.*, 2000) and the heterogeneity associated with its expression in adulthood (Leinonen *et al.*, 2001). From a more clinical perspective, researchers associated with the NMI have investigated issues such as co-morbidity of other pathologies with dyslexia including attention deficit disorder (Närhi and Ahonen, 1995; Räsänen and Ahonen, 1995; for a review see Lyytinen *et al.*, 1998).

Aro *et al.* (1999) and Holopainen *et al.* (2000) have described how phonological skills are connected to the acquisition of decoding skills in a regular orthography. Finnish children acquire reading skill by learning to assemble reading items (including words not known to them in advance or pseudowords) by blending the letter sounds based on single phoneme–grapheme identities rather than using any larger units by analogy (Holopainen *et al.*, 2002). This is very understandable taking into account the $G = P / P = G$ regularity which has few exceptions (see above). Holopainen *et al.* (2001) searched for the pre-reading skills that could predict the instruction time required to attain accurate and fluent decoding skills in a random sample of about 100 children. Although the well-known association of pre-school phonological measures (phonemic awareness and pseudoword repetition) with early reading was very significant, pre-school phonological awareness was not the best predictor of failure to acquire the expected reading accuracy or speed during the first two to three years of reading instruction. Apparently, orthographic regularity, in conjunction with the systematic phonics instruction very commonly applied in teaching, supports even the poorest readers in their attainment of phonemic awareness and thus facilitate mechanical reading. In turn, this assists performance (via letter knowledge and orthographic images) on phonological tasks, consequently reducing their role in predicting further reading acquisition. Instead, digit span and naming speed measured at pre-school emerged as the most successful predictors until 4th grade, even after controlling for IQ and reading level at 1st grade. It is worth noting, however, that pre-school visual analogical reasoning scores significantly differentiated these delayed readers from early readers and contributed independently towards the prediction. This invites one to speculate whether some still less well-specified components of cognitive abilities unrelated to phonology may indeed be prerequisites of a successful reading career.

One-third of Finnish children learn to read without formal training before school and most acquire accurate reading skill within three to five months of reading instruction. This is due to mastery of the 'easy' translation rules which suffice for accurate decoding, even of unfamiliar words. However, according to the follow-up study illustrated in the papers by Holopainen *et al.* (referred to in this article), 8 per cent of Finnish children require more than two years to attain accuracy. In addition, approximately 5 per cent of Finnish children experience difficulties in the automatization of their reading skill towards normal fluency. According to an examination of the reading of more than eight thousand parents screened for the afore-mentioned JLD study, approximately 6 per cent of Finnish adults have reading and writing difficulties; half of this number also have several relatives with reported reading difficulties. Substantially more report having experienced problems at school but are acceptably good readers according to assessment at adult age (Lyytinen *et al.*, 1995). Reading dysfluency (as opposed to inaccuracy), is a substantially more common problem than noted in the English context (Leinonen *et al.*, 2001).

Children with dyslexia who are referred from schools to clinically-oriented research centres usually have multiple problems. Almost without exception, they are also already affected by extended experiences resulting from their failure to acquire reading at a normal rate. In a context where most children learn basic decoding skills soon after the beginning of instruction, slow acquisition leads to a 'social diagnosis' due to the difference from classmates, even when the difficulty is mild. This may have a clear secondary effect. Oral reading practices during the first grade soon make the child in difficulty painfully aware of the problem. Children learn to be sensitive, even to implicit feedback received at school, not only from the teacher, but also from their classmates. A portion of those who are vulnerable to this type of self-perception may adopt e.g. an avoidance strategy concerning reading training and may even begin to lose motivation in wider domains of school learning. This may expose them to a vicious circle of difficulties and also produce resistance to treatment in the core domain as shown by Niemi *et al.* (1999). Elaboration of this phenomenon has led Niemi and his colleagues to emphasize the importance of motivational influences. In both the CLR and NMI, these influences have been interpreted as secondary phenomena based on experiences resulting from primary deficit(s) associated with dyslexia (Lyytinen *et al.*, 1998; Niemi *et al.*, 1999). However, there are some Finnish empirical data that also support an interpretation whereby individual strategic factors could play a role in the generation of learning problems (Vauras *et al.*, 1999; Onatsu-Arvilommi and Nurmi, 2000; Aunola *et al.*, 2002). In a cross-lag follow-up examination of the data from pre-school to 1st or 2nd grade, these latter two studies reveal slightly higher associations among a random sample of readers in the direction of strategic measures (such as task avoidance) to reading than from reading to strategic behaviour. However, a very recent longitudinal study by Poskiparta *et al.* (in press) in which children were followed from pre-school to the end of the second grade, quite convincingly supports the role of such achievement-related behaviours as secondary factors. This was evidenced through observations by both teacher and researchers that the critical differences associated with strategic and motivational issues only developed after the beginning of school and were significantly more likely to affect poor than normally reading children.

The first part of this chapter revealed that it must be relatively easy for a Finnish child to learn the basic G–P rules and thus to master mechanized reading. However, it does not necessarily follow that the number of children in need of additional support during the early school years is low. Approximately 15 per cent of pupils receive the services of special education during the first school years and even more (close to 25 per cent) are rated by their teachers to be in need of additional support during the pre-school and first two years of school in Finland. Problematic reading is the most common learning disorder at school although it is also usual for this to be associated with other problems such as attention-related disorders. However, a systematic phonics-approach to teaching and, when needed, tolerant small group or individual intervention, is sufficient to help most of those who fail to optimally acquire basic reading to overcome the problem. This can also reduce the reading-related mental strain, a source that also fuels problems related to attention, motivation and emotions. It is thus no surprise that such strain may also be exacerbated by the perception of one's position among classmates, most of whom are very good readers as revealed by the recent PISA study which shows that an average Finnish pupil is, in international comparison, a top-level reader.

ACKNOWLEDGEMENTS

This work is part of the Finnish Centre of Excellence Programme (2000–2005), and has been supported by the Academy of Finland and the University of Jyväskylä. We would like to thank Matti Leiwo for important comments concerning Finnish, and Jane Erskine for valuable notes concerning the comparison of languages. We are also grateful to her and Jenny Thomson for polishing our English.

NOTES

1 The short η-sound would be an exception to this principle, since it is marked with *n* that also corresponds to /n/. However, since short /ŋ/ always precedes /k/, one could also consider it as an allophone (variant) of /n/. In practice, /ŋk/ is often taught as a phoneme combination for beginning readers; both *nk* and *ng* are presented as graphemes.
2 For stop consonants *t*, *k* and *p*, the duration of the phoneme is not actually lengthened, but the stop before the explosion of the sound is lengthened.
3 The exception here is again /ŋ/, whose long duration is marked with the bigraph *ng*.
4 In loan words other syllable types can also be found.
5 Except in some loan words like *strategia*, *psalmi*, *traktori*.
6 Even the loan words follow this rule strictly; *posti* (post), *pankki* (bank), *kirahvi* (giraffe).
7 As a practical example of the straightforward assembly of pronunciation, Finnish dictionaries do not contain phonemic transcriptions.

REFERENCES

Aro, M., Aro, T., Ahonen, T., Räsänen, T., Hietala, A. and Lyytinen, H. (1999) The development of phonological abilities and their relation to reading acquisition: Case studies of six Finnish children. *Journal of Learning Disabilities*, 32(5), 457–463.

Aro, M. and Wimmer, H. (in press) Learning to read: English in comparison to six more regular orthographies. *Applied Psycholinguistics*.

Aunola, K., Nurmi, J-E., Niemi, P., Lerkkanen, M-K. and Rasku-Puttonen, H. (2002) Developmental dynamics of achievement strategies, reading performance, and parental beliefs. *Reading Research Quarterly*, 37(3), 310–327.

Dufva, M., Niemi, P. and Voeten, M.J.M. (2001) The role of phonological memory, word recognition, and comprehension skills in reading development: From preschool to grade 2. *Reading and Writing*, 14(1–2), 91–117.

Guttorm, T., Leppänen, P., Richardson, U. and Lyytinen, H. (2001) Event-related potentials and consonant differentiation in newborns with familial risk for dyslexia. *Journal of Learning Disabilities*, 34(6), 534–544.

Hari, R. and Kiesilä, P. (1996) Deficit of temporal auditory processing in dyslexic adults. *Neuroscience Letters*, 205, 138–140.

Hari, R. and Renvall, H. (2001) Impaired processing of rapid stimulus sequences in dyslexia. *Trends in Cognitive Neuroscience*, 5(12), 525–532.

Hari, R., Renvall, H. and Tanskanen, T. (2001) Left mini-neglect in dyslexic adults, *Brain*, 124, 1373–1380.

Hari, R., Sääskilahti, A., Helenius, P. and Uutela, K. (1999) Non-impaired auditory phase locking in dyslexic adults, *Neuroreport*, 10(11), 2347–2348.

Helenius, P., Salmelin, R., Service, E. and Connolly, J. (1999a) Semantic cortical activation in dyslexic readers. *Journal of Cognitive Neuroscience*, 11, 535–550.

Helenius, P., Tarkiainen, A., Cornelissen, P., Hansen, P.C. and Salmelin, R. (1999b) Dissociation of normal feature analysis and deficient processing of letter strings in dyslexic adults. *Cerebral Cortex*, 9, 476–483.

Helenius, P., Uutela, K. and Hari, R. (1999) Auditory stream segregation in dyslexic adults. *Brain*, 122, 907–913.

Holopainen, L., Ahonen, T. and Lyytinen, H. (2001) Predicting delay in reading achievement in a highly transparent language. *Journal of Learning Disabilities*, 34(5), 401–413.

Holopainen, L., Ahonen, T. and Lyytinen, H. (2002) The role of reading by analogy in first-grade Finnish readers. *Scandinavian Journal of Educational Research*, 46(1), 83–98.

Holopainen, L., Ahonen, T. and Lyytinen, H. (submitted) Characteristics of delayed readers in a highly orthographically regular language.

Holopainen, L., Ahonen, T., Tolvanen, A. and Lyytinen, H. (2000) Two alternative ways to model the relation between reading accuracy and phonological awareness at preschool age. *Scientific Studies of Reading*, 4(2), 77–100.

Karlsson, F. (1999) *Finnish: An Essential Grammar*. London: Routledge.

Karma, K. (1989) Auditive structuring as a basis for reading and writing. In H. Breuer and K. Ruoho (eds), *Pädagogisch-psychologische Prophylaxe bei 4–8 jährigen Kindern*. Jyväskylä: Jyväskylä Studies in Education, Psychology and Social Research, 71.

Kinnunen, R., Vauras, M. and Niemi, P. (1998) Comprehension monitoring in beginning readers. *Scientific Studies of Reading*, 2, 353–375.

Kujala, T., Karma, K., Ceponiene, R., Belitz, S., Turkkila, P., Tervaniemi, M. and Näätänen, R. (2001) Plastic neural changes and reading improvement caused by audiovisual training in reading-impaired children. *PNAS*, 98(18), 10509–10514.

Kujala, T., Myllyviita, K., Tervaniemi, M., Alho, K., Kallio, J. and Näätänen, R. (2000) Basic auditory dysfunction in dyslexia as demonstrated by brain-activity measurements. *Psychophysiology*, Special Report, 37, 262–266.

Kujala, T. and Näätänen, R. (2001) The mismatch negativity in evaluating central auditory dysfunction in dyslexia. *Neuroscience and Behavioral Reviews*, 25(6), 535–543.

Kyöstiö, O.K. (1980) Is learning to read easy in a language in which the grapheme-phoneme correspondences are regular? In J.F. Kavanagh and R.L. Venezky (eds), *Orthography, Reading, and Dyslexia*. Baltimore, MD: University Park Press.

Laasonen, M., Service, E. and Virsu, V. (2002) Cross-modal temporal order and processing acuity in developmentally dyslexic young adults. *Brain and Language*, 80(3), 340–354.

Laasonen, M., Tomma-Halme, J., Lahti-Nuuttila, P., Service, E. and Virsu, V. (2000) Rate of information segregation in developmentally dyslexic children. *Brain and Language*, 75(1), 66–81.

Landerl, K., Wimmer, H. and Frith, U. (1997) The impact of orthographic consistency on dyslexia: A German-English comparison. *Cognition*, 63, 315–334.

Lehtinen, E., Vauras, M., Salonen, P., Olkinuora, E. and Kinnunen, R. (1995) Long-term development of learning activity: motivational, cognitive, and social interaction. *Educational Psychologist*, 30(1), 21–35.

Leinonen, S., Müller, K., Leppänen, P., Aro, M., Ahonen, T. and Lyytinen, H. (2001) Heterogeneity in adult dyslexic readers: relating processing skills to the speed and accuracy of oral text reading. *Reading and Writing: An Interdisciplinary Journal*, 14, 265–296.

Leppänen, P.H.T., Richardson, U., Pihko, E., Eklund, K.M., Guttorm., T.K., Aro, M. and Lyytinen, H. (2003) Brain responses reveal speech processing differences in infants at risk for dyslexia. *Developmental Neuropsychology*, 22(1), 407–422.

Lieberman, I., Liberman, A.M., Mattingly, I. and Shankweiler, D. (1980) Orthography and the beginning reader. In J.F. Kavanagh and R.L. Venezky (eds), *Orthography, Reading, and Dyslexia*. Baltimore, MD: University Park Press.

Lyytinen, H. (1997) In search of precursors of dyslexia: A prospective study of children at risk for reading problems. In M. Snowling and C. Hulme (eds), *Dyslexia: Biology, Cognition and Intervention*. London: Whurr Publishers.

Lyytinen, H., Ahonen, T., Aro, M., Aro, T., Närhi, V. and Räsänen, P. (1998) Learning disabilities: A view of developmental neuropsychology. In R. Licht, A. Bouma, W. Slot and W. Koops (eds), *Child Neuropsychology: Reading Disability and More . . .* Delft: Eburon.

Lyytinen, H., Ahonen, T., Eklund, K., Guttorm, T.K., Laakso, M-L., Leinonen, S., Leppänen, P.H.T., Lyytinen, P., Poikkeus, A-M., Puolakanaho, A., Richardson, U. and Viholainen, H. (2001a) Developmental pathways of children with and without familial risk for dyslexia during the first years of life. *Developmental Neuropsychology*, 20(2), 535–554.

Lyytinen, H., Ahonen, T. and Räsänen, P. (1994) Dyslexia and dyscalculia in children – risks, early precursors, bottlenecks and cognitive mechanisms. *Acta Paedopsychiatrica*, 56(1), 179–192.

Lyytinen, H., Leinonen, S., Nikula, M., Aro, M. and Leiwo, M. (1995) In search of the core features of dyslexia: Observations concerning dyslexia in the highly orthographically regular Finnish language. In V. Berninger (ed.), *The Varieties of Orthographic Knowledge II: Relationships to Phonology, Reading, and Writing*. Dordrecht: Kluwer.

Lyytinen, H., Leppänen, P.H.T., Richardson, U. and Guttorm, T. (2003) Brain functions and speech perception in infants at risk for dyslexia. In V. Csepe (ed.), *Dyslexia: Different Brain, Different Behaviour*. Dordrecht: Kluwer.

Lyytinen, P., Poikkeus, A-M., Laakso, M-L., Eklund, K. and Lyytinen, H. (2001b) Language development and symbolic play in children with and without familial risk for dyslexia. *Journal of Speech, Language and Hearing Research*, 44(4), 873–885.

Närhi, V. and Ahonen, T. (1995) Reading disability with and without Attention Deficit Hyperactivity disorder: Do attentional problems make a difference? *Developmental Neuropsychology*, 11(3), 337–349.

Niemi, P., Kinnunen, R., Poskiparta, E. and Vauras, M. (1999) Do pre-school data predict resistance to treatment in phonological awareness, decoding and spelling? In I. Lundberg, F.E. Tönnessen and I. Austad (eds), *Neuropsychology and Cognition: Dyslexia: Advances in Theory and Practice*. Dordrecht: Kluwer Academic Publishers.

Onatsu-Arvilommi, T. and Nurmi, J.-E. (2000) The role of task-avoidant and task-focused behaviors in the development of reading and mathematical skills during the first school year: A cross-lagged longitudinal study. *Journal of Educational Psychology*, 92, 478–491.

Poskiparta, E., Niemi, P., Lepola, J., Ahtola, A. and Laine, P. (in press) Motivational-emotional vulnerability and difficulties in learning to read and spell. *British Journal of Educational Psychology*.

Poskiparta, E., Niemi, P. and Vauras, M. (1999) Who benefits from training in linguistic awareness in the first grade and what components of it show training effects? *Journal of Learning Disabilities*, 5, 437–446, 456.

Poskiparta, E., Vauras, M. and Niemi, P. (1998) Promoting word recognition, spelling and reading comprehension skills in a computer-based training program in grade 2. In P. Reitsma and L. Verhoeven (eds), *Problems and Interventions in Literacy Development*. Dordrecht: Kluwer Academic Publishers.

Räsänen, P. and Ahonen, T. (1995) Arithmetic disabilities with and without reading difficulties: A comparison of arithmetic errors. *Developmental Neuropsychology*, 11(3), 275–295.

Salmelin, R., Service, E., Kiesilä, P., Uutela, K. and Salonen, O. (1996) Impaired perception of visual word form in dyslexia revealed with magnetoencephalography. *Annals of Neurology*, 40(2), 157–162.

Seymour, P., Aro, M. and Erskine, J. (2003) Foundation literacy acquisition in European orthographies. *British Journal of Psychology*, 94, 143–174.

Thorstad, G. (1991) The effect of orthography on the acquisition of literacy skills. *British Journal of Psychology*, 82, 527–537.

Van der Leij, A., Lyytinen, H. and Zwarts, F. (2001) The study of infant cognitive processes in dyslexia. In A.J. Fawcett and R.I. Nicolson (eds), *Dyslexia: Theory and Good Practice*. London: Whurr.

Vauras, M., Rauhanummi, T., Kinnunen, R. and Lepola, J. (1999) Motivational vulnerability as a challenge for educational interventions. *International Journal of Educational Research*, 31, 515–531.

Wimmer, H. and Goswami, U. (1994) The influence of orthographic consistency on reading development: Word recognition in English and German children. *Cognition*, 51, 91–103.

9

DYSLEXIA RESEARCH IN GERMAN-SPEAKING COUNTRIES

Gerd Schulte-Körne

INTRODUCTION

During the past ten years a great amount of empirical research on dyslexia from different fields, e.g., psychology and medicine, has been carried out in Germany. A broad spectrum of research from genetic and neurobiological causes to prevention and intervention has been covered. However, only a few cross-linguistic studies have been published on the linguistic influence on dyslexia. The following review is a personal selection of research which will hopefully give the reader an overview of research activities in Germany.

LONGITUDINAL STUDIES

Follow-up studies of reading and spelling disorder have shown that the prognosis is unfavourable. Klicpera *et al.* (1993) investigated the development of reading and spelling skills from the 1st to the 8th Grade in a large epidemiological sample in Vienna. Reading and spelling skills proved to be highly stable. Only a small percentage of the children having problems in the 2nd Grade performed at an average reading and spelling level at the 8th Grade. The poorest readers read at the same level at the end of the 4th Grade as average readers did at the end of the 1st Grade. At the end of the 8th Grade these children had attained the level of average readers at the end of the 2nd Grade. The same results were revealed for spelling disabled. The underlying problem of the reading difficulties of these children might be due to persistent problems with phonological recoding (Klicpera and Gasteiger-Klicpera, 1994).

Behind the cognitive development of reading and spelling disorders there are a lot of other aspects like comorbidity and occupational status which have a great impact on the development of the disorder.

International Book of Dyslexia: A Cross-Language Comparison and Practice Guide. Edited by Ian Smythe, John Everatt and Robin Salter.   ISBN 0471498416   © 2004 John Wiley & Sons, Ltd.

Esser and Schmidt (1993) found in a German epidemiological sample that children with a specific reading retardation had a bad school performance at the age of 13 as well as at the age of 18. The number of psychiatric symptoms was enhanced at ages 8, 13 and 18. In particular, conduct disorders were more frequent and the rate of juvenile delinquency was enhanced. Strehlow *et al.* (1992) examined the longitudinal development from an out-patient population derived from the Department of Child and Adolescent Psychiatry of Heidelberg University.

At 12 years follow-up, 59 out of 115 male patients who had been diagnosed as dyslexic (mean age: 10.1 years) were examined. About half of the patients had participated in a specific spelling training programme that had lasted more than six months, but at follow-up no effect of therapy could be demonstrated. Spelling skills at follow-up were more that one standard deviation below the norm of the subjects' age. They found that the dyslexic children were severely impaired in their school career: although their average IQ was 112 and all of them came from middle-class families with well-educated parents, only 6 out of 59 had a secondary education. The dyslexic adolescents chose occupations often requiring practical skills rather than reading or spelling. Patients who had completed no more than the nine obligatory years at school were less content with their work than expected based on a normative sample.

Recently, the development of spelling skills, intelligence, the psychosocial development as well as the socio-economic status were evaluated in our follow-up study of dyslexic children who attended a boarding school (Schulte-Körne *et al.*, 2003a). Some 29 children with spelling disorders were examined 20 years after leaving school. Spelling ability was measured by the Mannheimer Spelling Test (MRT), psychiatric symptoms by the Symptom Checklist by Derogatis (SCL-90), the occupational level by the Magnitude-Prestigeskala by Wegener, intelligence by the Culture Fair Intelligencetest (CFT 20). A self-constructed questionnaire was used to register subjects' self-perception of reading and spelling ability, the role of reading and spelling at work and the influence of reading and spelling on the choice of employment. The main findings were that spelling skills at follow-up were more than 0.5 standard deviation above the spelling skill when entering school. The occupational level is rather high. There is no evidence for a significant number of psychiatric symptoms in these dyslexic adults. The general finding was the favourable development of children with a spelling disorder 20 years after attending a special boarding school for dyslexic children. The high IQ, the high socio-economic status of these dyslexic adults and their parents, and the long-lasting remedial work at the school all taken together might be the relevant factors explaining this development.

VISUAL AND AUDITORY PROCESSING IN DYSLEXIA

Auditory processing – phonological processing

Phonological processing refers to the concept of a variety of perceptual and cognitive abilities which play a major role in the development of reading and spelling. It is beyond the scope of this review to give more details about the development of phonological processing, correlation and intervention studies, however. The focus here will be on demonstrating the similarities and differences between a transparent orthography such as German and a non-transparent orthography such as English.

The role of phonemic awareness in reading and spelling has been shown for different languages (e.g., Lundberg *et al.*, 1980; Wagner and Torgesen, 1987; Cossu *et al.*, 1988; Wimmer *et al.*, 1991; Caravolas and Bruck, 1993). However, for onset-rime awareness (which is strongly correlated with reading [Bradley and Bryant, 1983; Bryant *et al.*, 1990] in English), no predictive value for reading development was found for German children (Wimmer *et al.*, 1994). This result might be explained by the structure of the English orthography: Goswami (2000) hypothesizes that rimes (as opposed to vowels) have a high consistency of spelling-sound relations and therefore onset-rime awareness is a strong predictor of learning to read English.

There is some empirical evidence that a phonemic deficit is less marked in children who are learning to read and spell an orthography that is more transparent than English. Phonemic recoding is often measured by a nonsense word reading task. This task requires the exact mapping of graphemes to phonemes. Rack *et al.* (1992) revealed a non-word reading deficit for English-speaking children and adults. Wimmer (1996) found that German dyslexic children needed more time to read nonsense word lists than controls, but they did not commit more reading errors. German dyslexic children are much better at reading nonsense words than English dyslexic children (Landerl *et al.*, 1997). However, Klicpera and Gasteiger-Klicpera (2000) could not replicate this finding. They found that phonological recoding (measured by a task of spelling words with voiced versus unvoiced stop consonants, with consonant cluster and pseudowords) is the main source of spelling difficulties in German. Schulte-Körne (2001a) found further evidence for the importance of phonological recoding in the reading and spelling ability of German adolescents and adults. The correlation between pseudoword reading and spelling ranged from 0.58 to 0.68 and remained significant if word reading was partialled out. Thus it is questionable whether German reading and spelling disabled overcome their initial difficulties in phonological recoding, as was suggested by Landerl and Wimmer (2000).

Auditory processing – speech perception

Deficits in phonological processing have been shown (see above) to play a major role in the aetiology of dyslexia, and speech perception was found to be a prerequisite for phonological processing (Watson and Miller, 1993; McBride-Chang, 1995; Schulte-Körne *et al.*, 1999b). In several studies, significant group differences have been found between dyslexic children and normals regarding the categorical perception of synthetic /ba/–/da/–/ga/ syllables (Godfrey *et al.*, 1981; Manis *et al.*, 1997; Werker and Tees, 1987). These studies used stimulus identification and discrimination tasks, which required the subjects to focus on the relevant stimulus dimensions. These cognitive processes could have been influenced by attention, motivation, and memory-span performance, all of which have been demonstrated to be abnormal in dyslexia (Jorm, 1983; Schulte-Körne *et al.*, 1991). Thus it remains unclear whether the deficits in speech perception demonstrated represent an underlying deficit in dyslexia, reflect a secondary effect, or are caused along with dyslexia by the same underlying, as yet unknown, deficit. Therefore, the question arises as to whether the speech perception deficit described in dyslexics occurs on the level of sensory perception which is characterized by pre-attentive and automatic processing.

A neurophysiological paradigm well suited to examining pre-attentive and automatic central auditory processing is the mismatch negativity (MMN). This is a negative component of the event-related brain potential (ERP), elicited when a detectable change occurs in a sequence of repetitive homogeneous auditory stimuli (Näätänen, 1992). The most commonly described MMN occurs at 100–300 ms post-stimulus onset although other studies have found later MMNs between 300 and 600 ms (Kraus *et al.* 1996). The MMN is elicited by any change in frequency, intensity or duration of tone stimuli, as well as by changes in complex stimuli such as phonetic stimuli (Näätänen, 1992). It is assumed to arise as a result of a mechanism that compares each current auditory input with a trace of recent auditory input stored in the auditory memory. The MMN usually reaches its amplitude maximum over the fronto-central scalp (ibid.).

In a study with dyslexic children we demonstrated that the late component of the MMN elicited by passive speech perception was attenuated in comparison to a control group (Schulte-Körne *et al.*, 1998a). This attenuation was detected only with speech but not with tone stimuli, supporting the hypothesis that dyslexics have a specific speech processing deficit at a sensory level. Further evidence for a specific speech processing deficit in dyslexic children and adults came from the studies by Watson and Miller (1993) and Schulte-Körne *et al.* (1998b, 1999b). They found no influence of the ability to discriminate tone stimuli or detect a gap between bursts on reading and spelling ability.

It is well known that dyslexic children often continue to have difficulties into adulthood, especially with spelling (Dilling *et al.*, 1991); however, the role of speech perception in dyslexia in adults has not yet been extensively examined. Dyslexics have been shown to have difficulties in speech identification and discrimination tasks (Libermann *et al.*, 1985; Steffens *et al.*, 1992; Cornelissen *et al.*, 1996), but tasks in all of these three studies required subjects to focus on the stimuli, thus the results may have been influenced by factors such as motivation and attention. In a second study Schulte-Körne *et al.* (2001a) found evidence for a speech processing deficit in dyslexic adults. The results of this study and the study with dyslexic children (Schulte-Körne *et al.*, 1998a) provide strong evidence that the speech discrimination difficulties of dyslexics occur already before conscious perception. The findings that speech perception has developed in early years of childhood (Kuhl *et al.*, 1992) and that infants at risk due to a familial background of reading problems process auditory temporal cues of speech sounds differently from infants without such a risk even before they learn to speak (Leppänen *et al.*, 2002) suggest that deficits in pre-attentive speech processing are a basic dysfunction in dyslexics which continues to have an important impact in dyslexia into adulthood.

Temporal processing

Many of the features distinguishing speech sounds, like voice onset time and formant transitions, require the detection of timing differences of complex auditory patterns in just a few milliseconds. In recent years the hypothesis of an underlying auditory temporal processing deficit in dyslexia has become very popular (Farmer and Klein, 1995). Tallal (1980) described a deficit in dyslexics regarding the processing of brief, rapidly changing auditory stimuli. The finding that dyslexics are mainly impaired in processing stop consonants (Cornelissen *et al.*, 1996; Manis *et al.*, 1997) which are characterized by brief and rapid spectral changes supports the role of temporal processing for speech perception in dyslexics. Following this, evidence was published that repeated short sequences of auditory stimuli are recognized and analysed as auditory patters at a very early pre-attentive stage of signal processing (Alain *et al.*, 1994; Winkler and Schröger, 1995).

Schulte-Körne *et al.* (1999c) examined the hypothesis that dyslexics have an attenuated

MMN (see above) for changes in auditory temporal patterns. We used tonal patterns (standard and deviant) in the experimental condition. The difference between the two patterns is that two segments of identical frequency but different duration have been exchanged, thus the patterns differ only regarding the duration but not the frequencies of the tones. Because the frequencies of the exchanged segments were identical, the change could not have been detected without a representation of the temporal structure of the patterns. Thus it can be concluded that temporal information is indeed included in the memory traces indexed by the MMN, supporting the hypothesis that patterns are represented as unified auditory events. Our hypothesis was that dyslexics have difficulties in processing temporal patterns, resulting in an attenuated MMN. This hypothesis was confirmed. The standard and deviant patterns used in our study do not differ regarding the frequencies of the tones; the difference between the deviant and standard stimuli is that two segments of identical frequency, but of different duration, have been exchanged. Thus it can be concluded that the temporal difference between the patterns triggered the MMN in both groups, but the dyslexics had a significantly attenuated MMN because they could not process the temporal information adequately.

In earlier studies Schulte-Körne *et al.* (1998b) found that dyslexics have an attenuated MMN for speech stimuli, but not for tone stimuli (see above), leading to the conclusion that their deficit was specific to speech perception. However, as distinguishing speech sounds requires the processing of temporal information (Kojima *et al.*, 1997), Schulte-Körne *et al.* (1999c) hypothesized that it may be the temporal information embedded in speech sounds, rather than phonetic information *per se*, that resulted in the attenuated MMN found in dyslexics in previous studies. This would also concur with the finding of Tallal *et al.* (1996) that training with temporally modified speech results in significant improvements in speech discrimination and language comprehension in language learning-impaired children. Regarding the high association between speech impairment and dyslexia, this might suggest that such a training programme might also help dyslexics.

Visual processing – orthographic awareness

In an alphabet-based language system there exists a very particular orthographic structure. For example, the possibility of a specific letter following another specific letter in any given syllable is not always the same. Some letter combinations are not even possible (Hultquist, 1997). Skilled readers and writers, therefore, have implicit knowledge of what letter combinations are orthographically legitimate. This also means that the orthographic process in word identification is very much word specific. Orthographic knowledge involves remembering specific spelling patterns to identify individual words or parts of words (Barker *et al.*, 1992). Thus it seems very plausible that the orthographic structure of a language has an influence on orthographic knowledge.

Schulte-Körne *et al.* (1997a) examined the influence of phonological recoding, orthographic knowledge and IQ on the spelling ability of German adults. They found that phonological recoding had the greatest influence on spelling whereas orthographic knowledge was of minor relevance. The influence of IQ was negligible.

More recently, Klicpera and Gasteiger-Klicpera (2000) investigated the development of orthographic knowledge in 2nd and 4th Grade children by recognition and production of critical spelling patterns in words whose correct spelling could only be found through word-specific knowledge or through knowledge of morphometric connections. These results were compared with the development of phonological recoding in the same sample (see above). The main results were that poor spellers lagged behind average spellers in the same grade in phonological recoding as well as in orthographic knowledge. The comparison with reading level-matched 2nd Grade children revealed that the 4th Grade poor spellers have greater problems with phonological recoding than orthographic knowledge. Although orthographic knowledge seems to be a problem for poor spellers until the end of primary school, problems in phonological recoding seem to be of more relevance for children suffering from a spelling disorder.

Visual processing – magnocellular and parvocellular system

Visual processing is currently seen as comprising two separate but interactive subsystems with different spatio-temporal response characteristics (Merigan and Maunsell, 1993). The magnocellular system, which arises from cells widely distributed across the retina, projects via the ventral lateral geniculate nucleus (LGN) to the visual cortex and thereafter largely to the parietal cortex. It preferentially mediates movement, fast temporal resolution, low contrast, and low spatial frequencies. The parvocellular system originates in cells concentrated in the fovea and projects via the dorsal LGN to the visual cortex and then mainly to the temporal cortex. It is responsible for colour resolution, high contrast, and high spatial frequencies (Merigan and Maunsell, 1993).

Considerable evidence has been put forward in favour of the magnocellular deficit theory in dyslexia (Stein and Walsh, 1997). Contradictory findings, however, have resulted in a continuing debate as to its role in the pathogenesis of dyslexia. According to the magnocellular system deficit theory, the processing of low spatial frequency and low contrast stimuli presented with high temporal frequency is disturbed in dyslexics. This theory could be confirmed by psychophysiological and neurophysiological studies. Schulte-Körne et al. (1999a) investigated the influence of high and low spatial frequencies and contrasts on the VEP in dyslexics and controls.

They found a lateralization of two components of the VEP, the P1 and P2. These positive components of the VEP with latencies of 100–250 ms reflect early perceptual processing and pattern recognition (Hillyard et al., 1998). For all contrasts and spatial frequencies, activity in the right hemisphere was greater than in the left. This result suggests that the magno- and parvocellular processing of contrasts and spatial frequencies is preferentially located in the right hemisphere. Additionally, the significant interaction of lateralization with spatial frequency demonstrates that this functional asymmetry is even greater for low spatial frequencies, which means that this magnocellular function (sensitivity to low spatial frequencies) is preferentially processed in the right hemisphere. The results of Schulte-Körne et al. (1999a) show no influence of contrast and spatial frequency variations on VEP amplitudes of dyslexics. This result does not support the magnocellular deficit theory in dyslexia.

INTERVENTION

The Marburg Spelling Training Programme

As has been mentioned above, German orthography is more consistent than English. Applying spelling rules is a good strategy to avoid spelling errors. For example, 66 per cent of the spelling errors of children in 2nd Grade could have been avoided by the proper use of spelling rules (Glogauer, 1970). The development of a spelling training programme has to take into account the developmental status with regard to the reading and writing capabilities of 3rd and 4th Grade students. Third Grade students often have little or no concept of spelling rules, or at least they cannot reliably make use of them. This means they may know the rules when asked, but they do not apply them in everyday writing.

The consequence of this phenomenon is that – beside teaching the rules themselves – a training programme also has to incorporate problem-solving strategies in order to ensure that the children really apply the rules. These areas of spelling addressed by the Marburg Spelling Training Programme (Schulte-Körne and Mathwig, 2001b) are those which commonly cause problems for dyslexic children in late primary school years. One common kind of spelling error in German is confusing the use of small and capital initial letters. Other common problems are violations of the so-called 'Dehnung' and 'Schärfung' rules.

There are now three evaluation studies of this training programme available (Schulte-Körne *et al.*, 1997b, 1998c, 2001b, 2003b). The first study assessed the benefit of the Marburg Spelling Training Programme in a parent–child training situation. Nineteen children (14 boys and 5 girls) with a spelling disorder were recruited. Mean age was 9.7 (SD = 0.9) and intelligence was in the normal range. The training programme was administered by the parents, who were supervised by an experienced therapist. The training was applied for half an hour per day, two or three times a week. The training programme helped the children to develop new language strategies for spelling. They were taught systematic rules to recognize specific features of words and algorithms to find the correct solutions.

At one-year follow-up, a significant improvement in specific areas targeted by the programme was found. At two-year follow-up, the specific areas practised had further improved and this benefit had generalized into a significant benefit in the overall spelling ability. In addition, the children reported more self-confidence in related areas such as writing on the blackboard and reading aloud in front of the class. This study demonstrates the value of a low-cost intervention for children with a specific spelling disorder. It demonstrates the potential value of including parents in a programme helping them to a better understanding of the disorder, and also potentially strengthening the parent–child relationship. The improved self-confidence of the children is likely to be an important protective factor against developing the associated emotional problems which are not uncommon with this disorder.

In a second study the Marburg Spelling Training Programme was administered to a sample of ten spelling-disabled primary school students (2nd–4th Grade) over three months in an individual setting. In comparison to the parent training study, the intensity of tutoring was much higher. Statistical analyses yielded significant improvements in spelling and reading test performances after three months (Schulte-Körne *et al.*, 2001b).

In a third study the Marburg Spelling Training Programme was evaluated as a school-based intervention method (Schulte-Körne *et al.*, 2003a). The Marburg Spelling Training Programme has already been evaluated in non-school settings but not in school-based ones. As a control condition we used a computer training program that was already in use in the school. A total of 37 students (2nd and 3rd Grade) had been rated as spelling disabled by their respective teachers and took part in the study. The students were tutored in small groups of five to six children in addition to normal teaching. Tutoring comprised two additional lessons per week. After two years, the training groups had significantly improved their spelling and reading regardless of the method used. This effect could be proved by tests as well as teachers' and parents' ratings. The emotional situation of the children did not change significantly though. The central conclusions were that training of spelling disabled students in small tutoring groups in school is an effective method of improving spelling and reading abilities.

PREDICTION

Early prediction is important since the development of dyslexic children is often faulty (see longitudinal studies). The major aim of the Bielefeld Longitudinal Study was to find specific predictors of reading and spelling ability in the first three grades (Marx and Jansen, 1999). Children were examined ten and four months before entering the 1st Grade, respectively. The screening procedure consisted of eight sub-tests in two domains: phonological awareness (recognition of rhyming words, syllable segmentation, sound blending, phoneme–word matching) and attention and memory (repeating words, rapid naming of colours, visual word matching). The prediction (total correct rate) based on a composite score from the screening of spelling was 86.3 per cent. For reading the rate was 90.2 per cent. The combined literacy achievement was predicted at a total rate of 92.2 per cent. These impressive results show that the identification of children at risk prior to school entrance is validly possible. Further, this study strengthens the importance of phonological awareness for reading and spelling in a transparent orthography.

PREVENTION

There are several German training studies examining whether training in phonological awareness with kindergarten children could improve phonological awareness and letter knowledge, and whether such an improvement would have positive effects on the acquisition of reading and spelling skills in school (Schneider *et al.*, 1997, 1999, 2000). Training studies in the UK and the United States have shown the benefit of phonological training on later reading and spelling development (Ball and Bachman, 1988; Bradley and Bryant, 1985; Byrne and Fielding-Barnsley, 1995). However, phonological awareness was taught while the children were already learning to read. Therefore, it is difficult to infer the causal effects of phonological awareness on reading and spelling because the acquisition of phonological awareness was confused in an unpredictable way with the acquisition of reading. However, training studies in Germany did not suffer from these problems because German children do not receive formal reading instructions in kindergarten. Schneider *et al.* (1997) found that phonological awareness can successfully be taught and developed before learning to read and spell. These results strengthen the role of phonological awareness as a prerequisite of the acquisition of literacy. More recently, Roth and Schneider (2002) have reported on the long-term effects of the kindergarten training study. Children at risk for dyslexia underwent different training procedures in kindergarten and were then followed up during the early school years. These children's reading and spelling development was compared with that of a randomly selected control group. Findings obtained at the end of the 3rd Grade indicate that a procedure combining phonological awareness training with letter–sound correspondence training turned out to be most effective. Children at risk who were in a group given this combined training performed at about the same level as the normal controls, thus confirming the phonological linkage hypothesis. A large percentage of taught children at risk for dyslexia did not show any problems regarding reading or spelling in elementary school.

REFERENCES

Alain, C., Woods, D.L. and Ogawa, K.H. (1994) Brain indices of automatic pattern processing. *Neuroreport*, 6, 140–144.

Ball, E.W. and Bachman, B.A. (1988) Phoneme segmentation training: effect on reading readiness. *Annals of Dyslexia*, 38, 208–225.

Barker, T.A., Torgesen, J.K. and Wagner, R.K. (1992) The role of orthographic processing skills on five different reading tasks. *Reading Research Quarterly*, 27, 334–345.

Bradley, L. and Bryant, P.E. (1983) Categorising sounds and learning to read: A causal connection. *Nature*, 310, 419–421.

Bradley, L. and Bryant, P.E. (1985) *Rhyme and Reason in Reading and Spelling*. Ann Arbor, MI: University of Michigan Press, International Academy for Research in Learning Disabilities, No 1.

Bryant, P.E., MacLean, M., Bradley, L. and Crossland, J. (1990) Rhyme and alliteration, phoneme detection and learning to read. *Developmental Psychology*, 26, 429–438.

Byrne, B. and Fielding-Barnsley, R. (1995) Evaluation of a programme to teach phonemic awareness to young children: A 2- and 3-year follow-up and a new preschool trial. *Journal of Educational Psychology*, 87, 488–503.

Caravolas, M. and Bruck, M. (1993) The effect of oral and written language input on children's phonological awareness: a cross-linguistic study. *Journal of Experimental Child Psychology*, 55, 1–30.

Cornelissen, P.L., Hansen, P.C., Bradley, L. and Stein, J.F. (1996) Analysis for perceptual confusions between nine sets of consonant-vowel sounds in normal and dyslexic adults. *Cognition*, 59, 275–306.

Cossu, G., Shankweiler, D., Liberman, I.Y., Katz, L. and Tola, G (1988) Awareness of phonological segments and reading ability in Italian children. *Applied Psycholinguistics*, 9, 1–16.

Dilling, H., Mombour, W. and Schmidt, M.H. (1991) *International Classification of Mental Disease, ICD-10* (German edition), Bern: Huber.

Esser, G. and Schmidt, M. (1993) Die langfristige Entwicklung von Kindern mit Lese-Rechtschreibschwäche. *Zeitschrift für Klinische Psychologie*, 22, 100–116.

Farmer, M.E. and Klein, R.M. (1995) The evidence for a temporal processing deficit linked to dyslexia. *Psychological Bulletin and Review*, 2, 460–493.

Glogauer, W. (1970) Die quantitative und qualitative Rechtschreibfehler-Analyse bei 7/8 jähren Schülern. *Schule und Psychologie*, 17, 225–234.

Godfrey, J.J., Syrdal-Lasky, K., Millay, K.K. and Knox, C.M. (1981) Performance of dyslexic children on speech perception tests. *Journal of Experimental Child Psychology*, 32, 401–424.

Goswami, U. (2000) Phonological representations, reading development and dyslexia: Towards a cross-linguistic theoretical framework. *Dyslexia*, 6, 133–151.

Hillyard, S.A., Teder-Salejarvi, W.A. and Münte, T.F. (1998) Temporal dynamics of early perceptual processing. *Current Opinion in Neurobiology*, 8, 202–210.

Hultquist, A.M. (1997) Orthographic processing abilities of adolescents with dyslexia. *Annals of Dyslexia*, 47, 89–114.

Jorm, A.F. (1983) Specific reading retardation and working memory: A review. *British Journal of Psychology*, 74, 311–342.

Klicpera, C. and Gasteiger-Klicpera, B. (1994) Die langfristige Entwicklung der mündlichen Lesefähigkeit bei guten und schwachen Lesern. *Zeitschrift für Entwicklungspsychologie und Pädagogische Psychologie*, 26, 278–290.

Klicpera, C. and Gasteiger-Klicpera, B. (2000) Sind Rechtschreibschwierigkeiten Ausdruck einer phonologischen Störung? [(Are spelling difficulties the expression of a phonological deficit?)] *Zeitschrift für Entwicklungspsychologie und Pädagogische Psychologie*, 32, 134–142.

Klicpera, C., Schabmann, A. and Gasteiger-Klicpera, B. (1993) Lesen- und Schreibenlernen während der Pflichtschulzeit: Eine Längsschnittuntersuchung über die Häufigkeit und Stabilität von Lese- und Rechtschreibschwierigkeiten in einem Wiener Schulbezirk. [Learning to read and write in compulsory education: A longitudinal study of the incidence and stability of reading and writing difficulties in a Vienna school district.] *Zeitschrift für Kinder- und Jugendpsychiatrie*, 21, 214–225.

Kojima, H., Hirano, S., Shoji, K., Naito, Y., Honjo, I., Kamoto, Y., Okazawa, H., Ishizu, K., Yonekura, Y., Nagahama, Y., Fukuyama, H. and Konishi, J. (1997) The role of the temporal coding system in the auditory cortex on speech recognition. *Neuroreport*, 8, 2395–2398.

Kraus, N., McGee, T., Carell, T., Zecker, S., Nicol, T and Kock, D. (1996) Auditory neurophysiologic response and discrimination deficits in children with learning difficulties. *Science*, 273, 971–973.

Kuhl, P.K., Williams, K.A. and Lacerda, F. (1992) Linguistic experience alters phonetic perception in infants by 6 months of age. *Science*, 255, 606–608.

Landerl, K. and Wimmer, H. (2000) Deficits in phoneme segmentation are not the core problem of dyslexia: Evidence from German and English children. *Applied Psycholinguistics*, 21, 243–262.

Landerl, K., Wimmer, H. and Frith, U. (1997) The impact of orthographic consistency on dyslexia: A German-English comparison. *Cognition*, 63, 315–334.

Leppänen, P.H., Richardson, U., Pihko, E., Eklund, K.M., Guttorm, T.K., Aro, M. and Lyytinen, H. (2002) Brain responses to changes in speech sound durations differ between infants with and without familial risk for dyslexia. *Developmental Neuropsychology*, 22, 407–422.

Libermann, P., Meskill, R.H., Chatillon, M. and Schupack, H. (1985) Phonetic speech perception deficits in dyslexia. *Journal of Speech and Hearing Research*, 28, 480–487.

Lundberg, I., Wall, S. and Olofsson, A. (1980) Reading and spelling skills in the first school years predicted from phonemic awareness skills in kindergarten. *Scandinavian Journal of Psychology*, 21, 159–173.

Manis, F.R., McBride-Chang, C., Seidenberg, M.S., Keating, P., Doi, L.M., Munson, B. and Petersen, A. (1997) Are speech perception deficits associated with developmental dyslexia? *Journal of Experimental Child Psychology*, 66, 211–235.

Marx, H. and Jansen, H. (1999) Möglichkeiten und Grenzen der Früherkennung und Vorhersage von Lese-Rechtschreibschwierigkeiten. *Forum Logopädie*, 6, 7–16.

McBride-Chang, C. (1995) Phonological processing, speech perception, and reading disability: An integrative review. *Educational Psychologist*, 30, 109–121.

Merigan, W.H. and Maunsell, J.H.R. (1993) How parallel are the primate visual pathways? *Annual Review of Neuroscience*, 16, 369–402.

Näätänen, R. (1992) *Attention and Brain Function*. Hillsdale, NJ: Lawrence Erlbaum.

Rack, J.P., Snowling, M.J. and Olson, R.K. (1992) The nonword reading deficit in development dyslexia: A review. *Reading Research Quarterly*, 27, 29–53.

Roth, E. and Schneider, W. (2002) Langzeiteffekte einer Förderung der phonologischen Bewusstheit und der Buchstabenkenntnis auf den Schriftspracherwerb. [Long-term effects of training phonological awareness and letter-knowledge on literacy acquisition.] *Zeitschrift für Pädagogische-Psychologie*, 16, 99–107.

Schneider, W., Ennemoser, M., Roth, E. and Küspert, P. (1999) Kindergarten prevention of dyslexia: Does training in phonological awareness work for everybody? *Journal of Learning Disabilities*, 32, 429–436.

Schneider, W., Küspert, P., Roth, E. and Visé, M. (1997) Short- and long-term effects of training phonological awareness in kindergarten: Evidence from two German studies. *Journal of Experimental Child Psychology*, 66, 311–340.

Schneider, W., Roth, E. and Ennemoser, M. (2000) Training phonological skills and letter knowledge in children at risk for dyslexia: A comparison of three kindergarten intervention programs. *Journal of Educational Psychology*, 92, 284–295.

Schulte-Körne, G. (2001a) *Lese-Rechtschreibschwäche und Sprachwahrnehmung*. [Dyslexia and Speech Perception.] Münster: Waxmann Verlag.

Schulte-Körne, G., Bartling, J., Deimel, W. and Remschmidt, H. (1999a) Attenuated hemispheric lateralisation in dyslexia: Evidence of a visual processing deficit. *Neuroreport*, 10, 697–701.

Schulte-Körne, G., Deimel, W., Bartling, J. and Remschmidt, H. (1998a) Auditory processing and dyslexia: Evidence for a specific speech deficit. *Neuroreport*, 9, 337–340.

Schulte-Körne, G., Deimel, W., Bartling, J. and Remschmidt, H. (1998b) The role of auditory temporal processing for reading and spelling ability. *Perceptual and Motor Skills*, 86, 1043–1047.

Schulte-Körne, G., Deimel, W., Bartling, J. and Remschmidt, H. (1999c) The role of phonological awareness, speech perception, and auditory temporal processing for dyslexia. *European Child and Adolescent Psychiatry*, Supplement 3, 28–34.

Schulte-Körne, G., Deimel, W., Bartling, J. and Remschmidt, H. (1999c) Pre-attentive processing of auditory patterns in dyslexic human subjects. *Neuroscience Letters*, 276, 41–44.

Schulte-Körne, G., Deimel, W., Bartling, J. and Remschmidt, H. (2001a) Speech perception deficit in dyslexic adults as measured by mismatch negativity (MMN). *International Journal of Psychophysiology*, 40, 77–87.

Schulte-Körne, G., Deimel, W., Hülsmann, J., Seidler, T. and Remschmidt, H. (2001b) Das Marburger Rechtschreib-Training – Ergebnisse einer Kurzzeit-Intervention. [The Marburg Spelling Training – Evaluation of a short time intervention.] *Zeitschrift für Kinder- und Jugendpsychiatrie und Psychotherapie*, 29, 7–15.

Schulte-Körne, G., Deimel, W., Jungermann, M. and Remschmidt, H. (2003a) Nachuntersuchung einer Stichprobe von lese-rechtschreibgestörten Kindern im Erwachsenenalter. [Development of spelling disabled children. Results of a follow-up examination in adulthood.] *Zeitschrift für Kinder- und Jugendpsychiatrie und Psychotherapie* (in press).

Schulte-Körne, G., Deimel, W. and Remschmidt, H. (1997a) Die Bedeutung von phonologischer Rekodierfähigkeit und orthographischem Wissen für die Rechtschreibfähigkeit Erwachsener. [The importance of phonological decoding and orthographic knowledge on spelling ability in adults.] *Zeitschrift für Klinische Psychologie*, 26, 210–217.

Schulte-Körne, G., Deimel, W. and Remschmidt, H. (1998c) Das Marburger Eltern-Kind-Rechtschreibtraining: Verlaufsuntersuchungen nach zwei Jahren. [The Marburg parent–child spelling training – follow-up studies after two years.] *Zeitschrift für Kinder- und Jugendpsychiatrie und Psychotherapie*, 25, 151–159.

Schulte-Körne, G., Deimel, W. and Remschmidt H. (2003b) Das Marburger Rechtschreibtraining in schulischen Fördergruppen – Ergebnisse einer Evaluationsstudie in der Primarstufe. *Zeitschrift für Kinder- und Jugendpsychiatrie und Psychotherapie*, 31 (in press).

Schulte-Körne, G. and Mathwig, F. (2001b) *Das Marburger Rechtschreibtraining Programm*. [(The Marburg Spelling Training Programme)]. Bochum: Winkler Verlag.

Schulte-Körne, G., Remschmidt, H. and Warnke, A. (1991) Selective visual attention and continuous attention in dyslexic children: An experimental study. *Zeitschrift für Kinder- und Jugendpsychiatrie*, 19, 99–106.

Schulte-Körne, G., Schäfer, J., Deimel, W. and Remschmidt, H. (1997b) Das Marburger Eltern-Kind-Rechtschreibtraining – Erste Befunde. [The Marburg parent–child spelling training programme.] *Zeitschrift für Kinder- und Jugendpsychiatrie*, 25, 151–159.

Steffens, M.L., Eilers, R.E., Gross-Glenn, K. and Jallad, B. (1992) Speech perception in adult subjects with familial dyslexia. *Journal of Speech and Hearing Research*, 35, 192–200.

Stein, J. and Walsh, V. (1997) To see but not to read; the magnocellular theory of dyslexia. *Trends in Neuroscience*, 20, 147–152.

Strehlow, U., Kluge, R., Möller, H. and Haffner, J. (1992) Der langfristige Verlauf der Legasthenie über die Schulzeit hinaus: Katamnesen aus einer Kinder psychiatrischen Ambulanz. [Long-term course of dyslexia beyond the school years: catamnesis from child psychiatric ambulatory care.] *Zeitschrift für Kinder- und Jugendpsychiatrie*, 20, 254–265.

Tallal, P. (1980) Auditory temporal perception, phonics, and reading disabilities in children. *Brain and Language*, 9, 182–198.

Tallal, P., Miller, S.L., Bedi, G., Byma, G., Wang, X., Nagarajan, S.S., Schreiner, C., Jenkins, W.M. and Merzenich, M.M. (1996) Language comprehension in language-learning impaired children improved with acoustically modified speech. *Science*, 271, 81–84.

Wagner, R.K. and Torgesen, J.K. (1987) The nature of phonological processing and its causal role in the acquisition of reading skills. *Psychological Bulletin*, 101, 192–212.

Watson, B.U. and Miller, T.K. (1993) Auditory perception, phonological processing, and reading ability/disability. *Journal of Speech and Hearing Research*, 36, 850–863.

Werker, J.F. and Tees, R.C. (1987) Speech perception in severely disabled and average reading children. *Canadian Journal of Psychology*, 41, 48–61.

Wimmer, H. (1996) The nonword reading deficit in developmental dyslexia: Evidence from children learning to read German. *Journal of Experimental Child Psychology*, 61, 80–90.

Wimmer, H., Landerl, K., Linortner, R. and Hummer, P. (1991) The relationship of phonemic awareness to reading acquisition: More consequence than precondition but still important. *Cognition*, 40, 219–240.

Wimmer, H., Landerl, K. and Schneider, W. (1994) The role of rime awareness in learning to read a regular orthography. *British Journal of Developmental Psychology*, 12, 469–484.

Winkler, I. and Schröger, E. (1995) Neural representation for the temporal structure of sound patterns. *Neuroreport*, 6, 690–694.

10

READING, SPELLING AND DYSLEXIA IN GREEK
Research on the role of linguistic and cognitive skills

Costas D. Porpodas

INTRODUCTION

The aim of this chapter is to summarize the existing evidence from empirical research on the role of linguistic and cognitive factors upon reading, spelling and dyslexia in Greek. The chapter will begin with a section on the main features of the Greek writing system and its implications for literacy acquisition and dyslexia. Then, a brief overview of the short history of dyslexia and research on literacy acquisition by dyslexic and normally achieving children in Greece will be given. Finally, a summarized review of the main research findings will be presented, related to the role of language and cognitive skills on reading, spelling and dyslexia.

THE GREEK WRITING SYSTEM AND THE LEARNING OF READING AND SPELLING

The Greek writing system was the first system to which the alphabetic principle was applied when it was discovered around the tenth century BC. Since then some aspects of the spoken form of the Greek language (as is the case in many other languages) have undergone some evolutionary and developmental changes. Those changes can be observed in the phonetic identity of words, in morphology, in syntax and in the pronunciation of

International Book of Dyslexia: A Cross-Language Comparison and Practice Guide. Edited by Ian Smythe, John Everatt and Robin Salter.   ISBN 0471498416   © 2004 John Wiley & Sons, Ltd.

new words. However, in comparison with other Indo-European languages, the changes which the Greek language has undergone through the centuries have been quite moderate. Thus, many aspects of the spoken form have remained almost unchanged throughout its long history. Among the aspects that have remained constant are the pronunciation of many words, many grammatical forms, various elements used in the construction of new words, some elements of syntax and a great number of morphemes (Tombaidis, 1987).

On the other hand, the written form of the Greek language did not follow those (even moderate) changes in the spoken language and has remained essentially unchanged through-out its long history. As a result of the difference in the changes between the oral and the written forms, the Greek language is now written not as it is pronounced today but as it prob-ably was pronounced almost twenty-five centuries ago. So between its spoken and written forms a number of inconsistencies exist. Some of those inconsistencies are as follows (cf. Triantaphyllidis, 1913; Tombaidis, 1987; Zakestidou and Maniou-Vakali, 1987):

- Some phonemes are written with different letters or letter combinations. For example:
  - The phoneme [i] is written with the letters η, ι, υ, ει, οι, υι (e.g. *συνειρμικός / sinir-mikos, οικιστής / ikistis, υιικός / iikos*).
  - The phoneme [o] is written with the letters ο, ω, (e.g. *όμως / omos, ώμος / omos*).
  - The phoneme [e] is written with the letter ε and the letter combination αι (e.g. *φαίνεται / fenete*).
  - The phoneme [u] is written with the letter combination ου (e.g. *ουρανού / uranu*).
  - The phoneme [s] is written with the letters σ, ς, σσ (e.g. *σύσσωμος / sisomos*).
- Some letters, depending on the context, represent different phonemes. For example:
  - The letter υ is pronounced as:
    [i] (e.g. *κύβος / kivos*),
    [f] (e.g. *ευχαριστώ / efharisto*),
    [v] (e.g. *αύριο / avrio*),
    or it is almost silent (e.g. *εύφορος / eforos*).
  - The letter τ is pronounced as:
    [t] (e.g. *κάτω / kato*),
    or as [d] (*πέντε / pede*).
- In some cases some letters are not pronounced and they are almost voiceless. For example:
  - The letter υ (e.g. *Εύβοια / Evia*).
  - The double consonants: λλ, κκ, ββ, μμ, etc. (e.g. *κάλλος / kalos, λάκκος / lakos, Σάββατο / Savato, γράμμα / grama*).
  - The letter π in the consonant cluster μπτ (e.g. *πέμπτη /pemti*).

As a result of this situation, modern Greek spelling cannot be characterized either as a phonetic or a phonological orthography but rather as a historic orthography, which reflects the initial phonetic identity and etymology of words (Babiniotis, 1980, p. 95).

In conclusion, Greek, like English, is a morphophonemic script but is much more trans-parent than English in the representation of phonology. The English spelling system has variable and inconsistent grapheme–phoneme relationships due to many irregular spellings and it is considered a *deep* orthography, with higher level morphological constraints (Chomsky and Halle, 1968). The Greek spelling system, however, is much more consistent in grapheme–phoneme correspondences (approaching the 1:1 mapping from graphemes to phonemes) and can be characterized as a *shallow* orthography where, as a rule, pronunciation is predictable from print. The grapheme–phoneme inconsistencies existing in Greek (mainly applying to digraph spelling patterns) are to a large extent rule-learned and apply in almost every case in which the particular spelling pattern occurs. It would be expected, therefore, that the existing systematic relationship between individual letters and individual phonemes would enable Greek children to develop a fully specified orthographic lexicon in which representations would be underpinned at the phonemic level. Consequently, it would also be expected that in learning to read the Greek language, Greek children would build on the nature of their writing system and would learn to read by a sequential decoding process.

In spelling, however, Greek is phonologically opaque since there is a 1:many phonemes–graphemes mapping and, therefore, spelling cannot always be predictable from phonology. So in a number of cases (mainly those following the historic orthography spelling rules, according to which the spelling of a word is derived from its initial or etymological basis), a word's phonemic structure can be represented by more than one graphemic alternative. Since most of such spelling patterns are explained by etymological and grammatical knowledge, spelling can be assisted by gradually learned rules based on morphology and lexical information.

A BRIEF HISTORICAL OVERVIEW OF DYSLEXIA AND READING/SPELLING RESEARCH IN GREECE

The issue of dyslexia has only a brief history in the Greek psychological and educational literature. It seems highly likely that the first systematic presentation of dyslexia theory and research was Porpodas' (1981) book entitled *Dyslexia*, which was based on his PhD research under the title *Experimental Approaches to the Study of Developmental Dyslexia* (1980). Prior to that, a short presentation of dyslexia had appeared in Chassapis (1976), while the first mention of dyslexia in the Greek educational literature was probably made by Kallantzis (1957).

The situation seems to be the same in the scientific study of reading and spelling and the analysis of the cognitive and linguistic factors that contribute to literacy acquisition by normally achieving and/or dyslexic vhildren. One of the first experimental studies on reading the Greek language seems to be Porpodas' (1976) investigation of some aspects of reading comprehension. Since then, it could be argued that the systematic research on reading, spelling and dyslexia in the Greek language began in the 1980s, first at the University of Patras (in the Research and Diagnostic Unit of Dyslexia, Reading and Spelling) and later in other Greek universities. However, the scientific study of reading and spelling development of Greek by dyslexic and normally achieving children is still limited. For this reason, the systematic investigation of every aspect of the issue 'how Greek children (dyslexic and normally achieving alike) read and spell' constitutes a scientific and educational necessity.

RESEARCH ON READING, SPELLING AND DYSLEXIA IN GREEK

The role of phonology in learning to read and spell

In view of the existing differences in the orthographic systems and their classification as deep or shallow orthographies, it could be assumed that the degree to which a writing system represents phonology (by which a system is classified as deep or shallow orthography) is highly likely to be related to the way the word recognition process takes place. This is in fact what Katz and Frost (1992) have suggested in their orthographic depth hypothesis. According to this hypothesis, a reader of a deep orthography is likely to be led (by the nature of the orthography) to process word recognition by using morphological information from the visual-orthographic structure of the written word. However, the reader of a shallow orthography is likely to be encouraged by the high degree of transparency in the representation of phonology to process word recognition by using the phonological information.

In view of this, it could be argued that the most decisive step in the process of learning to read seems to be the acquisition of phonological recoding, that is, 'the ability to translate printed words independently into their spoken equivalents'. Following the above account, it could be assumed that Greek children should not face much difficulty in acquiring phonological recoding as a procedure for accurate word recognition. Based on the consistency of orthography, the grapheme–phoneme recoding is expected to be reliable, provided that the lexical item presented conforms to the code (as is normally the case) or that the basics for the rule-read words have been learned. Success in phonological recoding is enhanced by the fact that Greek children are normally taught using an analytico-synthetic phonics method that directly facilitates phonological recoding as a means of word recognition.

In Greek this hypothesis is supported by Porpodas (2001, in press). In these studies he evaluated the reading strategies used by first graders after a period of schooling and literacy instruction and found that good as well as weak readers relied heavily on the alphabetic process.

As far as the learning of spelling is concerned, various models (such as those by Frith, 1980, 1985; Marsh *et al.*, 1981) have proposed that English spelling develops in a series of stages or periods. Those models postulate a period in which spelling is based on a coding strategy of phonological basis. The phonological analysis strategy is followed by a period in which the spelling strategy is based on lexical analogies, during which visual memory plays a primary role. During this period, spelling of a word is produced because it looks right, it is independent of sound or because there is a shift from the phonemic encoding strategy to a strategy based on analogy. The investigation of spelling in the Greek language has shown that Greek children seem to learn to spell by relying mainly on phonological information (Porpodas, 1989a, 1989b, 1990). As for the teaching of spelling to dyslexics, Mavrommati and Miles (2002) have proposed a pictographic method instead of the method employing the phonology and etymology of words.

The role of phonological awareness

The relationship between phonological awareness and success in literacy acquisition of Greek seems to have started being investigated by Porpodas in 1987 (Porpodas, 1989c, 1990, 1991a, 1991b, 1995a, 1999). The main findings of those investigations can be summarized as follows: first, syllabic awareness is much easier than phonemic awareness at the pre-reading stage. Second, children who at the pre-reading stage had acquired phonological awareness at a satisfactory level were achieving a better level of literacy development, at the end of the first primary class, compared to their classmates whose level of phonological awareness was low at the pre-reading stage. However, another interesting observation was that by the end of primary two class, the difference in literacy development was closing between those two groups of children.

The last point was also observed in the only systematic training study on phonological awareness that has been conducted so far in Greek. More particularly, in that training study Porpodas and Palaiothodorou (1999a, 1999b) not only have provided evidence for a causal relationship between phonological awareness and literacy acquisition but, in addition, have found that the advantage in literacy acquisition gained in the first primary class had disappeared by the end of the third primary class. (A similar finding has also been reported in Finnish by Niemi *et al.*, 2001.)

In the past few years more Greek researchers have shown an interest in the investigation of the relationship between phonological awareness and literacy acquisition in Greek. In particular, the pre-readers' greater capability in acquiring syllabic rather than phonemic awareness of Greek was also reported by Aidinis and Nunes (2001). Those researchers also found that the children were experiencing less difficulty in the phonemic analysis of the initial than the final phonemes of each word. Along the same lines, Nikolopoulos and Porpodas (2001), Chitiri and Porpodas (2002), Tafa (1997) and Papoulia-Tzelepi (1997) have found a strong relationship between phonological awareness and literacy acquisition in Greek.

Finally, the strong role of phonological awareness deficit (and especially at the phonemic level) in dyslexia in the Greek language has been reported by Porpodas (1995a, 1996, 1997) and Porpodas and Dimakos (2002).

The phonological representations hypothesis and the role of speech perception

The phonological representations hypothesis (adopted by Goswami, 2000, see also her contribution in this volume) was used to further investigate the causal role of developmental deficit hypothesis in developmental dyslexia. According to this hypothesis, the quality of segmental organization of representations supporting spoken word recognition and production should be related to speech perception parameters (Joanisse *et al.*, 2000) and phonological memory skills (Porpodas, 1999). In addition, it should be reflected in the level of difficulty in retrieving the phonological codes of representations from the mental lexicon as well as the ability to manipulate and be aware of the phonological structure of those representations (Swan and Goswami, 1997a, 1997b). It is therefore expected that this skill is likely to determine the level of reading and spelling ability.

This hypothesis was investigated in Greek by Panteli (in preparation) and Panteli and Porpodas (in preparation). In that research a battery of tasks was used to assess the auditory perception of non-speech stimulus, auditory discrimination, perception of rhythm in acoustic signals, phonological short-term memory, word-finding ability and phonological awareness skills. The results obtained so far seem to indicate that the dyslexic children's deficit in phonological processing arises from a lack of distinctness of phonological representations. This difficulty in forming precise representations of the phonological structure of words seems to be partly explained in terms of difficulties in the perception of the rhythm of acoustic signals.

Working memory

The decisive role of working memory in reading acquisition has been well documented in the literature (e.g. Baddeley, 1986; Baddeley *et al.*, 1981; Hulme, 1981). In the case of reading Greek, Porpodas (1991a) has found a direct relationship between the level of phonetic representaion in short-term memory at the pre-school level and the reading level achieved at the end of primary one class. In addition, Porpodas (1993) investigated the role of short-term memory storage of linguistic information in the process of reading. The main finding of that research was that the functional difficulties of the articulatory loop of working memory seem to inhibit the learning of reading.

Learning to read and spell Greek: a conclusion

On the basis of the existing data derived from empirical research and in view of the nature of the Greek spelling system, it is suggested that Greek dyslexic children tend to find learning to read easier than learning to spell. However, this does not mean that all children acquire reading skills easily. On the contrary, some have to struggle in completing phonological recoding in word reading. This is reflected in the dyslexics' reading performance where (and contrary to what happens in English) the most important index of their reading performance seems to be the reading processing time rather than reading accuracy (Porpodas, 1995a, 1995b, 1996, 1997; Porpodas and Karantzis, 1995).

FUTURE PROSPECTS

As was mentioned, research on reading spelling and dyslexia in the Greek language is still limited and fragmentary. This is probably due to the fact that psychological research until recently has not been orientated to the analysis of cognitive functions of those processes, while educational practice on literacy acquisition and dyslexia was developing, regardless of such research evidence. In addition, until recently, only very few researchers have shown an interest in the analysis of the cognitive functions of reading, spelling and dyslexia in Greek.

However, in the past few years the situation seems to have improved. Besides the ongoing research which has been taking place at the Research and Diagnostic Unit of Dyslexia, Reading and Spelling of the University of Patras, new academic researchers at other Greek universities have started working on some basic aspects of those issues. So it seems highly likely that the research on literacy acquisition and dyslexia will gradually increase and will improve, with positive consequences for the diagnosis of dyslexia and the teaching and education of young Greek children, normally achieving and dyslexic alike.

REFERENCES

Aidinis, A. and Nunes, T. (2001) The role of different levels of phonological awareness in the development of reading and spelling in Greek. *Reading and Writing: An Interdisciplinary Journal*, 14, 145–177.
Babiniotis, G. (1980) *Theoretiki Glossologia.* Athens. (In Greek.)

Baddeley, A.D. (1986) *Working Memory*. Oxford: Oxford University Press.

Baddeley, A.D., Eldridge, M. and Lewis, V.J. (1981) The role of subvocalization in reading. *Quarterly Journal of Experimental Psychology*, 33, 439–454.

Chassapis, I. (1976) *The Psychopathology of Infancy*. Athens: Vassilopoulos. (In Greek.)

Chitiri, F. and Porpodas, C. (2002) Phonological awareness and its relations to learning of reading and spelling as well as to linguistic ability and comprehension of Greek. Research paper (in preparation). Laboratory of Cognitive Analysis of Learning, Language and Dyslexia, University of Patras.

Chomsky, N. and Halle, M. (1968) *The Sound Pattern of English*. New York: Harper & Row.

Frith, U. (1980) Unexpected spelling problems. In U. Frith (ed.), *Cognitive Processes in Spelling*. London: Academic Press.

Frith, U. (1985) Beneath the surface of developmental dyslexia. In K.E. Patterson, J.C. Marshall and M. Coltheart (eds), *Surface Dyslexia*. London: Lawrence Erlbaum Associates.

Goswami, U. (2000) Phonological representations, reading development and dyslexia: Towards a cross-linguistic theoretical framework, *Dyslexia*, 6, 133–151.

Hulme, C. (1981) *Reading Retardation and Multi-sensory Teaching*. London: Routledge and Kegan Paul.

Joanisse, M.F., Manis, F.R., Keating, P. and Seidenberg, M.S. (2000) Language deficits in dyslexic children: Speech perception, phonology and morphology, *Journal of Experimental Child Psychology*, 77, 30–60.

Kallantzis, K. (1957) *Language Disorders in Childhood*. Athens: I. Kampanas. (In Greek.)

Katz, L. and Frost, R. (1992) Reading in different orthographies: The orthographic depth hypothesis. In R. Frost and L. Katz (eds), *Orthography, Phonology, Morphology and Meaning*. Amsterdam: North-Holland.

Marsh, G., Friedman, M., Welch, U. and Desberg, P. (1981) A cognitive-developmental theory of reading acquisition. In G.E. MacKinnon and T.G. Waller (eds), *Reading Research: Advances in Theory and Practice*, vol. 3. New York: Academic Press.

Mavrommati, T. and Miles, T.R. (2002) A pictographic method for teaching spelling to Greek dyslexic children. *Dyslexia*, 8(2), 86–102.

Niemi, P., Poskiparta, E. and Vauras, M. (2001) Benefits of training in linguistic awareness dissipate by Grade 3? *Psychology*, 8(3), 330–337.

Nikolopoulos, D. and Porpodas, C. (2001) Pre-cursors of reading and spelling in the regular Greek orthography. Paper presented at the 5th British Dyslexia Association International Conference 'Dyslexia: At the Dawn of the New Century', University of York, UK, 18–21 April 2001.

Panteli, M. (in preparation) Phonological representation and the role of speech perception in normal and dyslexic readers of Greek. Doctoral dissertation, University of Patras, Greece.

Panteli, M. and Porpodas, C. (in preparation) The role of speech perception in reading and spelling of Greek by dyslexic and non-dyslexic children. Research report, University of Patras, Greece.

Papoulia-Tzelepi, P. (1997) Analysis of phonological awareness in preschool children. *Glossa*, 41, 20–41. (In Greek.)

Porpodas, C.D. (1976) The effect of depth of reading comprehension upon processing time and recall in relation to age and sex. MEd thesis, University of Dundee, Department of Psychology.

Porpodas, C.D. (1980) Experimental approaches to the study of developmental dyslexia. PhD thesis. University of Dundee, Department of Psychology.

Porpodas, C.D. (1981) *Dyslexia*. Athens: Morfotiki. (In Greek.)

Porpodas, C.D. (1989a) The phonological factor in reading and spelling of Greek. In P.G. Aaron and R.M. Joshi (eds), *Reading and Writing Disorders in Different Orthographic Systems*. Dordrecht: Kluwer.

Porpodas, C.D. (1989b) Spelling by first grade children in relation to linguistic and memory abilities. *Psychologica Themata*, 2, 201–214. (In Greek.)

Porpodas, C.D. (1989c) The relation between phonemic awareness and reading and spelling of Greek words in the first school years. Paper presented at the 3rd European Conference for Research in Learning and Instruction, Madrid, Spain, 4–7 September 1989. Also published in M. Carretero, M. Pope, R.J. Simons and J. Pozo (eds) (1993) *Learning and Instruction*. Vol. 3. Oxford: Pergamon Press.

Porpodas, C.D. (1990) 'Linguistic awareness and learning to read Greek'. Paper presented at the 9th World Congress of Applied Linguistics, Halkidiki, 15–21 April 1990.

Porpodas, C.D. (1991a) Linguistic awareness, verbal short-term memory and learning to read Greek. Paper presented at the 4th European Conference for Research on Learning and Instruction, Turku, Finland, 24–28 August 1991.

Porpodas, C.D. (1991b) Cognitive-linguistic parameters in learning to read and spell Greek. Paper presented at the international conference on Cognitive neuropsychology of reading and writing disabilities: Differential diagnosis and treatments, Château de Bonas, Toulouse, France, 30 September–12 October 1991.

Porpodas, C.D. (1993) Phonetic short-term memory representation in children's reading of Greek. In R. Malatesha Joshi and C.K. Leong (eds), *Reading Disabilities: Diagnosis and Component Processes*. Dordrecht: Kluwer.

Porpodas, C.D. (1995a) Learning to read and spell Greek: Their relation to phonological awareness and memory factors. Paper presented at the IV European Congress of Psychology, 2–7 July 1995, Athens.

Porpodas, C.D. (1995b) Toward a method for the diagnosis and treatment of Dyslexia in the Greek language. Paper presented at the symposium, Cognitive and Linguistic Analysis of Dyslexia: Effects on Diagnosis and Treatment, IV European Congress of Psychology, 2–7 July 1995, Athens.

Porpodas, C.D. (1996) Reading and dyslexia in the Greek language: Research evidence for an explanation based on phonological awareness – Educational implications. Keynote paper presented at the 5th Panhellenic Conference of Psychological Research. 23–26 May, University of Patras, Greece. (In Greek.)

Porpodas, C.D. (1997) Dyslexia: A cognitive perspective. Keynote paper presented at the 6th Panhellenic Conference of Psychological Research, 29 May–1 June, Panteion University, Athens, Greece.

Porpodas, C.D. (1999) Patterns of phonological and memory processing in beginning readers and spellers of Greek. *Journal of Learning Disabilities* (Special Issue: Prevention and Treatment of Dyslexia), 32(5), 406–416.

Porpodas, C.D. (2001) Cognitive processes in first grade reading and spelling of Greek. *Psychology: The Journal of the Hellenic Psychological Society*: a special issue devoted to research on reading, spelling and dyslexia in Europe, 8(3), 384–400.

Porpodas, C.D. (in press) Cognitive strategies in learning to read Greek: Doubts regarding the importance of the logographic process. In A. Kantas, Th. Veli and A. Hantzi (eds), *Societally Significant Applications of Psychological Knowledge*. Athens: Ellinika Grammata.

Porpodas, C. and Dimakos, J. (2002) Two case-studies of Greek dyslexic children. Research manuscript. Dyslexia Unit, University of Patras, Greece.

Porpodas, C. and Karantzis, J. (1995) Working memory in children with and without reading and arithmetic difficulties. Paper presented at the IV European Congress of Psychology, 2–7 July, Athens.

Porpodas, C. and Palaiothodorou, A. (1999a) Phonological training and reading and spelling acquisition. Paper presented at the 4th European Conference on Psychological Assessment, University of Patras, Greece, 25–29 August 1999.

Porpodas, C. and Palaiothodorou, A. (1999b) A training study on phonological awareness and its effect on learning to read and spell the Greek language. Paper presented at the European Conference on Developmental Psychology, Spetses, Greece, 2–5 September 1999.

Swan, D. and Goswami, U. (1997a) Picture naming deficits in developmental dyslexia and the phonological representations hypothesis. *Brain and Language*, 56, 334–353.

Swan, D. and Goswami, U. (1997b) Phonological awareness deficits in developmental dyslexia and the phonological representations hypothesis, *Journal of Experimental Child Psychology*, 66, 18–41.

Tafa, E. (1997) *Reading and Writing in the Preschool Education*. Athens: Ellinika Grammata. (In Greek.)

Tombaidis, D. (1987) *A Concise History of the Greek Language*. Athens: OEDB. (In Greek.)

Triantaphyllidis, M. (1913) *Our Orthography*. Athens: Estia. (In Greek.)

Zakestidou, S. and Maniou-Vakali, M. (1987) Orthographic problem in grades 1 and 2 of the high school. *Nea Paideia*, 42, 80–93 and 43, 98–110. (In Greek.)

11

DEVELOPMENTAL DYSLEXIA IN THE HEBREW LANGUAGE

David L. Share and Mark Leikin

INTRODUCTION

This chapter summarizes the research evidence of developmental dyslexia in Hebrew. The first section provides an overview of the unique features of the Hebrew language and its orthography, with special emphasis on Semitic morphology (the 'root-plus-pattern' system) and the consonantal alphabet in both its 'pointed' (fully vowelled) and 'unpointed' (partly vowelled) forms. The next section reviews several studies investigating sources of individual differences in reading ability. The third section examines the characteristics of diagnosed dyslexics. Our review concludes by considering the similarities and dissimilarities between dyslexia in Hebrew and English.

HEBREW MORPHOLOGY AND ORTHOGRAPHY

The most characteristically Semitic feature of Hebrew is its derivational morphology (Berman, 1985). Almost all content words consist of a primarily consonantal 'root' and vocalic 'pattern'. The root is the semantic core of a word and usually consists of three consonants. Specific words are produced only when a root is embedded in a pattern consisting of vocalic infixes, and mostly syllabic prefixes and/or suffixes. For example, some of the verb forms derived from the triconsonantal root קלט = KLT include: קָלַט = KaLaT (he grasped) נִקְלַט = niKLaT (was grasped/absorbed), and הִקְלִיט = hiKLit (he recorded). A number of studies have indicated that knowledge of Hebrew morphology is important in reading acquisition (Ben-Dror et al., 1995; Birnboim, 1995; Levin et al., 1998; Rothschild-Yakar, 1989).

International Book of Dyslexia: A Cross-Language Comparison and Practice Guide. Edited by Ian Smythe, John Everatt and Robin Salter. ISBN 0471498416 © 2004 John Wiley & Sons, Ltd.

Morphological knowledge is likely to be a source of individual differences in reading ability because roots are phonologically highly opaque, manifest at the surface level in a variety of syllable forms. Whereas most root morphemes in English are integral units (consisting of both consonants and stem-internal vowels) and can therefore be heard and pronounced, Hebrew roots are uniformly unpronounceable. This problem is further compounded in the orthography by extensive affixation. For example, the two-word sentence נאכל בבוקר (NOXAL BABOKER) becomes six English words 'We will eat in the morning'. This morphological density demands considerable 'unpacking' on the part of the reader and creates an additional source of homography.

Probably because the semantic core of a word (the root) is consonantal, Hebrew orthography is a predominantly consonantal system with either no vowels or vowels represented in a subsidiary manner. Owing to its distinctive morphology, full representation of vowels in Hebrew, at least for the skilled reader, may well be unnecessary in contrast to Indo-European languages such as English that use vowel distinctions to mark basic morphemic contrasts. The major drawback of Hebrew's consonantal script, however, is the abundance of homographs all deriving from the same consonantal root (Bentin *et al.*, 1984; Navon and Shimron, 1984). For example, כתב (KTV) could represent 'journalist', 'orthography', 'he wrote', and more.

Two distinct supplementary systems of vowelling exist today. The first system called 'mothers of reading', employs four of the consonantal letters ((א ה ו י)) to serve the dual function of signifying vowels as well as consonants. This system, however, is both inconsistent and incomplete (Shimron, 1993; Yanay and Porat, 1987). Standard printed Hebrew appearing in today's books, newspapers and magazines is partly and inconsistently vowelled by means of the mothers of reading.

A second system of vowelization employs a complex system of diacritical marks ('points'). So-called pointed Hebrew is restricted largely to poetry, sacred texts and children's books but, in contrast to the mothers of reading, this diacritical system provides a complete and unambiguous representation of the vowels by means of tiny dots and dashes appearing mostly under letters. For example: דִ = /di/, דֹ = /do/, דֻ = /du/, דַ = /da/, דֶ = /de/. Although vowel diacritics help young readers resolve the ambiguity of unpointed text when reading aloud (Ravid, 1996; Shimron and Navon, 1981–1982), diacritics remain a source of difficulty as witnessed by the fact that most reading errors, even in pointed text, are vowel errors (Birnboim, 1995; Rothschild-Yakar, 1989).

Children learn to read in pointed Hebrew, which has almost perfect one-to-one grapheme-to-phoneme correspondence (Navon and Shimron, 1984), hence decoding is mastered very rapidly (Birnboim, 1995; Geva *et al.*, 1993; Shatil, 1997). Indeed, the accuracy of decoding pointed Hebrew in Grade 1 matches the level achieved in English only in Grade 5 (Geva *et al.*, 1993). Unlike grapheme-to phoneme correspondence, phoneme-to-grapheme relationships are frequently variable, with a number of pairs of (once phonemically distinct) graphemes now representing the same phoneme. The vast majority of Hebrew words, therefore, contain phonemes with alternate spellings. Not surprisingly, attaining spelling proficiency is a much greater challenge than learning to decode, and consistently lags behind that of English (ibid., 1993).

As the name square alphabet suggests, letter architecture, relative to the Latin alphabet, is more uniformly block-like. Not only are the letters less distinctive, but word length and word shape are also quite uniform.

SOURCES OF INDIVIDUAL DIFFERENCE IN HEBREW READING ABILITY

A modest number of Hebrew-language studies have examined factors associated with individual difference in reading skill across a range of ability. Because it is now recognized that dyslexia lies on the normal continuum of reading ability, these correlational studies are also relevant to understanding Hebrew reading difficulties.

In a longitudinal study of 63 kindergarten children, Meyler and Breznitz (1998) found that both visual STM (Stanford-Binet Object and Read Memory) and verbal STM (digit span, letter span and nonsense-syllable span) predicted significant variance in Grade 2 decoding skills even after controlling for IQ. WISC-R Block Design in kindergarten also correlated significantly with later decoding (r = .47).

A second longitudinal study (Shatil, 1997) assessed a variety of cognitive and psycholinguistic abilities in a sample of over 300 kindergarten children. The battery of 30 individual measures covered four domain-specific sets of variables (visuo-spatial processing, phonological awareness, phonological memory and early literacy), and three domain-general sets (general intelligence, metacognitive functioning, and oral language). Word recognition and reading comprehension were assessed one year later at the end of Grade 1. Collectively, the domain-general block explained a marginal 5 per cent of the variance in word recognition skill, but individual domain-specific sets of variables each accounted for significant amounts of decoding variance (visuo-spatial processing – 11 per cent, phonological awareness – 11 per cent, phonological memory – 16 per cent and early literacy – 19 per cent).

Phonological awareness

Several predictive/longitudinal and training studies have demonstrated that phonological awareness is an important determinant of individual differences in Hebrew reading acquisition, and furthermore, that the connection is causal.

Bentin and Leshem (1993) assessed the phonemic segmentation abilities of over 500 kindergarten children then randomly assigned the lowest scoring 100 children to one of four matched training groups. Interventions consisted of phoneme segmentation plus letter identity, general language skills, and non-specific training. At the end of Grade 1, both groups trained in phonemic awareness were well ahead of the other groups in reading words and pseudowords.

Kozminsky and Kozminsky (1993/94) randomly assigned two entire kindergarten classes to experimental and control groups. Training in the experimental group focused on syllabic, sub-syllabic and phonemic awareness, while the control class received a programme of visuo-motor integration. The group trained in phonological awareness demonstrated significantly superior reading comprehension not only at the end of Grade 1 but also when assessed again three years later at the end of Grade 3.

These longitudinal investigations of phonological awareness in Hebrew concur with the English language findings: difficulty in accessing phonemes is a significant predictor of later reading difficulties and, when taught, has a significant and durable impact on later reading ability. But the strength of the relationship may not be as powerful at that observed in English: correlation coefficients between reading and phonological awareness are typically lower in Hebrew than those reported in the English-language literature (Bentin and Leshem, 1993; Geva et al., 1993; Shatil, 1997). One possible explanation for this difference is simply that most children have attained mastery in decoding by the end of Grade 1, hence the correlation is attenuated by the greater range restriction in reading scores. Alternatively, the highly consistent orthography and/or Hebrew's relatively simple syllable structure may be responsible for an intrinsically attenuated relationship. Either or both of these factors may reduce the cognitive complexity involved in learning to decode pointed Hebrew script.

Morphology

Levin et al. (1998) examined the longitudinal relationships between early writing and knowledge of morphological structures that are characteristic of high-register written language in a sample of 40 pre-schoolers followed from kindergarten to the end of Grade 1. Morphology and writing were correlated both in kindergarten and at Grade 1 around the .50 mark. Moreover, kindergarten morphology predicted Grade 1 writing and remained a significant predictor even after controlling for kindergarten writing. Data reviewed in the next section confirm the conclusion that morphology is an important source of individual differences in early literacy.

CHARACTERISTICS OF DIAGNOSED DYSLEXICS

Morphological awareness among dyslexics

Ben-Dror et al. (1995) compared the semantic, phonological and morphological skills of Grade 5 disabled readers to both age-matched and younger control readers. The strongest differences between the groups were obtained on a morphological task in which children decided whether two words shared a common root. Cohen et al. (1996) also found that disabled readers in Grades 3 to 6 produced poorer oral and written narratives with regard to a variety of linguistic measures including morphology.

Two ERP (brain Event-Related-Potential) studies by Leikin and Breznitz (Breznitz and Leikin, 2000; Leikin and Breznitz, 2001) also revealed morphological deficiencies in dyslexics' sentence processing. Both normal and dyslexic readers' syntactic parsing was found to be dependent on the ability to use lexico-morphological information to identify a word's grammatical functions. However, dyslexics demonstrated reduced sensitivity to this information. The authors proposed that dyslexics' difficulties using lexico-morphological information to identify a word's grammatical functions lead to impaired syntactic processing.

These studies, together with the Levin et al. longitudinal investigation, converge on the conclusion that morphological deficiencies appear to play a causal role in reading and writing difficulties in Hebrew. To date, however, no experimental training study in morphology has yet been conducted.

Phonological skills among Hebrew dyslexics

Both Breznitz (1997) and Ben-Dror *et al.* (1995) reported pseudoword reading (accuracy and speed) and phonological awareness performance levels in dyslexic children that were significantly below younger normal controls. Thus, as a group, Israeli dyslexics, like English-language dyslexics, are characterized by severe phonological deficits.

Brande (1997) examined both phonological and orthographic skills in two groups of adolescent and pre-adolescent dyslexics and their chronological age-matched control readers. Overall, differences between controls and dyslexics were stronger on phonological abilities than on orthographic processing. Among the older dyslexics, differences were smaller relative to younger dyslexics on several measures related to meaning, comprehension, and orthographic processing. The gap between disabled and non-disabled readers in phonological abilities, however, did not narrow with age, and in several cases actually widened. These data accord with the English-language findings, demonstrating weakness in phonological processing co-existing with relative strengths in orthography and meaning (Share, 1995; Stanovich and Siegel, 1994). This pattern of phonological weakness and relative orthographic strengths has also been confirmed both behaviourally and electrophysiologically in a series of neuropsychological studies of Hebrew-speaking dyslexics conducted by Breznitz and colleagues.

Speed of processing (SOP)

Breznitz (submitted, a, b; Breznitz and Meyler, in press) undertook a series of studies investigating the sources of reading rate differences between dyslexic and normal readers. Breznitz hypothesized that speed of processing within and/or between the information processing sub-systems involved in word recognition may be a cause of reading rate deficits among dyslexics. Behavioural and electrophysiological data from a range of low-level auditory and visual tasks as well as high-level phonological and orthographic tasks, pointed to the predominance of a domain-specific phonological SOP deficit within the context of a general SOP deficit. Breznitz also proposed that the integration of phonological and visual/orthographic information may fail among disabled readers owing to excessive separation ('asynchrony') of faster visual processing and slower auditory processing.

Sub-types of dyslexia

To date, only one single Hebrew-language study has expressly searched for sub-types of dyslexia. Lamm and Epstein (1994) administered a battery of reading, spelling, and cognitive measures to 320 dyslexic children from Grades 3 to 10 referred to a private clinic. Cluster analysis revealed three homogeneous groups and a fourth mixed group. The largest groups (43 per cent), were classified not as phonological dyslexics but as 'surface/lexical' dyslexics. This developmentally delayed group were characterized by bottom-up letter-by-letter decoding, homophone confusions in spelling, and inferior visual/serial cognitive performance relative to normal visuo-spatial abilities. These children's reading and spelling errors were predominantly visual confusions. Performance on the visuo-spatial tests was also poor in this group.

Perhaps the most surprising outcome of the Lamm and Epstein sub-type analysis was the tiny proportion (4.4 per cent) classified as 'phonological' dyslexics. This group displayed severe difficulties in grapheme–phoneme translation. Lamm and Epstein described this group as having 'an extraordinarily severe reading deficit . . . with only a vague conception of the relations between phonology and orthography' (ibid., p. 763).

Lamm and Epstein's findings present several intriguing results. The large proportion of visuomotor dyslexics diverge from the current picture emerging from English-language research regarding the paucity of a visual or visuo-spatial subtype of dyslexia (see, e.g., Rayner *et al.*, 1995) but appear to converge with the Hebrew-language finding regarding the importance of visuo-spatial factors in early reading (Meyler and Breznitz, 1998; Shatil, 1997).

The most surprising outcome of this sub-typing study was the rarity of phonological dyslexics. Elsewhere, Lamm (1989) has claimed that Hebrew has few phonological dyslexics because systematic phonics instruction is virtually universal in Grade 1, and because pointed script is so highly regular. However, few studies reviewed above directly investigating phonological factors in reading ability[1] have, in each and every case, converged on the conclusion that substantial portions of early reading variance are attributable to phonological factors.

It is possible to reconcile Lamm and Epstein's seemingly conflicting data with the recent reconceptualization of surface dyslexia as a mild phonological deficit (Castles *et al.*, 1999; Manis *et al.*, 1996; Stanovich *et al.*, 1997). The presence of subtle phonological deficits when learning to read a highly regular orthography taught via systematic phonics methods may permit a child to attain a relatively high level of decoding accuracy (relative to English) if not speed, yet with difficulties in developing the orthographic representations typical of surface dyslexia. These surface or lexical deficits appear to be attributable not to usual deficits but to higher order aspects of decoding that require the string of decoded elements to be efficiently synthesized and integrated with lexical and morphological knowledge. Elsewhere, Lamm (1989) observes that most 'surface/lexical' dyslexics seem unable to make the transition from bottom-up, letter-by-letter phonological recoding (*kriya metzarefet*) to direct automatic visual/orthographic recognition.

An alternative account of Lamm and Epstein's surface/lexical dyslexics relates to morphology, in particular, morphophonology. Recently, Lamm (in preparation) found evidence that Hebrew surface dyslexics may have both subtle phonological deficits and lexico-morphological deficits. This study reported evidence that Hebrew surface dyslexics suffer a reduced sensitivity to both lexical and morpho-phonemic constraints in word decoding, consistent with the findings of Leikin and Breznitz discussed above.

Difficulties negotiating the transition from pointed to unpointed orthography

As already noted above, children begin learning to read with pointed text, but are gradually exposed to unpointed text in a systematic manner around Grade 3. Two studies (Bentin *et al.*, 1990; Deutsch and Bentin, 1996) have demonstrated that certain children have unique difficulties negotiating the transition from pointed to unpointed script.

Bentin *et al.* (1990) hypothesized that some poor readers may have difficulties making this transition owing not to inadequate knowledge of grapheme–phoneme correspondences but because of weaknesses in exploiting contextual information hypothesized to be critical for reading the phonologically ambiguous unpointed text. One group of disabled readers (selected on the basis of poor decoding ability of both pointed and unpointed text) were found to have inferior sensitivity to basic syntactic structures. A second group with a selective deficit in reading unpointed text demonstrated impairments not in sensitivity to basic syntactic structures but an inability to use syntactic knowledge in a productive way. In a follow-up study, Deutsch and Bentin (1996) replicated the earlier finding and traced the source of the syntactic deficits in disabled readers to the reduced efficiency of an attention-based inhibitory component of contextual processing.

Both these studies of syntactic processing, together with Cohen *et al.*'s (1996) findings, are important in suggesting that some children experience difficulties bridging the gap between pointed and unpointed text because of inadequate syntactic knowledge and/or inefficient use of this knowledge.

As discussed above, another source of difficulty in negotiating the transition to the deeper orthography may be a failure to acquire the root-based orthographic representations necessary for efficient reading in unpointed script owing possibly to deficient lexico-morphological knowledge. A reader who has difficulties establishing orthographic representations in memory may still cope satisfactorily with pointed print, albeit in a strictly bottom-up (surface) manner, but would be at a relative loss in unpointed script. The transition from pointed to unpointed orthography would appear to be an important topic for future research.

CONCLUSION

This chapter has highlighted both universal and language-specific aspects of developmental reading difficulties in Hebrew. The data converge with findings from other languages indicating that phonological skills appear to be a universal source of individual difference in learning to read. In Hebrew, as in English, deficiencies in phonology are counter-balanced by relative strengths in non-phonological aspects of reading such as contextual and orthographic processing that have important implications for remediation. Alongside these continuities, however, there exists a certain discontinuity with regard to the magnitude of the relationship between phonemic awareness (and phonological factors generally) and early reading, possibly owing to the highly regular orthography (taught via systematic phonics instruction) that may reduce the cognitive complexity of early decoding.

Several studies converge on the conclusion that morphological deficiencies have a special significance in understanding reading problems in Hebrew. Awareness of structural regularities across lexical items would seem to be especially important in view of both the high degree of morphemic density of written Hebrew, and a writing system uniquely designed to convey the abstract consonantal roots that constitute the semantic core of Hebrew words. The diacritical system, therefore, seems well adapted to the task of marking vowels while preserving the orthographic integrity of consonantal roots. Unfortunately, diacritics seem to be a relatively inefficient system.

The potentially problematic transition from the shallow pointed script to the deeper unpointed script represents another issue requiring further attention. Data on homograph confusions and the difficulties certain readers seem to experience utilizing syntactic context to resolve lexical ambiguity suggest that the transition from the shallower pointed script to the deeper, unpointed script represents another potential pitfall, particularly for children with weak morpho-syntactic skills.

NOTE

1 It should be noted that Lamm and Epstein (1994) did not directly test either pseudoword reading or phonological awareness.

REFERENCES

Ben-Dror, I., Bentin, S. and Frost, R. (1995) Semantic, phonologic, and morphologic skills in reading disabled and normal children: Evidence from perception and production of spoken Hebrew. *Reading Research Quarterly*, 30, 876–893.

Bentin, S., Bargai, N. and Katz, L. (1984) Orthographic and phonemic coding for lexical access: Evidence from Hebrew. *Journal of Experimental Psychology: Learning, Memory and Cognition*, 10(3), 353–368.

Bentin, S., Deutsch, A. and Liberman, I.Y. (1990) Syntactic competence and reading ability in children. *Journal of Experimental Child Psychology*, 48, 147–172.

Bentin, S. and Leshem, H. (1993) On the interaction of phonologic awareness and reading acquisition: It's a two-way street. *Psychological Science*, 2, 271–274.

Berman, R. (1985) Hebrew. In D.I. Slobin (ed.), *The Crosslinguistic Study of Language Acquisition*. Hillsdale, NJ: Lawrence Erlbaum Associates.

Birnboim, S. (1995) Acquired surface dyslexia: The evidence from Hebrew. *Applied Psycholinguistics*, 16, 83–102.

Birnboim, S. and Share, D.L. (1995) Surface dyslexia in Hebrew: A case study. *Cognitive Neuropsychology*, 12, 825–846.

Brande, S. (1997) Ifyunei meyumanuyot hakriya bekerev dislectim bogrim behashva'a ledislectim tze'irim [Characteristics of reading skills among adult dyslexics in comparison to dyslexic children.] Unpublished master's thesis, University of Haifa.

Breznitz, Z. (1997) Enhancing the reading of dyslexic children by reading acceleration and auditory masking. *Journal of Educational Psychology*, 89, 103–113.

Breznitz, Z. (submitted, a) Speed of phonological and orthographic processing as a factor in dyslexia: Electrophysiological evidence. *Scientific Studies of Reading*. Manuscript submitted for publication.

Breznitz, Z. (submitted, b) At synchrony of visual-orthographic and auditory-phonological word recognition processes: An underlying factor in dyslexia. Manuscript submitted for publication.

Breznitz, Z. and Leikin, M. (2000) Syntactic processing of Hebrew sentences in normal and dyslexic readers: Electrophysiological evidence. *The Journal of Genetic Psychology*, 161(3), 359–380.

Breznitz, Z. and Meyler, A. (in press) Speed of lower-level auditory and visual processing as a basic factor in dyslexia: Electrophysiological evidence. *Brain and Language*. Manuscript submitted for publication.

Castles, A., Datta, H., Gayan, J. and Olson, R.K. (1999) Varieties of developmental reading disorder: Genetic and environmental influences. *Journal of Experimental Psychology*, 72, 73–94.

Cohen, A., Schiff, R. and Gillis-Carlebach, M. (1996) Hashva'at ha'osher hamorfologi, hatachbiri vehanarativi bein yeladim hamitkashim bekriya levein yeladim yod'ei kro. [Complexity of morphological, syntactic and narrative characteristics: A comparison of children with reading difficulties and children who can read.] *Megamot*, 37, 273–291.

Deutsch, A. and Bentin, S. (1996) Attention factors mediating syntactic deficiency in reading-disabled children. *Journal of Experimental Child Psychology*, 63, 386–415.

Geva, E., Wade-Woolley, L. and Shany, M. (1993) The concurrent development of spelling and decoding in two different orthographies. *Journal of Reading Behaviour*, 25, 383–406.

Kozminsky, L. and Kozminsky, E. (1993/94) Hahashpa's shel ha'imun bemudaut fonologit begil hagan al hahatslacha berechishat hakri'a bevet hasefer. [The effects of phonological awareness training in kindergarten on reading acquisition in school.] *Chelkat Lashon*, 15–16, 7–28.

Lamm, O. (1989) Dislexia hitpatxutit vehora'at kri'a – ha'omnam hapitaron hu bektse haxotem? [Developmental dyslexia and the teaching of reading.] Issues in *Special Education and Rehabilitation*, 6, 13–26.

Lamm, O. and Epstein, R. (1994) Dichotic listening performance under high and low lexical work load in subtypes of developmental dyslexia. *Neuropsychologia*, 32, 757–785.

Leikin, M. and Breznitz, Z. (2001) Effects of accelerated reading rate on syntactic processing of Hebrew sentences: Electrophysiological evidence. *Genetic, Social and General Psychology Monographs*, 127(2), 193–209.

Leikin, M. and Breznitz, Z. (in press) Sentence processing in dyslexic readers. *Educational Psychology Review*.

Levin, I., Ravid, D. and Rapaport, S. (1998) Developing morphological awareness and learning to write: A two-way street. In T. Nunes (ed.), *Integrating Research and Practice in Literacy*. Amsterdam: Kluwer.

Manis, F.R., Seidenberg, M.S., Doi, L.M., McBride-Chang, C. and Peterson, A. (1996) On the bases of two subtypes of developmental dyslexia. *Cognition*, 58, 157–195.

Meyler, A. and Breznitz, Z. (1998) Developmental association between verbal and visual short-term memory and the acquisition of decoding skill. *Reading and Writing*, 10, 519–540.

Navon, D. and Shimron, Y. (1984) Reading Hebrew: How necessary is the graphemic representation of vowels? In L. Henderson (ed.), *Orthographies and Reading: Perspectives from Cognitive Psychology, Neuropsychology, and Linguistics*. London: Lawrence Erlbaum Associates.

Ravid, D. (1996) Accessing the mental lexicon: Evidence from incompatibility between representation of spoken and written morphology. *Linguistics*, 34, 1219–1246.

Rayner, K., Pollatsek, A. and Bilsky, A. (1995) Can a temporal processing deficit account for dyslexia? *Psychological Bulletin and Review*, 2, 501–507.

Rothschild-Yakar, L. (1989) Bedikat tahalichei kri'a be'ivrit mitoch perspectiva hitpatchutit etsel talmidim halomdim beshtei shitot hora'a shonot. [A study of reading processes in Hebrew from a development perspective among children learning in two different instructional methods.] Unpublished doctoral dissertation, University of Haifa.

Share, D.L. (1995) Phonological recoding and self-teaching: Sine qua non of reading acquisition. *Cognition*, 55, 151–218.

Shatil, E. (1997) Predicting reading ability: Evidence for cognitive modularity. Unpublished doctoral dissertation, University of Haifa.

Shimron, J. (1993) The role of vowels in reading: A review of studies of English and Hebrew. *Psychological Bulletin*, 114, 52–67.

Shimron, J. and Navon, D. (1981–1982) The dependence on graphemes and on their translation to phonemes in reading: A developmental perspective. *Reading Research Quarterly*, 17, 210–228.

Stanovich, K.E. and Siegel, L.S. (1994) Phonotypic performance profile of children with reading disabilities: A regression-based test of the phonological-core variable-difference model. *Journal of Educational Psychology*, 86, 24–53.

Stanovich, K.E., Siegel, L.S. and Gottardo, A. (1997) Converging evidence for phonological and surface subtypes of reading disability. *Journal of Educational Psychology*, 89, 114–127.

Yanay, Y. and Porat, S. (1987) Haktav ha'ivri vehaktiv ha'ivrit: Ba'aya atika vehatza'at pitaron. [Hebrew script and Hebrew spelling: An ancient problem and a proposed solution.] *Mada*, 31, 18–23.

12

RESEARCH ON DYSLEXIA IN HUNGARIAN

Éva Gyarmathy

INTRODUCTION

The Hungarian language is spoken by some 10 million Hungarians in Hungary, and a further 2 million outside Hungary, mostly in Romania. While there has been a long tradition of research in psychology, it has tended to be published in Hungarian, or occasionally the other language used by Hungarian academics, German. There has not been a large amount of research into reading and writing difficulties for a long time, partly because for many decades psychology was not an accepted area of the science, partly because many felt that Ranschburg had answered most of the difficulties as early as 1916 from a psycholinguistic perspective. This chapter attempts to convey his findings, as well as more recent work in other areas which relates to reading and writing difficulties in this transparent language.

There has been an increased interest in dyslexia in Hungary since the 1970s and 1980s. Mainly speech-therapists have been dealing with the treatment of dyslexia, but also psychophysiologists, psychologists and linguistics scholars have taken part in the research. In this chapter the research studies are reviewed that have attempted a better understanding of the role of the Hungarian language in reading difficulties.

THE HUNGARIAN LANGUAGE

The Hungarian language is a phonetic, transparent language of the Finno-Ugric group, of which Finnish is said to be the closest relative. Consequently it is not difficult for dyslexics, yet there are many features of the language that cause serious difficulties.

International Book of Dyslexia: A Cross-Language Comparison and Practice Guide. Edited by Ian Smythe, John Everatt and Robin Salter. ISBN 0471498416 © 2004 John Wiley & Sons, Ltd.

Hungarian is an agglutinative language: prepositions do not stand alone but are simply added to the end of the noun, which gets bigger and bigger with the complexity of the concept being expressed, and any single word may have several morphemes. For example if you want to say 'for your children', it is one word in Hungarian: *gyermekeiteknek*. If English were suddenly to be transformed into such an agglutinative language, words like 'antidisestablishmentarianism' would become the rule rather than the exception.

In Hungarian the word order is not fixed, the suffixes indicate the construction of the sentence. Thus suffixes are of a greater importance in the understanding of the sentence.

The letters of the Hungarian language can be classified into three groups:

1 Only standard characters, which can be vowels and consonants alike, e.g. *a, o, b, m*.
2 Standard characters and accent, which can be only vowels, e.g. *á, é, ö, ű*.
3 A combination of the standard characters, which are only consonants, e.g. *sz, zs, ny, ty, gy*.

Their relative incidence is approximately 70-20-10 from 100 letters (Gósy, 1999). It means that most of the letters are easily identifiable, but letters with an accent and combined letters are always a challenge for dyslexic children.

STUDIES OF THE HUNGARIAN LANGUAGE AND DYSLEXIA

Ranschburg Pál was the first Hungarian researcher who dealt with the disturbances of the spoken and written language on the basis of its principles. In his works he described and analysed dyslexia at the beginning of the twentieth century. Ranschburg (1939) tried to understand linguistic functioning on a broader biological, physiological and psychological basis.

No matter how diversified the languages are and how much they change through the centuries, their development and further formation are influenced by physiological, neurophysiological and psychological laws. These laws play a leading role in the development of every language; however, the sensitivity of the language to these laws is different.

The first law is the *law of economy*. It says that occurrences follow the line of least resistance (Hamilton's law). Its manifestation in phonetics is to the advantage of stronger sounds and of those sounds which are more easily identifiable and phonetically feasible. Thus voiceless consonants (e.g. *f, k, s, sz, t*) have an advantage over voiced consonants (e.g. *v, g, zs, z, d*), the more closed *m* over the *n*. The vowel-like soft *l* and *r* never assimilate. Furthermore, *l* before a consonant is often dropped in running speech in Hungarian, e.g. *boldog* (happy) pronounced *bo:dog* (the same in the English 'palm'). Dyslexics have great difficulty with this concept.

In many languages, e.g. Hungarian, mostly the voiceless consonants are used, because they are produced with less effort. Thus many words sound differently in Hungarian in spite of its phonetic nature, e.g. *fogta* ('took') written as it is pronounced: *fokta*.

Avoidance of consonant clusters also helps simplification. Hungarian strongly tries to simplify speech by inserting vowels, e.g. 'Turkish' – *török*. An original Hungarian word never starts with two consonants, and consonants within words merge in pronunciation.

The second law is the *principle of homogenous inhibition* (the Ra-effect named after its describer, Ranschburg). It says that the more different the adjoining contents and processes of the mind are, the less they interfere with each other's development. This phenomenon operates in other areas, in our perception, speech and in our memory errors.

As a result, similar sounds lose their distinctive features in running speech and utterances easily unite. In Hungarian many consonants have a similar formation and acoustic appearance definitely distinguished in the written language. For example, *sz* and *s* in *egészség* ('health') is written as it is pronounced: *egésség*; or *z* and *sz* in *házszám* ('street number') is written as it is pronounced: *hászszám*. Dyslexics have trouble identifying the graphemes in these cases.

However, very different sounds exist in running speech in spite of the economy law. Thus, the sounds *g* and *d* in e.g. *vagdal* ('chop'), *t* and *k* in e.g. *vétkes* ('guilty') etc. keep their distinctive features when they meet. In that way, they provide the unbroken pronouncing of the word, its perspicuity, namely the task of the speech and language, while other mechanisms provide the economic functioning (Ranschburg, 1939).

According to Ranschburg, in Hungarian the different types of errors in writing and reading can be traced back to the above described two laws. The different types of error are:

1 Merging of homogenous elements, elimination of one of the similar letters:
   (a) Some 74 per cent of the letters merged or lost are vowels. For instance, the adjective *meleg* ('warm') as an adverb is *melegen* ('warmly'). It is often written incorrectly: *melgen*. The reason for this is that there are very few vowels, and thus there are more possibilities for uniformity and similarity. In Hungarian a single vowel defines the nature of a longer word to some extent making the vocals homogenous – low or high. Thus there are more possibilities for the formation of uniformity and similarity, which is the cause of many spelling mistakes.
   (b) In 79 per cent of the cases of two or more alike sounds, the second one dissolves into the first one differently from the rules of the merging in speech, because the actual sound is identified at the prospective sound's expense.
   (c) In cases of uniformity the weaker element dissolves, and will be omitted.
2 Mistakes originating from the prohibitory effect of the homogeneity:
   (a) Phoneme substitution: the phoneme is replaced by a similar phoneme, e.g. *jön* ('come'), written incorrectly *jöm*. There are numerous double consonants in Hungarian. It is a characteristic mistake, when the child dissociates them, e.g. *arany* ('gold') written incorrectly: *aranj*.
   (b) Similarity mistakes: similar sounds near to each other cause inhibition, thus omission or transformation will happen, e.g. *mind* ('all') written incorrectly: *mid*; *macska csengő* ('cat bell') written incorrectly: *macska csenkő*.
3 Permutation: this happens when there are visually, aural and/or motor homogenous engrams of double graphemes, e.g. *cserép* ('tile') written incorrectly: *scerép*; *ponty* ('carp') written incorrectly: *ponyt*.
4 Contamination: there are word and letter contaminations. This happens when a new joint formation originates through the bridge of two similar sounding words or similar featured letter, e.g. *asztal* ('table') written incorrectly: *asztd*.
5 Repetitive augmentation: the previously formed element persists, e.g. *szeptember* written incorrectly: *szezptember*.
6 Quantitative inhibition: this happens when more consonants congest, and one of them drops out, e.g. *ezüst* ('silver') written incorrectly: *ezüt*.

As a result of his work, Ranschburg created a school. Recent research and educational methods on dyslexia are mainly based on his results, although after a gap of many decades.

Meixner Ildikó was one of the leading Hungarian experts, who started to study dyslexia in the 1960s. She followed Ranschburg's way of looking at reading difficulties. She built her work mainly on his results and the practical observations speech therapists made while correcting speech and language disorders.

Meixner and other experts worked out new reading methods. One of the most important characteristics of these methods was to teach children to analyse and synthesize the words. In Hungarian it often happens that even one letter can make a significant change in the meaning, because single letters at the end of the word (sometimes hidden among other suffixes) inform, for instance, about plural or genitive relations. For example, the word *gyermek* ('child'), *gyermeked* ('your child'), *gyermekednek* ('for your child'), *gyermekeidnek* ('for your children'). Reading non-words helps children to learn to read carefully and analyse, which is essential in Hungarian.

However, the new teaching methods no longer use the traditional syllabification methods, and the newly developed methods have, step by step, followed a more whole word approach. Children had to recognize the meaning from the printed form at once, which increased the reading difficulties.

Increased incidence of the syndrome led to increased interest in dyslexia. Though many researchers turned to psychophysiological studies, there are also significant works on the psycholinguistic side.

At that time one of the most important dyslexia models was developed by Subosits. Subosits (1989) suggested that those suffering from deep dyslexia are unable to dismantle the whole word images, as they do not possess the phonological module, which is required for the analysis of words. In the case of surface dyslexia, only the phonological system is used, the person can identify the letters, but cannot form words.

In his reading model Subosits (1989) described reading analysed as a system process. The blocks of the process are the following:

1 Block of lexemes: a word inventory to store the images of the words.
2 Block of optical perception: this is responsible for the perception and processing of the shape of the word.
3 Semantic block: this contains the mental images which are the bases of the meaning of the words.
4 Block of syntax: this contains the grammatical rules.
5 Acoustic-motor block: this is the output and performs the neurophysiological organization of the reading.

Blocks are in a star-like connection with each other. The block of lexemes is in the middle of the star. It receives information from the semantical and syntactical blocks for processing the words, and the result is transferred to the acoustic-motor block, which accomplishes the reading. Disturbed reading is the result of any break or disturbance in the above-mentioned connections. Reading mistakes can be grouped according to the nature of the error:

1 *Optical mistakes* originate from the misperception of the shape of the word. There are many kinds of this mistake:
   (a) *Confusion*, when the child confuses similar letters, e.g. *forma–torma* ('shape–horseradish'), *láda–lába* ('box–his leg'), *ülök–ölök* ('I sit–I kill'). Accents play an

important role in Hungarian. Similar accents indicate similar sounding and similarly produced sounds. Vowels with accents are a special challenge for dyslexics. For example, adult dyslexics confuse the *ö* and *ü* characters. It is a great problem for them to write words correctly, where there are such sounds in the same word, such as in the word *különböző* ('different').

(b) *Reading in unit (conflation)*: when the child reads letters together, e.g. *vágja–vágya* ('cut–his desire'), *éjnek-épek* ('of the night–they are intact').

(c) *Metastasis*: When the child inverts letters, e.g. *korsó–kosró* ('jug'–non-word), *zsúr–szúr* ('party–sting'). There are numerous double letters in Hungarian, and the reverse of the letters *sz* indicates another sound. In that case reversal can happen easily.

2 *Acoustic-motor mistakes*

(a) *Repetitions* are mistakes when the child repeats the first syllable of the word (certainly dysphemia has to be differentiated from this phenomenon).

(b) The reversal of a syllable we call *metathesis*, e.g. *korom–komor* ('soot–morose'), *temet–tetem* ('bury–corpse').

(c) *Shortening or resection* is when the child omits the end of the word, e.g. *monda–mond* ('myth–says'), *kereset–keres* ('salary–seek'), or omits letters from the word. Sometimes the child not only omits letters, but also adds to it. There are additions, when the child inserts groups of words that do not belong there, e.g. *korsó–koporsó* ('jug–coffin').

(d) *Assimilation* is when the child reads a letter, as if it were the previous or following one, e.g. *közút–között* ('public road–between').

The optical and acoustic-motor mistakes belong to surface dyslexia, because they originate from the afferent and efferent branches of the neurolinguistic system.

The following semantic and grammatical mistakes designate deep dyslexia.

1 In the case of semantic mistakes it is suggested that the lexemes or the semantic blocks are processed inefficiently. The reader exteriorizes inner images because of figural or semantic interferences. Figural interference is a misreading such as *szolid* instead of *szelíd* ('steady–gentle'), or semantic interference e.g. *halad–szalad* ('go–run').

2 The grammatical mistakes are barely differentiable from the optical mistakes because of the agglutinal character of the Hungarian language. The several postpositions make the words very long and less analysable. There are two groups of grammatical mistakes:

(a) Mixing up similar shaped or similar sounding suffixes, e.g. *tálba–tálban* ('into the bowl–in the bowl'), *erdőből–erdőtől* ('out of the forest–from the forest').

(b) Misreading of verbs is when the child reads the tense incorrectly, or reads a declarative verb instead of an imperative verb, or vice versa, e.g. *örül–örült* ('is glad–was glad') and *örül–örülj* ('is glad–be glad').

Subosits classified the mistakes of dyslexics in a slightly different system than that of Ranschburg; however, the described types of mistakes can still be identified and matched to Ranschburg's types of mistakes.

Based on lengthy research the optimal model of reading for Hungarian was established by Gósy (1999). The model consists of three phases. First, the preparation is to make the child conscious of the sound–letter connection, to understand that the graphemes represent the phonemes. This is the phase when the child learns the traditional direction of the written language as well. In the second phase the child learns to connect the sounds to the letters, the pronounced words to the printed words, and learns to decode the words with the help of syllabification. In the third phase the process has to become automatic, the child looks at the word, and understands the meaning at once (Adamikné Jászó, 1993). Gósy (1999) found the perception and comprehension of the speech to be a crucial factor in reading. Deficits in the processing of the speech can lead to reading difficulties later.

The way of understanding a sentence is language-specific. Processing a Hungarian sentence requires a more context-dependent decision because of the free word order. Deciding the function of a given word in the sentence you have to rely on the endings of the words. Gósy (1988) found in her experiments that longer words with suffixes are more understandable than sentences consisting of one-syllable words. Although the latter may be grammatically correct, the words do not give the usual information about the whole sentence as is customary in Hungarian. Thus the suffixes carry more information in Hungarian than, for example, in English. Misreading the endings of the words causes greater misunderstanding for the dyslexic person in Hungarian.

COGNITIVE PROCESSING

There is a relative scarcity of research on the association between cognitive deficits and difficulties in the acquisition of literacy skills in Hungarian (see discussions in Gyarmathy and Smythe, 2000). Smythe et al. (2002) found that 8-year-old good and poor spellers (matched for age, gender, teaching environment and Ravens matrices) are differentiated by auditory factors (i.e. non-word repetition and, to a lesser extent, sound discrimination) and speed of processing (i.e. number naming and, to a lesser extent, object naming), together with the potential effects of phonological factors (i.e. rhyme).

Spelling

In a regression analysis Smythe et al. (in preparation a) found measures of alliteration skills accounted for 34 per cent of the variance in spelling for poor spellers, but only 11 per cent for good readers. However, a further 32 per cent was predicted by sound discrimination in the good spellers. These results, supported by similar results for non-word spelling, suggest that once the preliminary skills of segmentation are acquired, it is the ability to discriminate between sounds and hold them in memory that is important.

Reading

For dyslexics, reading speed was found to be strongly predicted by rapid naming of numbers, a task that accesses orthographic rather than a semantic/visual representation, whereas for controls, the main predictor was alliteration skills.

Results suggested that these Hungarian children with poor reading skills are constructing the words item by item, holding the intermediate construction in the phonological loop. However, for the controls, the predictor is rapid naming, which may be a reflection of the ability to perform the graphemic to phonological representation fast enough to provide a 'word' as opposed to a string of dissociated phonemes.

One possible explanation proposed by Smythe et al. (in preparation b) is that in

Hungarian the poor reader is constantly trying to build up each word on a letter-by-letter basis, and therefore will require repeated access to the orthographic lexicon, as indicated by the rapid naming of numbers task. Such individual letter access may be slower than that for the controls and, consequently, causes the discrepant reading. However, the good reader may use an alternative strategy related to the ability to segment words, and use analogies.

SPELLING ERRORS

Smythe *et al.* (in preparation a) found that phonological segmentation and assembly skills are less important than in an opaque language (e.g. English) for controls though moderately predictive for dyslexics. However, auditory tasks, such as sound discrimination and auditory memory, are significant predictors for the control group in spelling tasks.

In an investigation into spelling, Smythe *et al.* (in preparation b) suggest that there are differences in the types of errors made. An analysis of non-word errors suggests that the specific categories discussed by Subosits that created problems were mainly acoustic mistakes, metathesis, shortening and resection.

MORPHOLOGY

Cognitive profiling research does not include a measure of morphological knowledge. However, Hungarian provides a good testing ground to study some of the basic issues in lexical access and morphological decomposition in processing and representation. With its rich agglutinative structure accompanied with more or less productive allomorphy patterns, it offers ample opportunities to raise and quite straightforwardly test some of the issues that are central in the contemporary literature on morphology processing.

Pléh *et al.* (Pléh, 1990; Gergely and Pléh, 1994) started an ambitious programme to investigate such issues as how morphemes are integrated on a time scale during understanding. They are looking for representational differences between different morphemes both as a function of linear position and morpheme type.

One of the basic issues in their studies is to see how morphological decomposition is prevalent with different types of affixes, and whether there are signs of preferential processing orders in suffixes. Hungarian word formation rules allow the study of affixes that differ both positionally (prefixes and ordered suffixes), and functionally (derivational suffixes, plural and possessive markers, and case markers).

Their studies showed that in an agglutinative language, if lexical decisions involve both search and grammatical-semantic combinations, reaction times become extremely slow. It is apparent that in these cases one can only study secondary representation processes rather than lexical access itself and the role of morphological parsing in it.

PSYCHOPHYSIOLOGY

Csépe *et al.* investigated the psychophysiological side of dyslexia. The aim is to assess whether dyslexic children can be separated from controls on a high variability of acoustic and phonetic discrimination performance by measuring the mismatch negativity (MMN) component of event-related potentials (Csépe *et al.*, 2000, 2001).

In a recent study (Csépe *et al.*, 2000) the MMN elicited by pith, vowel and consonant–vowel (CV) contrasts was measured in dyslexics of 9 years of age and in two groups of age-matched controls. The most reliable MMN difference between dyslexics and controls were found in the CV condition where voicing and place of articulation were used as contrasting features. Furthermore, the MMN to CV contrasts recorded in dyslexics were found to be different when compared to the MMN recorded in controls of poor phoneme discrimination performance. Based on the MMN results, their suggestion and further research hypothesis are that the speech sound representation of dyslexics and age-matched children is different.

SUMMARY

Hungarian presents the following challenges to dyslexics:

- Dyslexic children forget to use accents, some of them do not use accents at all, though in Hungarian they are very important for comprehension (*sor* means 'row', *sör* means 'beer').
- The similar-looking and similar-sounding *ö* and *ü* are very often mixed up, even by adult dyslexics.
- Dyslexic children use false accents which change emphasis or even the sound (*ö* is a short vowel, *ő* is a long one, or *a* is pronounced like 'run', *á* is like 'rasp'. You can make serious mistakes, as for instance *bal* means 'left', *bál* means 'ball', 'dance', *szél* is 'wind', *szel* means 'cut', *túr* is 'dig', *tűr* is 'endure', etc.)
- Dyslexic children cannot properly use the past ending on verbs (in Hungarian tense indicators are put to the end of the words whether it is a suffix or marker of tense, except for the future). If the verb ends with a vowel or a vowel has been added to the end of the verb to help the pronunciation, *tt* should be used, but if the consonant remains, then *t* is correct.
- There are some double consonants such as *ny* (pronounced like the first sound of '*new*'), or *gy* (the first sound from the Russian *Ded Maroz*) and *ty* which are very similar. These combined consonants can easily be mixed up.
- Use of double consonants such as *sz* (s) and *zs* (similar to the first sound in the French word *jour*) is also confusing.
- There are two equally pronounced consonants: *j* and *ly*. They are pronounced like the start of the English word 'you'. These letters are often mixed up.
- Suffixes and post-positions cause many mistakes. Suffixes should be written together with the basic word, but post-positions should be written separately. As both stand at the end of the word, the child should differentiate whether it is a suffix or a post-position e.g. *házban* ('in the house') *ház előtt* ('in front of the house').
- Words can be very long and complex because Hungarian is an agglutinative language.
- As the word order is not fixed, suffixes carry more information for the meaning of the whole sentence than in languages where the position of the word shows its function. Thus the misreading of these endings (sometimes only one or two letters long) might hinder understanding.

REFERENCES

Adamikné Jászó, A. (1993) A fonetikai kutatás újabb eredményeinek és a kiejtés kapcsolatának gyakorlata. In M. Gósy and P. Siptár (eds), *Beszédkutatás '93*. Budapest: MTA Nyelvtudományi Intézet.

Csépe, V., Szűcs, D., Lukács, Á. and Osman-Sági, J. (2001) The role of reading acquisition methods in phoneme representation as shown by MMN changes. *International Journal of Psychophysiology*, 41(3), 209.

Csépe, V., Szűcs, D. and Osman-Sági, J. (2000) A fejlődési diszlexiára (FDL) jellemző beszédhang-feldolgozási zavarok eltérési negativitás (EN) korrelátumai. [Abnormal mismatch negativity to phonetic deviations in developmental dyslexia.] *Magyar Pszichológiai Szemle*, 55(4), 475–500.

Gergely, Gy. and Pléh, Cs. (1994) Lexical processing in an agglutinative language and the organization of the lexicon. *Folia Linguistica*, 28, 175–204.

Gósy, M. (1988) Sentence understanding: The role of the number of syllables. *Magyar Fonetikai Füzetek* 19, 18–28.

Gósy, M. (1999) *Pszicholingvisztika*. Budapest: Corvina.

Gyarmathy, É. and Smythe, I. (2000) Többnyelvűség és az olvasási zavarok. [Multilingualism and reading difficulties.] *Erdélyi Pszichológiai Szemle*, December, 63–76.

Meixner, I. and Justné Kéry, H. (1967) *Az olvasástanítás pszichológiai alapjai*. Budapest: Akadémiai Kiadó.

Pléh, Cs. (1990) Word order and morphonological factors in the development of sentence understanding in Hungarian. *Linguistics*, 28, 1449–1469.

Ranschburg, P. (1939) *Az emberi tévedések törvényszerűségei*. Budapest: Novák Rudolf és Társa.

Smythe, I., Gyarmathy, É. and Everatt, J. (2002) Olvasási zavarok különböző nyelveken: egy nyelvközi kutatás elméleti és gyakorlati kérdései. [Reading difficulties in different languages: Theoretical and practical issues of a cross-linguistic study.] *Pszichológia*, 22, 387–406.

Smythe, I., Gyarmathy, É. and Everatt, J. (in preparation a) Cognitive predictors of Hungarian spelling errors.

Smythe, I., Gyarmathy, É. and Gabor, G. (in preparation b) Comparison of spelling errors in good and poor Hungarian spellers.

Subosits, I. (1989) Az olvasás és írás zavarainak típusai. *Pedagógia Szemle*, Október.

13

DYSLEXIA IN ITALIAN

Patrizio Tressoldi

ITALIAN ORTHOGRAPHY

Italian orthography favours the recognition and the use of the orthographic-phonological rules. Regardless of the context in which they occur, each of the five vowels has only one orthographic rendition in Italian. Consonants have only one graphemic rendition and vice versa, except for a few stop consonants and affricates (i.e. /k/ and /g/; /tʃ/ and /dʒ/). In these cases, the same grapheme followed by different vowels has different phonological renditions. For instance, the letters (g) + (a) are rendered as /ga/, but (g) + (i) as /dʒi/; in order to obtain the voiced velar /gi/, we need to insert the letter h (ghi). A similar pattern applies to the voiceless velar /k/ as well.

In a few cases, the orthographic rendition of the word is phonologically unpredictable: the voiceless velar /k/ followed by the vowel /u/ which appear in /kuadro/ ('picture') are written as *quadro*, in /kuore/ ('heart') as *cuore* and in /akua/ ('water') as *acqua*. Similarly unpredictable, on rare occasions, is the spelling of the voiceless palatal /tʃ/, the voiced affricate /dz/ and the fricative /ʃ/ before the vowel /e/. The word /tʃeleste/ (light blue) and /tʃelo/ (sky), /dʒelo/ (frost) and /tʃiliedʒe/ (cherries) are rendered in orthography as *celeste* and *cielo*, *gelo* and *ciliegie*, respectively. In similar vein /tʃero/ ('candle') and /tʃeco/ ('blind'), /ʃena/ ('scene') and /ʃentsa/ ('science') are rendered as *cero* and *cieco*, *scena* and *scienza*, respectively. Apart from these few exceptions, Italian orthography is rendered by a fairly biunivocal correspondence between phoneme and grapheme (see Table 13.1).

Cossu *et al.* (1995) observed that first- and second-grade Italian children produced a reduced number of vowel errors in reading isolated words with respect to their English controls, but a higher number of consonant errors. This result was interpreted as a consequence of the difference between the syllable structure between the two languages: open-syllable, with few variations for Italian, closed-syllable with many variations, for English. A similar interpretation was put forward by Wimmer and Goswami (1994)

International Book of Dyslexia: A Cross-Language Comparison and Practice Guide. Edited by Ian Smythe, John Everatt and Robin Salter.   ISBN 0471498416   © 2004 John Wiley & Sons, Ltd.

TABLE 13.1 Correspondences between phonemes and graphemes in Italian

Phonemes ⇒	Letters	Phonemes ⇒	Letters
a	a	ʎ	gl (+ i)
e	e	ɲ	gn
i	i	–	h
o	o	l	l
u	u	m	m
b	b	n	n
k	c (+ a, o, u)	p	p
k	ch (+ i, e)	k	q (+ u)
tʃ	c (+ i, e)	r	r
d	d	s, z	s
f	f	ʃ	sc (+ i, e)
g	g (+ a, o, u)	t	t
dʒ	g (+ i, e)	v	v
g	gh (+ i, e)	ts, dz	z

comparing the superiority in reading non-words of German vs. English 7- to 9-year-old children.

This finding may be specific to Italian and to other regular orthographies allowing the subjects to read words and non-words using the same process. The use of the same cognitive process for reading words and non-words forces Italian readers to rely on the use of the phonological component at the beginning of their reading experience. This permits even reading-disabled subjects to read non-words at the same level as words.

Normal readers easily develop their orthographic component from the beginning of their reading experience (Cossu, 1999), whereas most reading-disabled subjects continue to rely on their phonological component, retarding the development of the direct or lexical component.

A recent cross-linguistic comparison among different European orthographies (Seymour et al., 2003), has confirmed that in languages with shallow orthographies, children become accurate and fluent both in reading simple words and non-words at the end of the first Grade, differently from children who must learn to read French, Danish and particularly English. The difference between a 'deep' orthography like English and a 'superficial' one like Italian has been also documented using a PET study by Paulesu et al. (2000). These authors revealed that different brain areas are activated when English and Italian students read lists of words and non-words. To summarize their findings, Italian students showed greater activation in left superior temporal regions, in contrast, English students showed greater activation, particularly for non-words, in left posterior temporal gyrus and anterior inferior frontal gyrus.

DIAGNOSIS OF DYSLEXIA IN ITALY

The MT battery (Cornoldi and Colpo, 1981) is the most popular and psychometrically valid instrument for measuring reading speed and accuracy in Italy from the 1st to the 8th Grade. It comprises different passages for each grade level with an increasing number of syllables per passage (from 250 in the 2nd Grade to 570 in the 8th Grade). The sample used for the standardization comprised more than 200 children for each grade from the second to the eighth. Mean test–retest coefficient for all Grades was .85. Construct and parallel validity evidence are satisfactory and are reported in the administration manual. The measure of speed is obtained by dividing the number of syllables by the seconds taken to read the passage. Accuracy corresponds to the number of words misread and omitted. The median correlation between speed and accuracy from the 2nd to the 8th Grade is .75.

Reading characteristics of the subjects, especially the relative efficiency of the orthographic and the phonological process of reading, are measured using the lists of words and non-words in the standardized battery of Sartori *et al.* (1995). Non-word reading relies upon the phonological skills more than the other reading tasks and represents the most sensitive measure of the phonological efficiency of the reading system (Rack *et al.*, 1992).

The list of words comprised 112 items, half of low frequency and the other half of high frequency according to the Italian count by Bortolini *et al.* (1972). Some 56 words were of two syllables, 28 of three and 28 of four syllables. The non-words were 48 items of two, three and four syllables, all drawn from words changing a letter in different positions in order to maintain the rules of Italian pronunciation. The norms are drawn from more than 100 subjects for each grade from the 2nd to the 8th. Test–retest reliability was .77, Crombach alpha .75.

According to the guidelines presented by the ICD-10 and DSM-IV manuals, a diagnosis of dyslexia is formulated when the reading performance is at least 2 SD below the fluency and/or accuracy norms expected.

Accuracy is the measure of reading efficiency most often used in English-speaking countries, given the disparity between English orthography and phonology. However, for Italian and other so-called transparent orthographies like Spanish and German, accuracy is a minor problem whereas low reading speed remains a core symptom of reading impairment (Wimmer, 1993; Wimmer and Goswami, 1994; Zoccolotti *et al.*, 1999).

DYSLEXIA SUB-GROUPS

For Italian, Job *et al.* (1984) and Sartori and Job (1982) presented data of single case subjects with characteristics of surface and phonological dyslexia. However, their data are not immune to the critiques regarding the criteria used for this classification: use of accuracy and not speed and the comparison of the performance of the two reading components within the subject and not with respect to a developmental model. In fact, as indicated by Castles and Coltheart (1993), in order to study the efficiency of the direct and the indirect component of reading it is necessary to compare the performance of dyslexic subjects with their chronological or grade-normal controls because the two components develop at different rates during reading development.

Recently, Zoccolotti *et al.* (1999), examining a group of four dyslexic adolescents, suggested that their core problem is the formation of an orthographic lexicon of whole words, a typical characteristic of surface dyslexia.

DYSLEXIA DEVELOPMENT

The 'natural' development of fluency and accuracy of reading of dyslexic children has recently been published by Tressoldi *et al.* (2001) and compared with that of normal

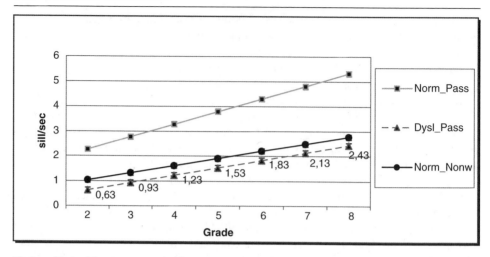

FIGURE 13.1 The 'natural' development of fluency reading a passage (Norm_Pass) and lists of non-words (Norm_Nonw) of normal reading children, compared with the development of fluency reading a passage of children with dyslexia (Dysl_Pass), expressed in syllables per seconds.

reading children published by Tressoldi (1996). The data regarding the fluency of passage reading is illustrated in Figure 13.1. The most interesting finding is that the fluency of dyslexic children, when they read texts, progresses at a rate comparable to that of normal readers when they read non-words and corresponds to roughly half that of normal readers, .3 vs .5 syll/sec. respectively.

DYSLEXIA TREATMENT

Only recently research related to the outcomes of treatment of Italian dyslexics has appeared in the international literature (Tressoldi *et al.*, 2000; Judica *et al.*, 2002; Lorusso *et al.*, submitted), even if some papers had already been published in Italian journals. What seems to be emerging is confirmation that accuracy, contrary to fluency, is not a particular problem to solve. However, this reading characteristic shows results amenable to treatment with improvement, obtained in 3–5 months with at least two sessions a week, of the same amount to those obtained in 12 months without specific interventions. The more efficacious treatments seem to be those aimed at automatizing the recognition of syllables and whole words presented tachistoscopically, isolated or in texts.

DYSLEXIA RESOURCES

The Italian Dyslexia Association (www.dislessia.it) is a new organization of scholars, professionals, parents and adults with dyslexia. It is affiliated to the European Dyslexia Association and represents a very important resource for all those interested in this problem. Its scientific committee has recently produced guidelines for the diagnosis of dyslexia, while the General Council is in discussion with the Minister of Public Health and the

Minister of Instruction regarding official recognition of this disability and consequently providing the necessary instructional facilities to all children affected by dyslexia. Another not-for-profit organization, the Association for Research and Intervention in the Psychopathology of Learning (www.airipa.piave.net) serves as another important resource for the dissemination to professionals of research related to this topic.

ACKNOWLEDGEMENTS

I greatly appreciate the collaboration of Professor G. Cossu who kindly supplied Table 13.1 and the information on Italian orthography. Special thanks also to the Editors for their revisions and suggestions to improve the chapter.

REFERENCES

Bortolini, U., Tagliavini, C. and Zampolli, A. (1972) *Lessico di frequenza della lingua italiana.* [Frequency lexicon of Italian.] Milan: Garzanti.

Castles, A. and Coltheart, M. (1993) Varieties of developmental dyslexia. *Cognition*, 47, 149–180.

Cornoldi, C. and Colpo, M. (1981) *La valutazione oggettiva della lettura.* [The objective evaluation of reading.] Florence: Organizzazioni Speciali.

Cossu, G. (1999) The acquisition of Italian orthography. In M. Harris and G. Hatano (eds), *Learning to Read and Write: A Cross-Linguistic Perspective.* New York: Cambridge University Press.

Cossu, G., Shankweiler, D., Liberman, I.Y. and Gugliotta, M. (1995) Visual and phonological determinants of misreadings in a transparent orthography. *Reading and Writing: An Interdisciplinary Journal*, 7, 237–256.

Job, R., Sartori, G., Masterson, J. and Coltheart, M. (1984) Developmental surface dyslexia in Italian. In R.N. Malatesha and H.A. Whitaker (eds), *Dyslexia: A Global Issue.* The Hague: Martinus Nijhoff.

Judica, A., De Luca, M., Spinelli, D. and Zoccolotti, P. (2002) Training of developmental surface dyslexia improves reading performance and shortens eye fixation duration in reading. *Neuropsychological Rehabilitation*, 12(3), 177–196.

Lorusso, M.L., Facoetti, A., Gazzaniga, I., Paganoni, P., Pezzani, M. and Molteni, M. (submitted) Treatment of developmental dyslexia: Visual hemispheric-specific stimulation and speech therapy.

Paulesu, E., McCrory, E., Fazio, F., Menoncelli, L., Brunswick, N., Cappa, F., Cotelli, M., Cossu, G., Corte, F., Lo Russo, M., Pesenti, S., Gallagher, A., Perani, D., Price, C., Frith, C.D. and Frith U. (2000) A cultural effect on brain function. *Nature Neuroscience*, 3(1), 91–96.

Rack, J., Snowling, M. and Olson, R. (1992) The nonword reading deficit in developmental dyslexia: A review. *Reading Research Quarterly*, 27, 29–53.

Sartori, G. and Job, R. (1982) Phonological impairment in Italian acquired and developmental dyslexia. Paper presented to the NATO conference on acquisition of symbolic skills, Keele University.

Sartori, G., Job, R. and Tressoldi, P. E. (1995) *Batteria per la diagnosi della dislessia e disortografia evolutiva.* [Battery for the diagnosis of the developmental dyslexia and dysgraphia.] Florence: Organizzazioni Speciali.

Seymour, P.H.K., Aro, M. and Erskine, J.M. (2003) Foundation literacy acquisition in European orthographies. *British Journal of Psychology*, 94, 143–174.

Tressoldi, P. E. (1996) L'evoluzione della lettura e della scrittura dalla 2a elementare alla 8a classe. [The development of reading and writing from the 2nd to the 8th grade.] *Età Evolutiva*, 53, 43–55.

Tressoldi, P.E., Lonciari, I. and Vio, C. (2000) Results of the treatment of specific developmental reading disorder, based on the single and dual-route models. *Journal of Learning Disabilities*, 33(3), 278–285.

Tressoldi, P.E., Stella, G. and Faggella, M.(2001) The development of reading speed in Italians with dyslexia: A longitudinal study. *Journal of Learning Disabilities*, 34(5), 67–78.

Wimmer, H. (1993) Characteristics of developmental dyslexia in a regular writing system. *Applied Psycholinguistics*, 14, 1–33.

Wimmer, H. and Goswami, U. (1994) The influence of orthographic consistency on reading development: Word recognition in English and German children. *Cognition*, 51, 91–103.

Zoccolotti, P., DeLuca, M., DiPace, E., Judica, A., Orlandi, M. and Spinelli, D. (1999) Markers of developmental surface dyslexia in a language (Italian) with high grapheme-phoneme correspondence. *Applied Psycholinguistics*, 20, 191–216.

14

LEARNING TO READ IN JAPANESE
Word to sentence reading

Jun Yamada

INTRODUCTION

Is developmental dyslexia virtually non-existent in Japan? Some researchers say yes (Makita, 1968; Sakamoto and Makita, 1973; Wydell and Butterworth, 1999), and others say no (Stevenson *et al.*, 1982; Hirose and Hatta, 1988; Yamada and Banks, 1994). Obviously these conflicting views reflect the complexity of the matter including the characteristic features of the Japanese writing system. The following summary made by Kess and Miyamoto (1999, p. 152), however, seems to represent the basic state of affairs:

> Some specific reading problems may indeed be associated with the orthographic type used in each respective linguistic culture, but other factors such as definition and attribution will also critically affect reports of incidence. It probably is true that it is easier to learn to read the inventory of words written in Japanese kana than it is to learn to read the inventory of words written in the English alphabet. But as soon as you add into the equation the necessity of learning to read kanji as well, the simple statement that learning to read in Japanese is easier than learning to read in English is simply a non-sequitur.

Implicated in this statement is difficulty in learning to read *kanji* (a logographic script). We therefore discuss this issue first. Learning to read *kanji*, however, is not sufficient for reading comprehension. We report the case of a boy who could adequately read single *kanji* but not whole sentences. While it is true that normal children at Grade 3 read whole sentences, this boy could not do so, as we will show, until the latter part of Grade 6. We will suggest that this kind of dissociation generally arises from an insufficient amount of reading activities at the text level. The only remedy for the dissociation is to learn to read by reading sentences in books. Learning to read *kanji* in the fullest sense of the term is

International Book of Dyslexia: A Cross-Language Comparison and Practice Guide. Edited by Ian Smythe, John Everatt and Robin Salter. ISBN 0471498416 © 2004 John Wiley & Sons, Ltd.

intertwined with learning to read sentences in a more integrated fashion than generally appreciated.

KANJI ARE NOT EASY TO LEARN

Akita and Hatano (1999, p. 217) state:

> After that [teaching of hiragana], kanji are taught. Beginning with eighty characters in the first grade and more in the higher grades, by the end of elementary school children have mastered 1,006 characters. In junior high school they master another 950. Thus, children master nearly 2,000 characters by the end of junior high school.

This description is simply incorrect or misleading at best. As a matter of fact, very few children, if any, master the 1,006 characters by the end of elementary school, and the 1,945 characters by the end of junior high school.

Two fundamental problems concerning mastery of *kanji* should be made clear here. First, a *kanji* character typically has two or more readings (i.e., pronunciations), one *kun* Japanese reading and one or more *on* Chinese readings. Some 2,000 readings are associated with the 1,006 characters, and some 4,000 readings are associated with the 1,945 characters. Hence, to master the entire set of 1,945 characters entails the learning of all of the 4,000 readings. The question is how many of these readings the average student in each grade knows. Although no comprehensive research seems to have been conducted (National Language Research Institute, 1988; 1994), preliminary findings indicate that the mastery rate is not very high.

Evidently, Akita and Hatano (1999) are using a rough and perhaps too lenient criterion. Even with this lenient criterion, however, the mastery level never nears 100 per cent. For example, the National Language Research Institute (1988) carried out an empirical study to learn how many of the 1,945 individual *kanji* presented in isolation average students were able to name (see Yamada, 1998). In this study, ten average seventh graders (elementary school graduates) and ten average tenth graders (junior high school graduates) were selected as subjects from a large population. The results showed that for the seventh graders, the mean percentage correct for 996 characters (assigned for learning in their school classes) was 91 per cent (N = 906), and for the tenth graders the mean percentage correct for the 1,945 characters was 86 per cent (N = 1,672). Such scores are inadequate for good reading. According to Hayashi (1982), for example, the first 1,000 high frequency *kanji* account for 90 per cent of tokens of *kanji* appearing in journals, and the first 1,500 high frequency *kanji*, for 96 per cent. Thus the reader who knows 1,500 *kanji* would encounter four unknown *kanji* in every 100 *kanji* in journal articles.

Second, and even more importantly, learning *kanji* in higher grades often involves learning new words with those *kanji*. It is true that, given the above lenient criterion, learning to read *kanji* is easy in lower grades. Steinberg and Yamada (1978–79) demonstrated that even 3-year-olds were able to learn to read visually complex *kanji* words. Thus, for example, some 3-year-olds learned *kanji* such as 花 /hana/'flower' and 海 /umi/'ocean' in a single trial in a paired associate learning paradigm. Similarly, first and second graders would enjoy *kanji* learning. However, many *kanji* introduced in higher grades are used as bound morphemes and are less meaningful, so that such *kanji* become far more difficult to learn. For example, both 短い 'short' and 所 'a place' are Grade 3 *kanji* and their speech forms, /mijika-i/ and /tokoro/, are well within the spoken vocabulary of third graders. So learning to read these *kanji* should be easy. However, the former *kanji* has another reading /tan/ and the latter another reading /sho/. These bound morphemes are combined to form a new idiom-like word 短所 /tansho/'a defect'. This two-*kanji* word appears in a sixth grade primer, and if the sixth grader does not know the word, he/she would have to learn three items of information at the same time, the speech form, the orthographic form (i.e., combination of characters), and the meaning. (Note that the new meaning, 'a defect', cannot be derived simply from the meanings of 'short' and 'a place'.)

In fact, these types of bound-morphemes *kanji* combine to generate tens of thousands of two- or more-*kanji* words. While the learning of these *kanji* can be viewed as an important part of vocabulary learning, the learning proceeds mainly through reading activities. This being the case, some children with limited reading experience will have great difficulty learning bound-morpheme *kanji* from one stage to another, and one consequence of this is impoverished reading vocabularies. Such children may be classified as poor readers, or developmental dyslexics.

WORD RECOGNITION TIMES LISTENING IS NOT READING

Suppose that a child knows a substantial number of *kanji* and many of their readings. Is such a child a good reader? Generally speaking, yes, but exceptionable cases are frequently observed. Stanovich (1996), for example, stated: 'it is possible for adequate word recognition skill to be accompanied by poor comprehension abilities' (p. 418). Thus, although Wydell and Butterworth (1999), working with an English-Japanese bilingual, observe that 'single word reading tests are used as diagnostic tools to identify children with reading impairments' (p. 279), such an assumption is unwarranted (and their conclusion concerning a 16-year-old boy's 'clear dissociation' between reading English and Japanese is questionable). On the other hand, it is commonly believed that the following equation obtains: word recognition times listening is reading. For example, in emphasizing the centrality of word recognition in reading, Gough and Hillinger (1980, p. 194) argue:

> Our view of reading, that it consists of decoding plus linguistic comprehension, may be too simple. If so, it should be easy to refute, for it holds that any child with normal comprehension who learns to decode with facility will know how to read, and if any child with normal comprehension fails to read, it is because he has not learned to decode with facility.

THE CASE OF TARO

In this regard, we would like to report the case of a Japanese boy, Taro (a pseudonym), who was a good *kanji* reader and a good listener, but continued to be a poor reader for a long period of time. Eventually, however, nearing the end of his sixth grade, he largely overcame his reading difficulty. The details and implications of this case will now be considered.

Taro's mother, a medical research assistant, referred her son's case to our Dyslexia Clinic at Hiroshima University, when he was a sixth grader (aged 11 years). She described him as follows:

> He is cheerful, somewhat hyperactive, dyslexic, but not awkward. Although he is talkative, his vocabulary is meagre. He is strongly right-handed and poor at copying figures. He is fond

of playing baseball. It is difficult to evaluate his performance in baseball because while he is rather less skilled, he always contributes to the game, trying hard and playing intelligently. He also loves to watch professional baseball games on TV. He surprises us by showing his remarkable ability to 'read' many 'difficult' kanji names of baseball players.

Taro's father, a first-rate medical researcher, almost regularly reads a book to him. Taro enjoys listening to the stories his father reads. He comprehends them perfectly. As far as listening comprehension is concerned, he has no problem whatsoever. He sometimes tries to read a book which looks interesting, but gives up quickly. He finds textbooks very difficult to read even though the contents themselves are not very difficult to understand. As a result, his school record has been very poor. His younger sister has no reading problem. Both parents are avid readers.

Taro's emotional and educational experience appeared to the author to be normal, with his parents exhibiting understanding and not driving him hard. His only problem was in reading.

When he was in Grades 4, 5, and 6, his mother took him to a child care centre to find out if he had any mental or intellectual problems. Nothing wrong was found. The child care centre administered the Japanese version of the Weschler Intelligence Scale for Children, Revised (WISC-R). The results indicated that his intelligence was above average. Taro's verbal IQ in Grades 4, 5, and 6 was 131, 112, and 117, respectively, and his full IQ in Grades 4, 5, and 6 was 122, 117, and 114, respectively. Overall, nothing from these results suggested that Taro has poor reading skills. For example, since the mean was 10, his spoken vocabulary scores in the WISC-R, i.e., 12, 13, and 14 points in Grades 4, 5, and 6, contrary to his mother's belief, were consistently well above average.

It seemed possible that the mother's evaluation of Taro's reading skill was an exaggeration, a typical evaluation of educated mothers. Given this situation, the author attempted to objectively assess his true reading ability. Two tests were done when he was in his sixth grade.

First testing at the end of Grade 6-1

This was done at the end of the first term of Grade 6, which was five months after Taro became a sixth grader. Under the guidance of the author, Taro's mother administered the Standardized Diagnostic Reading Test C (Sakamoto, 1966), which, though dated, contains only a few rare and obsolete words. The test consists of four subtests: Reading speed (7 min., no. items = 30), Reading comprehension (16 min., no. items = 50), Knowledge of *kanji* (5 min., no. items = 49 × 2), and Vocabulary (7 min., no. items = 52).

The results of this test are presented in Table 14.1 (G6-1). Taro's overall reading ability was at the level of the second term of Grade 5, which was one year behind his actual school year. More important, however, his reading speed and comprehension scores were

TABLE 14.1 Taro's reading grade level

	Grade 6-1	Grade 6-3
Reading Speed	G4, 2nd Term	Not given.
Reading Comprehension	G4, 1st Term	G6, 3rd Term
Kanji	G7, 2nd Term	G6, 3rd Term
Vocabulary	G5, 2nd Term	G6, 2nd Term
Criticisms/Interpretation	Not given	G5, 2nd Term
Overall	G5, 2nd Term	G6, 2nd Term

at the levels of the first and second terms of Grade 4, more than two years behind. In marked contrast with those low scores was the high score for *kanji*, which was one year ahead of the average!

Taro's ability to name the 1,006 characters for elementary school education was also examined under the supervision of the author. Each of the characters was written on a 8 cm × 8 cm card with a felt pen. The task was to orally name the *kanji* on the card. The tester was Taro's mother, who recorded his oral response on the reverse side of the card. The responses were also audio-taped. The mother and son had three sessions in three different days to complete the 1,006 *kanji* items. The total time spent was about one and a half hours. The results were satisfactory, i.e., he scored 80.1 per cent correct, naming 806 *kanji* correctly. It was noted, however, that he made many more visual errors (e.g., 貿→貨) than average children (cf. National Language Research Institute, 1988).

What was the problem?

Why was Taro so good at naming *kanji* words (Grade 7 level) but so poor at text reading (Grade 4 level)? Both word recognition and listening comprehension are necessary to read a text, but they are *not* sufficient. Something more is necessary. What is it?

It appears that Taro's reading experience was limited to the substantial number of *kanji* which was acquired through incidental exposure in everyday situations where *kanji* words appear, for example, on signboards, TV, and the name plates of his friends. That is to say, just as a child learns a new spoken word by hearing it in conversation, so Taro seems to have learned a new *kanji* word, being exposed to it in conversation. In this sense, his learning to read *kanji* was natural and probably less strenuous. But in another sense, his learning was 'abnormal' in that he did not learn *kanji* involved in written sentences, which is necessary in normal reading experience. Taro had to learn the *kanji* which he already knew but when they appeared in less familiar contexts, i.e., in written sentences.

Learning to read by reading sentences

To get Taro to read sentences, the author employed Smith's (1976) basic motto. The author instructed the parents to encourage Taro to read interesting books on his own. It was emphasized that interest-driven reading was the key to the development of reading fluency (e.g., Fink, 1998). The parents were told that skim reading was acceptable and that they should not worry about any errors that Taro made. That kind of suggestion, however, did not appear to effect his antipathy to reading books; he continued to lose interest in books. About that time, however, he happened to become a subscriber to *Baseball Magazine*, a weekly for baseball fans. He devoured it! He tried to read every phrase, sentence, and paragraph in the issue.

Second test at the end of Grade 6-3

Six months passed. As he was about to finish Term 3 of Grade 6, Taro was given another standardized reading test. This time the author instructed the parent to administer the Tatsumi and Kembo (1967) Standardized Reading Test, which is composed of four sub-tests: Reading comprehension (18 min., no. items = 22), Vocabulary (5 min., no. items =

20), Knowledge of *kanji* (3 min., no. items = 24), and Criticisms and interpretation (14 min., no. items = 14). (The Sakamoto test was not repeated because the period between the first test and the second test was short and consequently Taro might have remembered items from the first test.)

We also tested knowledge of *kanji* by using about 300 *kanji* cards specially selected from among the 1,006 cards which we used before. The cards consisted of the items which he had previously failed to respond to correctly or he showed some difficulty in recognizing.

The results of the reading test shown in Table 14.1 (G6-3) were surprising. The earlier strange dissociation largely disappeared, except for the Criticisms/Interpretation subtest's, Grade 5-2, which indicates that he was one year and one term below. This subtest required the testee to think critically of the passages and/or to consider possible implications of the stories. In any case, Table 14.1 shows that on the Reading Comprehension subtest Taro had progressed the equivalent of two or more years within a period of just six months, thereby catching up with his peers. His knowledge of *kanji* was also good, being 91.2 per cent correct (N = 917). Correspondingly, his school records became almost 'average' for the first time in his six years of elementary school education.

Discussion and implications

Somehow Taro had difficulty assembling written words efficiently to form a larger meaningful unit for comprehension even though he had no difficulty assembling spoken words for comprehension. However, we do not know exactly why or how this gap arose in Taro. We do not know what was the initial reason for Taro's poor reading skills. The many visual errors he made in naming *kanji* may have something to do with his initial difficulty. Such errors may suggest that he had difficulty grasping a whole–part relation of a visual stimulus. On this supposition, even a string of hiragana characters could cause trouble at the initial stage of reading. (Visual errors, however, also seem to be attributable at least in part to Taro's way of *kanji* learning, i.e., he did not need to pay attention to the details of the configuration of the characters when he learned to name a *kanji* which appeared on a signboard, for example.)

Another possibility involves Taro's vocabulary. His mother said that his vocabulary was small although the results from the WISC-R and reading subtests indicated otherwise. His mother might not have been entirely wrong, however. Miller and Gildea (1987) state: 'In about the fourth grade they begin to see written words they have not heard in coversation. At this point it is generally assumed that something special must be done to teach children these unfamiliar words' (p. 88). But nothing special was done for Taro. This would suggest that Taro's reading vocabulary was much smaller than his listening vocabulary although these vocabularies shared many words in common. Words from a reading vocabulary would begin to appear in conversation as children grow older. These might be the words that Taro had failed to understand in everyday conversations with his mother.

If such is the case, this discrepancy between listening and reading vocabularies may partially account for the dissociation of reading *kanji* from reading sentences. Many lexical items used in vocabulary subtests in the WISC-R and reading tests might have belonged in Taro's listening vocabulary. On the other hand, a few words which were interspersed in sentences in a reading comprehension subtest might not have been in Taro's vocabulary, thereby making the sentences difficult to understand. It would be unlikely, however, that Taro could miraculously increase his reading vocabulary size within six months. Rather, he might have learned to infer in intelligible contexts the meanings of unknown *kanji* words composed of the constituent *kanji* which he knew.

CONCLUSION

We pointed out two inter-related obstacles children with potential reading disorders in Japan tend to encounter. The first stumbling block is learning to read *kanji*, although *kanji* may be learned to some extent without having a good amount of text reading experience. The learning of *kanji* in its real sense is not easy even for a normal child and continues throughout one's life. At advanced stages learning *kanji* often becomes part of learning new words, i.e., the child has to learn a new usage of the *kanji* which he or she may (or may not) know. Such words are learned mainly in the process of overcoming the second, or ultimate obstacle, that is, reading at the text level. Taro seems to be a rare case, exhibiting a remarkable dissociation between word and sentence reading. However, there are many poor and dyslexic children who, albeit less remarkably, suffer this kind of dissociation which lasts for a number of years. Whatever the causes of this dissociation may be, if such children are normal listeners like Taro, learning to read by reading books must be essential.

ACKNOWLEDGEMENTS

The author thanks Taro and his mother for making our study possible and showing us many important aspects of reading difficulty. He is also grateful to Professor Danny Steinberg for his invaluable comments. This study was supported in part by the Japanese Ministry of Education (Grant No. 11610120-00; No. 1451014300).

REFERENCES

Akita, K. and Hatano, G. (1999) Learning to read and write in Japanese. In M. Harris and G. Hatano (eds), *Learning to Read and Write: A Cross-linguistic Perspective.* New York: Cambridge University Press.

Fink, R.P. (1998) Literacy development in successful men and women with dyslexia. *Annals of Dyslexia*, 48, 311–346.

Gough, P.B. and Hillinger, M.L. (1980) Learning to read: An unnatural act. *Bulletin of the Orton Society*, 30, 179–196.

Hayashi, O. (ed.) (1982) *Zusetu nihongo* [Japanese from a statistical perspective]. Tokyo: Kadokawa Shoten.

Hirose, T. and Hatta, T. (1988) Reading disabilities in modern Japanese children. *Journal of Research in Reading*, 11, 152–160.

Kess, J.F. and Miyamoto, T. (1999) *The Japanese Mental Lexicon: Psycholinguistic Studies of Kana and Kanji Processing.* Amsterdam: John Benjamins.

Makita, K. (1968) The rarity of reading disability in Japanese children. *American Journal of Orthopsychiatry*, 38, 599–614.

Miller, G.A. and Gildea, P.M. (1987) How children learn words. *Scientific American*, 257(3), 86–91.

National Language Research Institute (1988) *Jidoo seito no joyo kanji no shuutoku.* [Acquisition of joyo kanji by school children]. Tokyo: Tokyo Shoseki.

National Language Research Institute (1994) *Joyo kanji no shuutoku to shidoo* [Acquisition and teaching of joyo kanji]. Tokyo: Tokyo Shoseki.

Sakamoto, I. (1966) *The Standardized Reading Diagnostic Test, C.* Tokyo: Kaneko Shoboo.

Sakamoto, T. and Makita, K. (1973) Japan. In J. Downing (ed.), *Comparative Reading.* New York: Macmillan.

Smith, F. (1976) Learning to read by reading. *Language Arts*, 53, 297–299.

Stanovich, K.E. (1996) Word recognition: Changing perspectives. In R. Barr, M.L. Kamil, P. Mosenthal and P.D. Pearson (eds), *Handbook of Reading Research.* Vol. II. Mahwah, NJ: Lawrence Erlbaum Associates.

Stevenson, H.W., Stigler, J.W., Lucker, G.W., and Lee, S.Y. (1982) Reading disabilities: The case of Chinese, Japanese, and English. *Child Development*, 53, 1164–1181.

Steinberg, D.D. and Yamada, J. (1978–79) Are whole word kanji easier to learn than syllable kana? *Reading Research Quarterly*, 14, 88–99.

Tatsumi, T. and Kembo, G. (1967) *The Standardized Reading Test.* Tokyo: Kaneko Shoboo.

Wydell, T.N. and Butterworth, B. (1999) A case study of an English-Japanese bilingual with monolingual dyslexia. *Cognition*, 70, 273–305.

Yamada, J. (1998) Script makes a difference: The induction of deep dyslexic errors in logograph reading. *Dyslexia*, 5, 197–211.

Yamada, J. and Banks, A. (1994) Evidence for and characteristics of dyslexia among Japanese children. *Annals of Dyslexia*, 44, 105–119.

15

DYSLEXIA IN POLISH
Specific problems of dyslexic children in Poland

Marta Bogdanowicz

POLISH SCRIPT

In Polish an alphabetical script is used. This kind of script, in which letter signs correspond to phonemes, was first created around the eighth century BC and was brought to Poland together with Christianity (the Latin rite) in the tenth century CE. It took a few centuries to adapt Latin script to the range of Polish phonemes which is more than twice as large. That is why the first full text written in Polish dates from as late as the fourteenth century. The spread of print in the sixteenth century encouraged the standardization of the Polish script.

There are numerous discrepancies in descriptions of the modern phonological system of the Polish language. They concern e.g. the number of phonemes (one proposal: 37; Wróbel, 2001) or number of distinctive features that are the basis for differentiating the phonemes (e.g. 11 or 12; Wróbel, 2001; Laskowski, 1994). As there are more phonemes in Polish than letters in the Latin alphabet, specifically Polish letters with diacritical marks (e.g. 'ę' for nasal 'e') as well as letter dyads (e.g. 'sz' for the sound [ʃ]) appeared in our alphabet during the process of script creation. The modern Polish alphabet consists of 39 letter signs:

32 single letters:
   24 basic letters: a, b, c, d, e, f, g, h, i, j, k, l, ł, m, n, o, p, r, s, t, u, w, y, z
   8 letters with diacritical marks: ą, ć, ę, ń, ó, ś, ż, ź
7 letter dyads: ch, cz, dz, dż, dź, rz, sz.

Among them there are 9 vowels: a, ą, e, ę, i, o, ó, u, y; and 30 consonants: b, c, ć ch, cz, d, dz, dż, dź, f, g, h, j, k, l, ł, m, n, ń, p, r, rz, s, ś, sz, t, w, z, ż, ź (Gałkowski and Jastrzębowska 1999).

International Book of Dyslexia: A Cross-Language Comparison and Practice Guide. Edited by Ian Smythe, John Everatt and Robin Salter. ISBN 0471498416 © 2004 John Wiley & Sons, Ltd.

GRAPHEME–PHONEME CORRESPONDENCE

Unlike English, Polish script it is basically phonetic, however, there are a number of differences between speech and script:

1 a given letter may correspond to more than one phoneme;
2 a given phoneme may be coded with different letters;
3 a given phoneme may be coded with one or two letters;
4 a set of two following phonemes may be coded with one or two letters.

The above summary does not list all the reasons for discrepancies between speech and script.

More than half of the letters are multifunctional: they function as separate phonemes, as parts of phonemic dyads or can also be pronounced as its voiced/unvoiced equivalent depending on its position in the word. For example, the letter 'd' can function in 8 different phonemes: voiced [d], unvoiced [t] and phonemic dyads: [dz], [dż] and [dź] and their unvoiced equivalents: [c], [cz] and [ć]. Due to this fact, notation of many words is different from the phonetic transcription. Such discrepancies appear in other languages with different intensity (Jassem, 1973). The weakest grapheme–phoneme correspondence is observed in English and French. In Polish a considerable consistency in this correspondence is observed; however, it not as strong as in Slovak or Czech nor, above all, as in Finnish or Hungarian (ibid.).

The conservatism of the historically established graphic forms of words causes the slow transformation of the Polish written language into the ideographic one. This produces some set of words causing spelling problems. Some of them can be explained by certain orthographic rules. There are, however, also some words which have to be learned by heart in order to spell them.

Generally Polish orthography is based on four rules:

1 Phonetic rule (write as you speak and hear): this rule is used most generally.
2 Morphological rule (belonging to a certain category of words decides on the spelling): in each category the same morphemes are used, although appearing in different variations. This gives a clue to which version of homophonic spelling should be used in the case of letters that are read in exactly the same way (e.g. 'u' and 'ó').
3 Historical rule (write as it has been written up to now): this rule concerns mostly words that have to be learned by heart, as no orthographic rule can explain their spelling.
4 Conventional rule (write as it is agreed): from time to time Polish linguists decide on some spelling rules (e.g. which words should be written separately from pronouns or particles, or how to use capital letters) (Gałkowski and Jastrzębowska, 1999).

All the above rules cause much more problems in writing than in reading.

RESEARCH ON READING AND WRITING DIFFICULTIES IN POLAND

Since the 1950s multidisciplinary studies on specific difficulties in reading and writing have been conducted mainly at the University of Warsaw (Spionek, 1965). The results of

Spionek's research showed that psychomotor development of dyslexic pupils is non-harmonious – some functions develop with significant delay. This concerns:

- motor functions (26–58 per cent of examined children);
- perceptive functions: visual (61–68 per cent), auditory and language (69–87 per cent) (Spionek, 1965, 1973).

Some 63–76 per cent of dyslexics she tested had two or three functions disturbed. The disturbances of perceptive-motor functions cause the specific reading and writing difficulties.

In this chapter I will present some examples of research in this field.

Prevalence of cognitive difficulties

In 1968–69 Marta Bogdanowicz, Hanna Jaklewicz and Wirginia Loebl carried out research in an outpatient clinic for neurotic children in Gdansk in order to find out what the prevalence of dyslexic pupils in our schools was. A group of 395 children as a representative sample of 9,500 pupils in 4th Grade (age of 10) at the end of elementary level of primary school were tested.

The diagnosis of developmental dyslexia was based on the assessments of the psychologist and the educator who diagnosed: intellectual level, attention, perception and memory of visual, auditory, language function, general and fine motor skills, laterality and orientation in body and space schema. The assessment of reading and writing (copying, writing from memory and dictation) level was also conducted with use of the standard set of diagnostic tests and trials.

Some 51 subjects were diagnosed as dyslexic with reading and/or spelling problems (13.1 per cent). Children with reading and spelling difficulties made up 9.2 per cent. There were also some children who had isolated spelling problems (3.4 per cent). This means that most frequently among Polish pupils there are cases of difficulties in spelling (13.1 per cent), which we called dysorthography, and 3.8 per cent of subjects had problems with graphic level of writing. These results showed that the problem of dyslexia is very frequent and important in Polish schools, because in every grade there are 3–4 pupils suffering from developmental dyslexia. These findings so alarmed the school administration that they organized a system of remedial teaching for dyslexic pupils – so-called educational therapy (Bogdanowicz, 1978).

For the next stage of this study I carried out research in 1970–73 on a group of 100 dyslexic pupils in the 4th Grade in Gdansk. The aim of my investigation was psychological analysis of the writing and spelling process, its structure, its form as well as patomechanisms of the reading and writing difficulties. The results confirmed the data from Spionek's studies. Children who were properly mentally developed suffered from disturbances of visual functions (66 per cent), auditory and language functions (85 per cent) and motor function (22 per cent). Some 62 per cent of dyslexic subjects had disturbances of two or three functions. It was showed that language impairment was the most important cause of specific reading and spelling difficulties. It was confirmed that there existed a dependency between the type of mistakes in spelling and the disturbances of functions involved in the spelling process. It means that careful analysis of the written tasks of dyslexic pupils may provide information about the kind of difficulties and their causes, and can guide the therapeutic work (Bogdanowicz, 1978).

Difficulties statistics

The first follow-up study on dyslexia as the reason for difficulties in learning at school was carried out by Hanna Jaklewicz, Marta Bogdanowicz and Danuta Męcik. Its aim was to check whether the children diagnosed as dyslexics at the end of the elementary level of primary school still experienced difficulties in reading and spelling after two years of education.

Some 51 subjects were diagnosed as children with reading and spelling problems at the beginning of their 4th Grade, at the age of 10 (pre-test: September 1968). Two and a half years later at the end of 6th Grade of primary school (age of 12) a post-test was conducted (June 1971). During the period between primary diagnosis and post-test, the children were not subject to any form of therapy. In both tests we used the same methods as in the previous study. The results of the study show that pupils diagnosed earlier as dyslexics after two and a half years still experienced problems with reading (82.6 per cent) and spelling (89.1 per cent). These difficulties resulted in general school problems regardless of their good intellectual development (80.5 per cent). Also, many of these children suffered from emotional disorders which was the additional effect of the wrong situation at school (Jaklewicz, *et al.*, 1975).

Socio-economic implications

Another longitudinal study was conducted by Marta Bogdanowicz, Hanna Jaklewicz and Barbara Lewandowska in 1969 to 1979. It concerned difficulties in reading and writing as well as perceptual-motor function disorder and emotional disturbances. Its aim was to find out whether it is possible to 'grow out' of dyslexic problems. Within this research one hundred subjects were tested as primary school pupils (aged 8–10). Some 51 per cent of children suffered from psychomotor development disorders (visual, auditory, language and motor developmental disturbances), which resulted in developmental dyslexia. The other group of children (49 per cent) had no problems at school.

The follow-up study was conducted on the same group of children after a period of 8–10 years, when they were already adults (at the age of 18–20). The methods used in both tests were the same as in previous studies and also Cattell's 14-Factorial Personality Questionnaire for Adolescents.

The results of our study revealed difficulties in reading and writing were still appearing in adulthood as well as the disorders of perceptive and motor functions, causing dyslexic problems to remain within the ten years period. A small improvement in the previous developmental deficits was observed. However, these were eliminated completely only in cases of subjects who suffered from a very small range of disorders (concerning one or two functions) or when the disorder had not seriously developed. Also, it was proved that in some cases the adults (from 18 to 20 years old) were at the level of a 6 year old or even younger, regarding their visual and/or phonological functions. Some of them had also difficulties with laterality as well as body schema and space concerning the left and right direction. Reading and spelling disorders do not disappear on their own (except in a few cases) but they can even become more serious and last one's whole life.

Psychological and psychiatric research proves that those from the dyslexic group had additional emotional problems based on school failure, which lasted for a long time. On the other hand, the control group did not appear to suffer from such emotional problems. The dyslexic children who were not subject to the remedial teaching, suffered in their adult lives from a complex emotional disorder. Their school and then adult careers were far below their intellectual possibilities. Most of them did not continue their education and became only manual workers, in spite of being intelligent, sometimes even with above average intelligence levels. The situation when the problems with reading and writing disappear is not totally satisfying because the emotional disorder still exists and constantly influences the personality of such people. It was proved that all of these disorders have a negative and a lasting influence on a dyslexic child who does not receive help in time (Lewandowska and Bogdanowicz, 1982).

Heritability

This research was continued by Hanna Jaklewicz in 1989 and 1993/4. In the first stage of this 25-year follow-up study, the individuals who had been investigated since 1968 were asked to fill in a questionnaire on their interests, actual personal, financial and professional situation. The questions were answered by 28 dyslexics and 32 persons from a control group. Nobody from the dyslexic group occupied an important professional position and nobody took an active part in a social life compared to the majority of the control group. All dyslexics regarded their school-years as the most difficult time in their life (but the control group remembered this period as joyful). The majority of the dyslexics thought that they did not realize their ambitions and plans made in childhood. The dyslexics had a limited range of interests. They judged their family life to be a happy one but one problem, which exists in all families, is a difficult financial situation.

In the last stage of this study, 22 children (2nd to 4th Grade) from 18 families of earlier investigated dyslexics were included in the investigation. The diagnostic assessment revealed that 21 of the examined children had difficulties in spelling. The errors made in written tasks were specific and indicated disturbances of phonological skills and developmental dyslexia. One half of the group (12 children) showed specific difficulties in reading (1–2 years behind their chronological age). These results confirmed that reading and spelling disorders had a genetically determined and persistent character, and had limited the education, professional career and social achievements of these dyslexic persons. Their children constituted a group at risk of dyslexia, and needed a proper intervention programme (Jaklewicz, 1997).

Sensorimotor integration

In 1981–82 I undertook a study on the development of sensorimotor integration and its role in the acquisition of reading skills. The representative sample of 392 pupils was abstracted from the population of 7,500 children attending so-called '0' grade (preparatory class) in the kindergartens and primary schools of Gdansk. Based on the assessment of reading, two groups were chosen from this sample for further examination: one of them consisted of children 'at risk of dyslexia' (34 poor readers – 10 per cent), the other of 34 good readers. The methods for assessment of visual, auditory, language and motor functions were the same as those used in previous studies. Additionally, sensorimotor integration was assessed. The findings had both theoretical importance and practical use in diagnosis and therapy. It happened that 10 per cent of children in '0' grades revealed symptoms of risk of dyslexia and 4 per cent had serious difficulties in reading. It was found that sensorimotor integration developed: its significant progress was observed even during one year. Study allowed us to establish norms for diagnostic trials. The level of sensorimotor integration determines readiness to acquire reading skills and correlates with the reading level. It was established that a retardation of sensorimotor integration is one of the reasons for difficulties in learning to read, sometimes even being the main cause of these (Bogdanowicz, 1987, 1993a/b, 1997a–d).

Social emotional study

The research conducted in 1981–90 by Marta Bogdanowicz and Bożena Wszeborowska-Lipińska was a continuation of study 5 (detailed above). It concerned the development and school career of two groups of 34 children (poor and good readers) over a period of 9 years. The children were tested in three stages: in '0' grade (1981, at the starting point of education), 4th Grade (1986, at the end of elementary education level) and 8th Grade (1990, at the end of primary school).

The methods for assessment were the same as those used in study 5. Additionally, personality and behaviour were assessed by Cattell's 14-Factorial Personality Questionnaire for Adolescents and Unfinished Sentences Trial.

The psychological studies undertaken over nine years show that the disturbance of perceptive-motor functions and the lack of the sensorimotor integration, as well as reading and writing difficulties, are maintained among the children who in their '0' grade respectively found themselves in the subgroup of poor readers. As far as their school career is concerned, we noticed that dyslexic children had worse marks than the good readers. The dyslexics had specific learning problems in all subjects: Polish and foreign languages, geometry, chemistry, music (reading notes), geography (map orientation), physical activities. Moreover, the two compared groups had different attitudes towards the school. That is why the dyslexics often played truant all alone in order to avoid their school problems, and had many conflicts with teachers. As a result they were marked poorly for their behaviour at school. These marks differed from the controls on all levels of education.

The children from the control group eagerly took part in out-of-school activities, while the dyslexics did not have time for this because they usually spent more time (about one hour more a day) on their homework. On average, the dyslexics spent three hours a day on learning at home in the 3rd Grade and about six hours in the 8th Grade. They came to school much more often unprepared because of lack of time to do their homework as well as their negative attitude towards some subjects. The dyslexic children worked more slowly and needed much more help in their school work than their peers. Some of the children had severe problems moving up to the next class. School failure and low self-esteem influenced their further education. They chose less attractive types of schools (vocational and technical schools) than the controls. The negative experiences conducted with nine years of lasting failure during the primary school strongly influenced the personal development of these pupils. Future self-esteem and the self-image of dyslexic children were significantly decreased, the locus of control was external, their anxiety level was increased. Their fears were connected to school failure and with being rejected by grown-ups. Because of that, their plans were very modest in comparison with their real intellectual potential.

Good and poor readers were significantly different with regards to characteristics on the Cattell's 14-Factorial Personality Questionnaire for Adolescents. According to this test, the dyslexic children were realistic, and adapted to overcoming obstacles. They expected support from their peers to compensate for their bad relations with grown-ups (teachers, parents). To get that support they had to conform more, be more dependent on group opinion, and had to reduce their level of aspiration. Their long-lasting school failure seriously limited their individualism and creativity as well as their ambitions. According to the Polish phrase 'it cut their wings', just as in their childhood. Psychosomatic symptoms connected with school anxiety were characteristic for both groups. However, the Polish school environment may be blamed for this. In a group of poor readers these symptoms appeared only at school or just before going to school and they became more severe in the upper grades. In comparison to good readers, only dyslexics had the feeling of having an 'empty head' which appeared when asked a question by a teacher. The research suggests the neurotic personal development of many dyslexic pupils (Bogdanowicz, 1992; Bogdanowicz and Wszeborowska-Lipińska, 1992; Wszeborowska-Lipińska and Bogdanowicz, 1995).

Adolescent experiences

In 1985–93 Bożena Wszeborowska-Lipińska tried to find out whether the dyslexic adolescents experiencing specific difficulties in reading and writing at the end of the secondary school, who did not undergo any professional therapy, still had disturbances in the development of perceptual and motor functions in adulthood. A group of 130 people (100 of them suffering from dyslexia, plus 30 controls – good readers) aged 19 was first tested in the last grade of secondary school. They were questioned in the second stage (about eight years later) about their schools or professional careers as well as their interests, plans for future, reasons for their difficulties in reading and writing and occurrence of their emotional disturbances. The basic methods used in research were the same as described in previous studies. Additionally, personality was tested by the Cattell 16-Factor Personality Questionnaire, the Gough Adjectives Test and an interview concerning personality and information about their life, education, and career plans.

As a result, we observed that the disturbances of perceptual and motor functions as well as difficulties in spelling and, less frequently, in reading, still were present. On average, the dyslexics repeated a year at secondary school and changed schools much more often than their peers.

On the Intelligence Scale (Wechsler-Bellevue) they showed distinctly lower results in Coding, Picture Completion and Digit Span Subtest. In spite of being of above average level intelligence, the examined individuals' school careers were negatively influenced by their difficulties in reading and writing. Moreover, these difficulties had an influence on their choice of professions, interests and plans for future. Out of 100 people, 78 continued their studies (universities and technical colleges), 19 people worked and 3 were unemployed. The dyslexics chose mainly careers connected with engineering (33 per cent), economics (20 per cent), arts (12 per cent), law (9 per cent) and medicine (7 per cent). Here we found a difference in comparing the results of our previous study, which revealed that such an attempt was made only by 12 per cent of the dyslexic pupils finishing primary school. Only part of this group wanted to continue learning at secondary school (Bogdanowicz and Jaklewicz, 1982). The end of the primary school period was a very important, critical moment in the future of the dyslexic pupils affecting education, vocational career and their further personal life. The distribution of interests in both groups was remarkably different. The dyslexics preferred tourism, arts and technology; their peers more often preferred humanistic interests and learning foreign languages. These differences resulted from difficulties in reading and writing. Examination of the personality revealed a stronger need for achievement, for domination, for autonomy and the level of self-confidence, better realism and social skills, ego-power, stronger enthusiasm and willingness of dyslexics compared with the control group. This indicates that the group participating in our examination was a selective one, these were pupils who went through primary school successfully and continued to secondary school because of their high intellectual level as well as the support of their well-educated parents (Wszeborowska, 1995).

Cross-cultural study

In 1994–97 a cross-cultural study was conducted by Grażyna Krasowicz-Kupis, Marta Bogdanowicz and Peter Bryant (Krasowicz et al., 1997). The main aims of the research were to find an answer to the question whether the linguistic awareness of a child determines his or her progress in reading and spelling acquisition. The second aim was to compare the relationship between phonological and syntactical awareness and progress in reading acquisition in Polish and English children. The last aim was to explore the specificity of phonological and syntactical awareness in children at the ages of 6, 7 and 8.

This research concerned children at the age of 6–8. The first examination was carried out in kindergarten (a group of 6-year-olds), and the last in the second semester of the 2nd class. The size of the sample was 367 in the first assessment and 167 in the last one. Children came from three environments: a large city, a medium-sized city, and a small town. The controlled variables were: gender, parents' education, intellectual development and cognitive abilities according to WISC-R. The main independent variable was linguistic awareness, that is phonological and syntactical awareness assessed by specially prepared methods. The main dependent variables were the reading and spelling skills in accordance with the definition accepted.

We confirmed the importance of children's phonological skills in the early stages of reading and spelling. Generally more phonological skills were found for reading. This phonological connection is as important in learning to read in Polish as in several other languages, such as English. All the phonological scores predicted reading in the short term, even after quite stringent controls for differences in extraneous variables such as intelligence. The stronger predictors of reading in the long term were the phoneme tasks. The syllable scores were also connected to reading. The role of syntactic awareness was not similarly strong. Some connections between syntactic skill measures were found for text reading and reading understanding (Krasowicz and Bogdanowicz, 1997).

The studies presented here are only examples of the research on dyslexia conducted in Poland. In recent years at the UMCS University in Lublin and at the University of Gdansk some investigations on disorders of the phonological, semantic and syntactic aspects of language functions of dyslexic children were carried out. The authors of this research were: Zbigniew Tarkowski and Aneta Borkowska (1998), Barbara Koltuska (1988), Grażyna Krasowicz-Kupis (1997), Marta Bogdanowicz and Alicja Maurer (1997),

Urszula Oszwa (1999), Malgorzata Lipowska (2001). In 1995–98 Grażyna Krasowicz-Kupis in cooperation with Marta Bogdanowicz carried out research on phonological development of children aged 6–9 and its connection with the acquisition of reading and writing ability. This research confirmed that the development of language skills involved in the reading process of children in Poland proceeds in a different way from that of English children due to the specificity of the Polish language. The results of these investigations and the results of Grażyna Krasowicz-Kupis' research on the connection of phonological development and learning of reading were published in her monograph (Krasowicz-Kupis, 1999). Another subject for research is the development of children at risk of dyslexia. A study by Dorota Kalka revealed that these children cannot 'grow out of' their developmental disorders and school problems without remedial teaching. It appears that the Scale of Risk of Dyslexia test of Bogdanowicz can be helpful in screening and early intervention in these cases (Bogdanowicz, 1993, 1995; Kalka, 2001).

REFERENCES

Bogdanowicz, M. (1978) Psychologiczna analiza trudności w pisaniu u dzieci. Zeszyty Naukowe Wydziału Humanistycznego. *Psychologia*, 1, 89–100.

Bogdanowicz, M. (1983) *Trudności w pisaniu u dzieci*. Gdansk: University of Gdansk.

Bogdanowicz, M. (1985a) Therapeutic care of children with reading and writing difficulties in Poland. In D.D. Duane and C.K. Leong (eds), *Understanding Learning Disabilities: International and Multidisciplinary Views*. New York. Plenum Press.

Bogdanowicz, M. (1985b) *Metoda dobrego startu w pracy z dzieckiem od 5 do 10 lat*. Warsaw: WsiP.

Bogdanowicz, M. (1985c) Badania nad częstością występowania dysleksji, dysortografii i dysgrafii wśród polskich dzieci. Zeszyty Naukowe Wydziału Humanistycznego. *Psychologia*, 7, 143–156.

Bogdanowicz, M. (1987) *Integracja percepcyjno-motoryczna a specjalne trudności w czytaniu u dzieci*. Gdansk. University of Gdansk, Praca habilitacyjna.

Bogdanowicz, M. (1989a) A follow-up study of dyslexic children in Poland. In R.I. Brown and M. Chazan (eds), *Learning Difficulties and Emotional Problems*. Calgary: Detselig Enterprises Ltd.

Bogdanowicz, M. (1989b) Diagnosis and treatment of children with reading and writing difficulties in Poland. *International Journal of Disability: Development and Education*, 2, 151–161.

Bogdanowicz, M. (1991) Badania katamnestyczne nad rozwojem i edukacją szkolną dzieci z dysleksją i dysortografią. Zeszyty Naukowe Wydziału Humanistycznego *Psychologia*, 10, 63–78.

Bogdanowicz, M. (1992) Nine years follow-up study of dyslexic children. Paper presented at the First All-Greek Congress on Special Education. Ateny Ionios School, pp.1–9.

Bogdanowicz, M. (1993a) Dziecko ryzyka dysleksji – co to takiego. *Scholasticus*, 2, 39–45.

Bogdanowicz, M. (1993b) Sensorimotor integration and special difficulties in acquiring skills. *Bulletin Le Bon Départ*, 3, 1–18.

Bogdanowicz, M. (1994) *O dysleksji czyli specyficznych trudno[ţiach w czytaniu i pisaniu*. Lublin: Linea.

Bogdanowicz, M. (1995) Skala Ryzyka Dysleksji (SDR) w profilaktyce specyficznych trudności w czytaniu i pisaniu u dzieci. *Scholasticus*, 1, 45–53.

Bogdanowicz, M. (1996) The good start method. *Bulletin le bon départ*, 1, 38–46.

Bogdanowicz, M. (1997a) *Integracja percepcyjno – motoryczna. Teoria – diagnoza – terapia*. Warsaw: CMPP-P.

Bogdanowicz, M. (1997b) Six years of the Polish Dyslexia Association. *Dyslexia: An International Journal of Research and Practice*, 2, 109–111.

Bogdanowicz, M. (1997c) The early prediction of the ability to read and write according to the Scale of the Risk of Dyslexia. Paper presented at the 4th World Congress on Dyslexia. Abstracts. Halkidiki, p. 9.

Bogdanowicz, M. (1997d) The awareness of dyslexia in Poland. In J. Waterfield (ed.), *Dyslexia in Higher Education: Learning along the Continuum*. Dartington Hall. University of Plymouth.

Bogdanowicz, M. (1999) Model kompleksowej pomocy osobom z dysleksją rozwojową – ocena stanu aktualnego i propozycje zmian w świetle reformy systemu edukacji. *Psychologia Wychowawcza*, 3, 217–227.

Bogdanowicz, M. and Jaklewicz, H. (1989) A follow-up study of dyslexic children in Gdańsk primary schools. In R.I. Brown and M. Chazan (eds), *Learning Difficulties and Emotional Problems*. Calgary: Detselig Enterprises Ltd.

Bogdanowicz, M., Jaklewicz, H. and Loebl, W. (1969) Próba analizy specyficznych zaburzeń czytania i pisania. *Psychiatria Polska*, 3, 297–301.

Bogdanowicz, M. and Rocławski, B. (1989) Prevention of dyslexia. In H. Breuer and K. Ruoho (eds), *Padagogischpsychologische Prophylaxe bei 4-8 jährigen Kindern*. Jyvaskyla: Jyvaskylan Yliopisto.

Bogdanowicz, M. and Wszeborowska-Lipińska, B. (1992) Rozwój psychomotoryczny, kariera szkolna i osobowość młodzieży dyslektycznej. *Scholasticus*, 1, 35–39.

Bogdanowicz, M. and Wszeborowska-Lipińska, B. (1993) Follow-up study of adolescents with specific difficulties in reading and writing. *Journal of Philosophy of Medicine and Medical Psychology*, 1, 96.

Bogdanowicz, M. and Wszeborowska-Lipińska, B. (1995) Follow-up di adolescenti con difficolta specifiche nella lettura e nella scrittura. *International Journal of Adolescentology*, 1, 89–101.

Borkowska, A. (1998) *Analiza dyskursu narracyjnego u dzieci z dysleksją rozwojową*. Lublin: UMCS.

Gałkowski, T. and Jastrzębowska, G. (eds), (1999) *Logopedia*. Opole: Uniwersytet Opolski.

Jaklewicz, H. (1980) *Badania katamnestyczne nad dysleksją-dysortografią*. Gdansk: Inst. Med. Morskiej i Tropikalnej.

Jaklewicz, H. (1997) Twenty-five years of longitudinal studies on dyslexia. In B. Ericson and J. Ronnberg (eds), *Reading Disability and its Treatment*. Linkoping: Linkoping University.

Jaklewicz, H. and Bogdanowicz, M. (1982) Zaburzenia emocjonalne i ich wpływ na kształtowanie się niektórych cech osobowości, na podstawie badań katamnestycznych dzieci z dysleksją i dysortografią. Zeszyty Naukowe Wydziału Humanistycznego. *Psychologia*, 4, 19–28.

Jaklewicz, H., Bogdanowicz, M. and Męcik, D. (1975) Dysleksja i dysortografia jako przyczyny niepowodzeń w nauce szkolnej. In M. Chojecka (ed.), *Przyczyny niepowodzeń szkolnych*. Warsaw: WSiP.

Kalka, D. (2001) *Weryfikacja predyktywnej wartości wczesnej diagnozy ryzyka dysleksji*. Gdansk: University of Gdansk.

Kołtuska, B. (1988) Rola procesów lingwistycznych w zaburzeniach dyslektycznych. *Zagadnienia Wychowania a Zdrowie Psychiczne*, 3, 45–51.

Krasowicz, G. (1997) *Język, czytania i dysleksja*. Lublin: Agencja Wydawniczo – Handlowa AD.

Krasowicz, G. and Bogdanowicz, M. (1997) Assessment of linguistic abilities as a prediction of developmental dyslexia in Polish children: dyslexia-biological bases, identification and intervention. 25th Anniversary Conference, BDA, York.

Krasowicz, G., Bogdanowicz, M. and Bryant, P. (1997) Metalinguistic abilities as a predictor of reading acquisition in Polish children. In *New Trends in Developmental Psychology: Resume*. Eighth Conference Européenne de Psychologie du Devéloppement. Rennes.

Krasowicz-Kupis, G. (1999) *Rozwój metajęzykowy a osiągnięcia w czytaniu u dzieci 6 – 9 – letnich*. Lublin: Wydawnictwo UMCS.

Lewandowska, B. and Bogdanowicz, M. (1982) Trudności w czytaniu i pisaniu oraz zaburzenia funkcji percepcyjno-motorycznych u dzieci z dysleksją i dysortografią. Wyniki badań katamnestycznych. Zeszyty Naukowe Wydziału Humanistycznego. *Psychologia*, 4, 5–18.

Lipowska, M. (2001) *Profil rozwoju kompetencji fonologicznej dzieci w wieku przedszkolnym*. Kraków: Oficyna Wydawnicza Impuls.

Nartowska, H. (1980) *Różnice indywidualne czy zaburzenia rozwoju dziecka przedszkolnego*. Warsaw: WsiP.

Spionek, H. (1965) *Zaburzenia psychoruchowego rozwoju dziecka*. Warsaw: WsiP.
Spionek, H. (1973) *Zaburzenia w rozwoju uczniów a niepowodzenia szkolne*. Warsaw: WsiP.
Wszeborowska-Lipińska, B. and Bogdanowicz, M. (1995) Development, school career and personality of dyslexic children – nine years follow-up study. *Polish Quarterly of Developmental Psychology*, 1, 51–56.

16

RESEARCH ON THE ROLE OF PHONOLOGY, ORTHOGRAPHY AND COGNITIVE SKILLS IN READING, SPELLING AND DYSLEXIA IN BRAZILIAN PORTUGUESE

Fernando C. Capovilla and Alessandra G.S. Capovilla

RESEARCH ON THE ROLE OF PHONOLOGY

According to the phonological deficit hypothesis, meta-phonological difficulties hinder reading and writing acquisition. Therefore intervention programmes devoted to training phonology awareness and teaching grapheme–phoneme correspondences have been able to increase reading and spelling skills and decrease the incidence of dyslexia (Borstrom and Elbro, 1997). This has been corroborated for the first time in Brazil in a research programme involving the development of the first Brazilian standardized and validated phonological awareness test (A. Capovilla and Capovilla, 1997a; A. Capovilla, Capovilla and Silveira, 1998) and the first systematic procedures for training phonology awareness and teaching grapheme–phoneme correspondences (A. Capovilla and F. Capovilla, 2003a, 2003b).

The phonological awareness test assesses ten skills including segmentation, synthesis, manipulation, and transposition of both syllables and phonemes, as well as judgement of rhyme and alliteration. It has been used in a number of successful intervention studies showing that phonological awareness training and phonics instructions can systematically improve the reading and spelling skills of 6–8-year-old children (e.g., A. Capovilla and F. Capovilla, 2001).

International Book of Dyslexia: A Cross-Language Comparison and Practice Guide. Edited by Ian Smythe, John Everatt and Robin Salter.   ISBN 0471498416   © 2004 John Wiley & Sons, Ltd.

Two of the studies of the research programme were conducted in small groups with children with literacy acquisition difficulties (F. Capovilla and A. Capovilla, 1999; A. Capovilla and F. Capovilla, 2000a). After being exposed to the two-month phonological awareness training programme described in A. Capovilla and F. Capovilla (2003b), 4–8-year-old children who had performed poorly on the phonological awareness test achieved the highest phonological awareness performances of their classes. Further, 6–8-year-old children also exhibited strong reading and spelling gains, and became as good as the best students in their classes.

A third study was conducted individually with physically-impaired children with the purpose of allowing them to replace pictorial communication boards with alphabetic written communication (e.g., A. Capovilla, Capovilla, Silveira, Vieira and Matos, 1998). The training was successful in replacing pictogram communication with written communication, and substantially improved the integration of cerebral-palsied children at school (F. Capovilla, Capovilla and Macedo, 2001a).

A fourth study was conducted in the classroom by teachers especially trained to introduce the phonics method described in A. Capovilla and F. Capovilla (2003a, 2003b). Children taught to read under the phonics method achieved significantly higher reading and spelling competence than that of their peers who had been taught under the ideographic whole-language approach. In addition to that, the same study assessed reading competence of 345 first graders at the end of the year as a function of the proportion of time their teachers spent on either phonemes or text during the first semester. Performance on standardized tests showed that both single-word reading and sentence reading were direct functions of the time spent on phonemes, and inverse functions of the time spent on texts.

In addition to that, such research programmes corroborate previous findings with Portuguese-speaking Brazilian children, showing that:

1 Phonological awareness correlates positively with reading and spelling acquisition (A. Capovilla and F. Capovilla, 2003a; A. Capovilla and F. Capovilla, 1997b; A. Capovilla, Capovilla and Silveira, 1998; Cardoso-Martins, 1991), vocabulary development (A. Capovilla and F. Capovilla, 2003a; A. Capovilla, 1999; Portugal and Capovilla, 2002), school grades attributed by teachers of Portuguese (Portugal and Capovilla, 2002), and working memory skills (A. Capovilla and F. Capovilla, 1997b; F. Capovilla and Nunes, 2001; F. Capovilla and A. Capovilla, 2001a; Salles *et al.*, 1999).

2 Syllabic awareness precedes phonemic awareness and takes place before schooling (A. Capovilla and F. Capovilla, 2003a; A. Capovilla and F. Capovilla, 1997b; A. Capovilla, Capovilla and Silveira, 1998; Parente *et al.*, 1999).

3 Sensitivity to global phonological similarity (e.g., rhyme and alliteration) plays a relatively minor role in learning to read and spell in Portuguese compared to English (Cardoso-Martins, 1995).

4 Knowledge of the alphabet enables children to learn reading by processing and storing letter-sound correspondences in words (Abreu and Cardoso-Martins, 1998; A. Capovilla and F. Capovilla, 2003a).

A. Capovilla and F. Capovilla (2003a, 2003b) demonstrated the importance of the grapheme–phoneme correspondence training paired with phonological awareness training in improving reading and spelling skills in Portuguese. Before that, Abreu and Cardoso-Martins (1998) had already demonstrated that knowing letter-names facilitates the process of learning to read the phonetic spellings of target words. In the experiment, preschoolers who could not read words out of context were divided into two groups, those who knew letter-names, and those who did not. Both groups were taught to read two types of spellings: phonetic (i.e., a spelling whose letters correspond to sounds in the pronunciation of the target words, such as CRVA for the word 'cerveja'), and visual (i.e., a spelling whose letters did not correspond to sounds but were visually salient, such as XQKO for 'cerveja'). Children who knew letter-names learned to read phonetic spellings more easily, whereas those who did not know them learned to read visual spellings more easily.

RESEARCH ON THE ROLE OF ORTHOGRAPHY

The Portuguese script is a fairly transparent orthography with regular grapheme–phoneme correspondences and rules of pronunciation (Lemle, 1991) that account for most non-canonical correspondences. In Portuguese, the grapheme–phoneme exceptions pose a greater problem for spelling than they do for reading.

Reading and spelling processes in Portuguese have been analysed according to a dual-processing model of reading as a function of the Portuguese orthography (F. Capovilla, Capovilla and Macedo, 2001b; Lecours and Parente, 1997) and of psycholinguistic characteristics such as grapheme–phoneme regularity, extension, lexicality, and frequency of occurrence (A. Capovilla, Capovilla and Macedo, 1998; F. Capovilla, Macedo and Capovilla, 2002b; Pinheiro, 1994, 1995). A consensual finding is that the Portuguese orthography is relatively transparent with respect to reading.

Comparing the degree of grapheme–phoneme correspondences, Parente (1994) concluded that the Portuguese orthography is more similar to the fairly transparent Spanish orthography than it is to the more opaque English or French orthographies. The Portuguese orthography presents few grapheme–phoneme exceptions that pose problems for reading, but a number of phonemes with irregular grapheme representations that pose problems for spelling. Given the relative absence of exception words for reading in the Portuguese orthography, the grapheme–phoneme regularity effect is usually not present in reading, despite the presence of phonological regularization.

Such a conclusion is shared by Pinheiro (1997), who compared competent reading by English and Portuguese readers, and identified compatible as well as discrepant results. English and Portuguese readers present comparable results with respect to processing time and error rates for both words and non-words. However, the regularity effect is present in competent readers of English, whereas it is absent in competent readers of Portuguese.

Hosogi and Parente (1995) corroborate such a conclusion. Studying the use of the phonological route by patients with acquired morphemic dyslexia, they reported an absence of grapheme–phoneme regularity effects. Again, this lack of regularity effect in reading is attributed to the relative absence of exception words for reading Portuguese.

Therefore, once the phonological route has matured and readers have acquired competence, regularity effects are not expected in reading Portuguese orthography. That happens even when readers acquire morphemic dyslexia. However, during the process of maturation in the alphabetic stage, regularity effects are indeed expected, and have been found with respect to pronunciation segmentation in reading aloud tasks (F. Capovilla, Macedo and Capovilla, 2002b; F. Capovilla, Macedo, Capovilla and Charin, 1998). Capovilla and co-workers attribute the relative absence of regularity effects not only to the greater grapheme–phoneme transparency of the Portuguese orthography but also to the kind of measure usually chosen (i.e., reaction time) in the area. By collecting more temporal measures of utterances such as duration and segmentation frequency and analysing them as a function of orthographic and psycholinguistic characteristics, they have been able to demonstrate with greater precision the full range of those effects (F. Capovilla, Capovilla and Macedo, 2001b).

Such developments in basic research in Brazil have been recently followed by an effort toward developing psychometrical and neuropsychological instruments to assess reading competence in Portuguese orthography (F. Capovilla, Macedo and Capovilla, 2002a, 2002b). There is a growing awareness of the need for instruments capable of identifying reading and spelling acquisition problems, quantifying the degree of those problems, and interpreting their precise nature in terms of theoretical models so as to guide intervention procedures.

In order to identify problems with reading acquisition, quantify its degree, and interpret its nature, two computerized, standardized and validated tests have been developed: a reading aloud test (A. Capovilla, Capovilla and Macedo, 1998) and a silent reading test (A. Capovilla, Capovilla, Macedo and Duduchi, 2000). Given that they require different output mechanisms, their combination offers useful information for differential diagnosis of reading problems. As psychometric tests, they offer standardized norms that allow reading delay to be identified and measure its severity. As neuropsychological tests, they offer an interpretation of the delay in terms of the dual-process reading model of information processing in cognitive psychology (Ellis and Young, 1988), and of a developmental model of reading and spelling acquisition, and development dyslexia. According to Frith (1985, 1990) in reading and spelling development one can distinguish three fairly different stages: the logographic, the alphabetic, and the orthographic. Developmental dyslexia may be interpreted as the difficulty of progressing from one stage to the next. The majority of poor readers at the first grade present phonological difficulties and tend to present a logographic reading style with visual exchange errors, whereas the others present morphemic difficulties and tend to present a more phonological reading style with phonological regularization errors.

The reading aloud test (A. Capovilla, Capovilla and Macedo, 1998) offers a direct phonetic (i.e., speech articulation) measure of cognitive processing during reading aloud. According to dual-route reading models (Ellis and Young, 1988), in the lexical route pronunciation is retrieved as a whole from the lexicon, whereas in the perilexical route it is constructed via phonological decoding of syllabic segments. It assesses temporal parameters of pronunciation: reaction time (i.e., pronunciation latency), duration, and segmentation frequency (i.e., the number of energy peaks separated by the pauses in the waveforms) as a function of reading age and psycholinguistic variables. Examples of such variables include lexicality (words vs. non-words), regularity of grapheme–phoneme correspondence (regular vs. context dependent vs. exception items), extension (short vs. long items), and occurrence frequency in Portuguese (low vs. high frequency items). It may be programmed to present different lists of items, such as Pinheiro's (1996) computerized list of 28,742 words classified according to their frequency of occurrence for Brazilian children at different school levels. In the phonological route, the pronunciation is built segment by segment. Therefore, it is more segmented, slower and takes longer. In the lexical route for reading, the pronunciation is retrieved as a whole from the lexicon. Therefore, it is less segmented, faster and shorter. As children acquire literacy and evolve from the alphabetic to the orthographic stage, there is a shift in prevalence from the phonological route to the lexical route and, consequently, a systematic decline in all three temporal parameters. By assessing such decline, the test measures reading age. By comparing them under different psycholinguistic variables, it measures the relative efficacy of the routes. Since the reading aloud test is capable of assessing both the overall reading age and the relative efficacy of different reading strategies, it is an important instrument for the identification and differential diagnosis of dyslexia. Research (F. Capovilla, Macedo, Capovilla and Charin, 1998; F. Capovilla, Macedo and Charin, 2001) demonstrates that, as children mature from first to third Grade, there is a marked decline in the temporal parameters as well as a shift in the prevalence from phonological reading to lexical reading. Such a shift is marked by declining effects of regularity and extension (which indicate phonological reading), and increasing effects of lexicality and frequency (which indicate lexical reading). The test has been standardized for 6–8-year-old children (A. Capovilla and Capovilla, 2003b).

The computerized reading aloud test has also been used to analyse perilexical processing during reading aloud of 270 isolated non-words by 44 college students (F. Capovilla, Capovilla and Macedo, 2001b). Temporal parameters of pronunciation such as reaction time (RT), duration and segmentation frequency were analysed as a function of orthographic characteristics of the non-words. Results showed that: (1) the shortest and simplest syllables produced the highest reading speed and segmentation frequency; (2) the longest non-words produced the highest segmentation frequency, but the lowest reading speed; (3) digraphs (two letters: one phoneme) increased error frequency as well as duration and RT, but decreased segmentation frequency; (4) digraphs increased RT only when they occurred in the initial syllables; and (5) digraphs produced greater RT than did consonantal combinations (two letters: two phonemes), which, in turn, produced greater RT than did simple graphemes. Such findings increase the validity of the dual-process reading model, as well as the understanding of serial and parallel processes involved in the perilexical reading.

The silent reading test (A. Capovilla, Capovilla, Macedo and Duduchi, 2000) is based on Khomsi's test (1997), as improved by Braibant (1997). It presents 70 pairs, each composed of a written item and a picture. The examinee is asked to cross out inadequate pairs. There are seven pair-types, all of them randomly distributed over trials:

1 Correct grapheme–phoneme regular words.
2 Correct grapheme–phoneme exception words.
3 Semantically incorrect words (e.g., picture of an airplane mislabelled as eagle).
4 Non-words with visual exchanges (picture of a television – *televisão* – mislabelled as *taieuisão*).
5 Non-words with phonological exchanges (picture of a magician – *mágico* – mislabelled as *máchico*).
6 Homophone non-words (picture of a boy – *menino* – mislabelled as *mininu*).
7 Strange non-words (picture of a clown – *palhaço* – mislabelled as *meloce*).

Pair-types 1 and 2 are to be accepted, whereas pair-types 3–7 are to be rejected. Lack of lexical processing is indicated by failure in accepting pair-type 2, as well as by failure in rejecting pair-type 6. Lack of semantic lexical processing is indicated by failure to reject pair-type 3. Phonological difficulties (and lack of lexical processing) are indicated by failure to reject pair-type 5. Lack of phonological and lexical processing (i.e., logographic reading) is indicated by failure to reject pair-type 4. The test has been validated and standardized for 6–10-year-old children and norms have been generated for a general score, as well as for scores on each separate pair-type.

Results show that pair-types 7, 1, and 3 were easier than pair-types 2 and 4, which, in turn, were easier than pair-types 5 and 6. This is: rejecting strange non-words (task 7), accepting correct words (task 1), and rejecting semantically incorrect words (task 3) were approximately equivalent in difficulty, and far easier than all the others. Such tasks require only elementary reading skills at the phonological level and even at the logographic one. They reflect fairly elementary skills involved in a common reading repertoire. Thus, tasks 7, 1 and 3 were easier than both accepting correct grapheme–phoneme exception words (task 2) and rejecting non-words with visual exchanges (task 4). While task 2 requires some lexical processing, task 4 requires not only phonological decoding but also a relatively high degree of attention to the visual details involving letter shapes. Both of these tasks, 2 and 4, in turn, were easier than both rejecting non-words with phonological exchanges (task 5) and rejecting homophone non-words (task 6). Task 5 requires refined phonological decoding skills with precise phoneme representation, whereas task 6 requires an even higher processing, i.e., a refined lexical reading, with the retrieval of the adequate orthographic form from the lexicon and its comparison with the homophone non-word to be rejected. Thus, task 5 tends to be slightly easier than task 6. Such results are thoroughly compatible with Firth's model of reading acquisition and developmental dyslexia, and reinforce the validity of the test as an instrument for differential diagnosis of developmental dyslexia.

RESEARCH ON THE ROLE OF COGNITIVE SKILLS: DISCRIMINATION, MEMORY, PROCESSING SPEED, AND CENTRAL AUDITORY PROCESSING

There is considerable debate on the nature of the problems underlying reading and spelling difficulties. According to Morais (in press) the central problem stems from involuntary speech perception difficulties (i.e., phonological discrimination). According to Share (1995), it stems from temporal processing difficulties, which happen when one has to process stimuli of short duration or short inter-stimulus intervals (ISIs). According to Mody *et al.* (1997) such difficulties are limited to verbal material and phonetically similar stimuli.

A. Capovilla, Capovilla and Silveira (2000) studied the nature of the problems underlying reading and spelling difficulties in Portuguese-speaking Brazilian children, and assessed the differential involvement of discrimination and working memory variables. In the study 32 elementary public school children (16 good readers and 16 poor readers from 1st and 2nd Grades) were exposed to a computerized task involving judgement of whether a pair of syllables sounded identical or different. Children were first divided into good readers and poor readers based on their performance on a silent reading test (A. Capovilla, Capovilla, Macedo and Duduchi, 2000). Both groups were presented with five pairs of syllables with ISIs varying from 0–60 seconds (0, 20, 40, 60, 80, 100, 150, 200, 250, 300, 350, 400, 450, 500 milliseconds, 1, 2.5, 5, 15, 30, 60 seconds). The syllables of each pair were either identical or different. The difference involved consonants that differed with respect to either: (1) place (e.g., /ba/-/da/); (2) manner (/za/-/la/); (3) voicing (/fa/-/va/); or (4) all three (/sa/-/ma/). The hypotheses were that:

1 If poor readers had temporal processing difficulties, then they should perform worse than good readers at lower ISIs.
2 If poor readers had memory difficulties, then they should perform worse than good readers at higher ISIs.

3 If poor readers had discrimination difficulties, then they should perform worse on syllable pairs involving subtle consonantal differences (i.e., in only one dimension rather than in all three).

Results showed that poor readers performed worse than good readers did under all ISIs when syllables were phonetically similar, thus confirming their difficulty with phonological discrimination. In addition, it was found that their performance was even worse under short ISIs (i.e., temporal processing difficulties) and long ISIs (i.e., memory difficulties). The study not only identified the presence of phonological and memory problems in poor readers, but also helped validate the silent reading test (A. Capovilla, Capovilla, Macedo and Duduchi, 2000). Thanks to this series of studies, we now know that children identified as poor readers in the silent reading test may present problems with discrimination processing speed and working memory.

Temporary and repeated deprivation of auditory input during language acquisition due to recurrent conditions such as otitis media has been found to produce central auditory processing disorders (Bellis, 1996; Chermak and Musiek, 1997). Such disorders, in turn, have been found to reduce speech perception and produce persistent reading and spelling acquisition difficulties (Kraus *et al.*, 1996). Thus, assessing central auditory processing skills may help identify children at risk for literacy acquisition failure. It may also help reveal the nature of difficulties presented by poor readers. There are several screening batteries, such as SCAN (Keith, 1986) and others (e.g., Cherry, 1992). Based on SCAN, Zaidan (2001) developed a battery for screening central auditory processing in Portuguese-speaking Brazilian children. The battery is composed of three tasks: (1) repetition of competitive words presented under dichotic listening; (2) repetition of words presented under filtered speech (cutting frequencies above 1,000 Hz); and (3) repetition of words presented against background noise of conversation (signal to noise relationship of +5 dB). Using such a battery, F. Capovilla (2002) found evidence of central auditory processing deficits in 6–11-year-old children with reading acquisition difficulties. When compared to children with normal reading and spelling development, children with persistent phonological deficits were found to present central auditory processing deficits under all three tasks. By controlling age level as a covariant via ANOVAs, the study revealed that children with poor reading and spelling skills presented significant difficulty in the tasks of repeating spoken words that were presented under all three difficult hearing conditions: dichotic listening, filtered speech, and background conversation noise. Presently, the relationships between phonological awareness and central auditory processing are under experimental scrutiny.

DYSLEXIA RESEARCH

The International Dyslexia Test (Smythe and Everatt, 2000) assesses different cognitive abilities related to the acquisition of reading and writing, such as phonological awareness, auditory processing, visual processing, speed of processing, sequencing, motor abilities, reasoning, and arithmetic abilities. It has been translated into different languages and is used as a dyslexia diagnosis instrument in a number of countries. A Brazilian study (A. Capovilla, Smythe, Capovilla and Everatt, 2001) conducted with first graders aimed at adapting the test to Brazilian Portuguese and using it to assess the cognitive abilities in which good writers and poor writers present significant differences. Results showed that children with writing difficulties (i.e., poor writers) scored lower than did good writers in phonological awareness, auditory processing, sequencing, and speed of processing. However, their scores were comparable with respect to motor abilities, visual processing and arithmetic abilities. Such results are similar to those found in other alphabetic orthographies, such as English and German. This confirms the importance of phonological awareness, auditory processing and sequencing to the reading and writing acquisition of orthographies that map speech at the phonemic level.

A number of important syndromes have been studied in Brazilian readers, such as: phonological dyslexia (Caramelli *et al.*, 1994; Parente and Hosogi, 1999), deep dyslexia (Vidigal and Parente, 1995), neglect dyslexia (Vidigal and Parente, 1999), pure alexia (Parente, 1997), acquired morphemic dyslexia (Hosogi and Parente, 1995), letter-by-letter reading (Pinheiro and Parente, 1999; Silveira and Parente, 1995), dysgraphia (Cartery and Parente, 1998a, 1998b), and hyperlexia (Rego and Parente, 1999).

Silveira and Parente (1995) found that symptoms presented by Brazilian dyslexics with letter-by-letter reading do not differ from those presented by readers of less transparent orthographies such as English and French.

Pinheiro and Parente (1999) analysed the effects of word frequency and extension in peripheral dyslexia of the type letter-by-letter reading. According to them, the patient's reading of isolated words and non-words was very strongly affected by extension, frequency and lexicality. In addition, the patient demanded a considerably long processing time to pronounce words containing graphemes that require contextual clues for grapheme–phoneme conversion. However, the memories involved in lexical and phonological routes were preserved. The hypothesis of visual breakdown was confirmed by a greater difficulty in classifying graphically similar stimuli as being identical or different. The study suggests that the effect of extension and that the interference of contextual rules are a consequence of a letter-by-letter reading, whereas the effects of both frequency and lexicality (which would not be expected in this case) indicate the use of top-down strategies in letter processing.

Vidigal and Parente (1999) reported evidence in favour of the two-stage model of neglect dyslexia. According to that model, there are two stages in the perception of written words, the first in which it is centred on the perception of the object and the second in which it is centred on its representation. They have reported two case studies of Brazilian patients with neglect dyslexia due to damage to the right cerebral hemisphere. Results showed dissociation, so that while one of the patients was more sensitive to the physical properties of stimuli, the other was more sensitive to their linguistic properties.

Rego and Parente (1999) found evidence of hyperlexia in four adolescent patients with Asperger syndrome. All four showed greater use of the phonological route (i.e., based on grapheme–phoneme decoding) with limited access to meaning.

Cartery and Parente (1998a, 1998b) reported evidence of double dissociation between phonological spelling and lexical spelling in several patients with dysgraphia due to brain lesion. Results showed selective damage to one of the routes. This suggests that the dual-process reading model may also apply to spelling.

BILINGUALISM

Parente and Hosogi (1999) and Caramelli *et al.* (1994) reported evidence of relationships between reading deficits in Japanese and Portuguese in bilingual patients. A Nisei patient presenting breakdowns in the syllabic *kana* and maintenance of *kanji* was found to present a phonological dyslexia in Portuguese. That is, he was found to be able to read exception words, but not non-words. Such a case study indicates that the dual-processing model is universal, even though its manifestations depend on the characteristics of the reader's orthography.

Using the silent reading test, A. Capovilla, Machalous and Capovilla (2002) compared the effects of orthography (German versus Brazilian Portuguese) in 7- and 8-year-old bilingual children. Given the greater transparency of German as compared to Portuguese, as expected, results showed that, in bilingual children, there was a greater prevalence of the phonological strategy for processing the German orthography than for processing the Portuguese one. Thus, in pair-type 4 (non-words with visual exchanges), error frequency was lower in German than it was in Portuguese; whereas in pair-type 6 (homophone non-words), the opposite was found. Using the same silent reading test to compare deaf and hearing Brazilian readers, Capovilla and Viggiano (2003) found that, in pair-type 4, error frequency was higher for deaf readers than it was for hearing ones; whereas in pair-type 6, the difference between deaf and hearing readers disappeared. Such results give further support to the validity of using the silent reading test in the assessment of dual route processing.

F. Capovilla and Viggiano (2003) analysed reading and spelling acquisition in Portuguese by 850 6–45-year-old Brazilian deaf students who are bilingual in Portuguese and Brazilian Sign Language. Based on the Brazilian Sign Language dictionary (Capovilla and Raphael, 2001) and encyclopaedia (Capovilla, 2003), the authors found evidence that reading and spelling errors are mediated by phonological (i.e., cheremic) properties of Brazilian Sign Language signs such as specific combinations of hand-shapes, articulation place with respect to body, movement in signing space, and associated facial expression. The study also found evidence that such cheremic type of error is more frequent in deaf students whose mother language is Brazilian Sign Language (i.e., pre-lingual deaf students) than in those whose mother language is Portuguese (i.e., late deafened students). The study replicated previous findings (e.g., Bellugi *et al.*, 1989; Fok and Bellugi, 1986; Klima and Bellugi, 1979; Klima, Bellugi and Poizner, 1988) showing that paralexias and paragraphias made by deaf students are frequently mediated by underlying signs (F. Capovilla and A. Capovilla, 2001b). In addition to that, by comparing the relative contribution of different kinds of similarity (i.e., orthographic, semantic and cheremic ones), the study also found evidence that the errors made by late deafened students tend to be based mostly on orthographic similarity rather than on cheremic similarity.

In that study, in order to assess signing, reading and spelling skills, nine different tests were created or adapted with increasing complexity, so that from the second test on, each test was built on previously examined skills. For example, the first test assessed receptive vocabulary in Brazilian Sign Language using a test similar to the Peabody Picture Vocabulary Test (Dunn *et al.*, 1986), but instead of speaking, the examiner simply signed. In each trial, the examiner emitted one sign and children were supposed to choose, from among four alternative pictures, the one that corresponded to it. The second test assessed reading processing in Portuguese. On each trial, the examiner presented one test picture and children were supposed to choose, from among four alternative written words in Portuguese, the one that corresponded to it. In order to examine the underlying processes involved, out of the four alternative words for choice, one was the target (i.e., the written word that corresponded to the test picture) and the other three were distracters (i.e., one written word orthographically similar to the target word; one written word whose corresponding underlying sign was semantically related to the underlying target sign associated to the test picture, and one written word whose corresponding underlying sign was cheremically similar to the underlying target sign associated to the test picture – that is, the underlying distracter sign was similar to the underlying target sign with respect to cheremes such as hand shapes, articulation place, movement, and/or facial expression). The third test assessed receptive vocabulary in Brazilian Sign Language as related to reading processing in Portuguese. In each trial, the examiner emitted one sign, and children were supposed to choose, from among four alternative written words, the one that corresponded to it. Again, in order to examine the underlying processes involved, out of the four alternative words for choice, one was the target (i.e., the written word that corresponded to the test sign), and the other three were distracters (i.e., one orthographically similar to the word, one semantically similar, and one whose underlying sign was cheremically similar to the sign associated to the target word).

Among other things, the study demonstrated the importance of considering phonological processing in the visual modality (i.e., chereme processing) as a resource for making sense of apparently senseless paralexias and paragraphias made by deaf students when dealing with the alphabetic script.

REFERENCES

Abreu, M.D. and Cardoso-Martins, C. (1998) Alphabetic access route in beginning reading acquisition in Portuguese: The role of letter-name knowledge. *Reading and Writing: An Interdisciplinary Journal*, 10, 85–104.

Bellis, T.J. (1996) *Assessment and Management of Central Auditory Processing Disorder in the Educational Setting*. San Diego, CA: Singular.

Bellugi, U., Tzeng, O., Klima, E.S. and Fok, A. (1989) Dyslexia: Perspectives from sign and script. In A.M. Galaburda (ed.), *From Reading to Neurons: Issues in the Biology of Language and Cognition*. Cambridge, MA: Bradford Book and MIT Press.

Borstrom, I. and Elbro, C. (1997) Prevention of dyslexia in kindergarten: Effects of phoneme awareness with children of dyslexic parents. In C. Hulme and M. Snowling (eds), *Dyslexia: Biology, Cognition and Intervention*. London: Whurr Publishers Ltd.

Braibant, J.M. (1997) A decodificação e a compreensão: Dois componentes essenciais da leitura no segundo ano primário. [Decoding and understanding: Two essential components of reading in the second grade.] In J. Grégoire and B. Piérart (eds), *Avaliação dos problemas de leitura: Os novos modelos teóricos e suas implicações diagnósticas*. Porto Alegre, RS: Artes Médicas.

Capovilla, A.G.S. (1999) Leitura, escrita e consciência fonológica: Desenvolvimento, intercorrelações e intervenções. [Reading, spelling and phonological awareness: Development, interrelation and intervention.] Unpublished doctoral thesis, Universidade de São Paulo, SP.

Capovilla, A.G.S. and Capovilla, F.C. (1997a) O desenvolvimento da consciência fonológica em crianças durante a alfabetização. [The development of phonological awareness in children during literacy acquisition.] *Temas sobre Desenvolvimento*, 6(35), 15–21.

Capovilla, A.G.S. and Capovilla, F.C. (1997b) Treino de consciência fonológica e seu impacto em habilidades fonológicas, de leitura e ditado de pré-3 a 2a. série. [Phonological awareness training and its impact on phonological awareness, reading and spelling from pre-school to second grade.] *Ciência Cognitiva: Teoria, Pesquisa e Aplicação*, 1(2), 461–532.

Capovilla, A.G.S. and Capovilla, F.C. (2000) Efeitos do treino de consciência fonológica em crianças com baixo nível sócio-econômico. [Effects of phonological awareness training in low socio-economic status children.] *Psicologia: Reflexão e Crítica*, 13(1), 7–24.

Capovilla, A.G.S. and Capovilla, F.C. (2001) Intervenção em dificuldades de leitura e escrita com tratamento de consciência fonológica. [Intervention in reading and spelling difficulties: Phonological awareness training.] In M.T.M. Santos, A.L.P. Navas (eds), *Distúrbios de leitura e escrita: teoria e prática*. São Paulo, SP: Manole.

Capovilla, A.G.S. and Capovilla, F.C. (2002) Instrumentos para avaliar desenvolvimento dos vocabulários receptivo e expressivo, e consciência fonológica, normatizados de maternal a segunda série e validados com medidas de leitura e escrita. [Instruments for assessing the development of phonological awareness as well as receptive and expressive vocabulary standardized from pre-school to second grade and validated by reading and spelling measures.] In F.C. Capovilla (ed.), *Neuropsicologia e aprendizagem: Uma abordagem multidisciplinar.* São Paulo, SP: Sociedade Brasileira de Neuropsicologia, Scortecci.

Capovilla, A.G.S. and Capovilla, F.C. (2003a) *Alfabetização: método fônico.* [Literacy acquisition: Phonics method.] 2nd edn. São Paulo, SP: Memnon, Fapesp, CNPq.

Capovilla, A.G.S. and Capovilla, F.C. (2003b) *Problemas de leitura e escrita: Como identificar, prevenir e remediar numa abordagem fônica.* [Reading and spelling problems: How to identify, prevent and intervene in a phonics approach.] 3rd edn. São Paulo, SP: Memnon, Fapesp.

Capovilla, A.G.S., Capovilla, F.C. and Macedo, E.C. (1998) Validação do software CronoFonos para a análise de tempo de reação, duração e freqüência de segmentação locucionais na leitura em voz alta de itens isolados. [Validity of software CronoPhonos for assessing temporal parameters of pronunciation (reaction time, duration and segmentation frequency) during reading aloud.] *Ciência Cognitiva: Teoria, Pesquisa e Aplicação,* 2(3), 253–340.

Capovilla, A.G.S., Capovilla, F.C., Macedo, E.C. and Duduchi, M. (2000) Instrumentos neuropsicológicos e psicométricos para diagnóstico diferencial de distúrbio de aquisição de leitura e para avaliar leitura silenciosa e em voz alta. [Neuropsychological and psychometrical instruments for differential diagnosis of reading acquisition problems and for assessing silent reading and reading aloud performances.] In M.J. Gonçalves, E.C. Macedo, A.L. Sennyey and F.C. Capovilla (eds), *Tecnologia em (re)habilitação cognitiva: A dinâmica clínica, teoria e pesquisa.* São Paulo, SP: Edunisc, Sociedade Brasileira de Neuropsicologia.

Capovilla, A.G.S., Capovilla, F.C. and Silveira, F.B. (1998) O desenvolvimento da consciência fonológica, correlações com leitura e escrita, e tabelas de normatização. [Phonological awareness development, its correlation with reading and spelling, and standardisation tables.] *Ciência Cognitiva: Teoria, Pesquisa e Aplicação,* 2(3), 113–160.

Capovilla, A.G.S., Capovilla, F.C. and Silveira, F.B. (2000) Distúrbios de discriminação e memória fonológica em problemas de leitura e escrita. [Problems in reading and spelling acquisition: Evidence of the involvement of phonological discrimination deficits and memory deficits.] In M.J. Gonçalves, E.C. Macedo, A.L. Sennyey and F.C. Capovilla (eds), *Tecnologia em reabilitação cognitiva 2000: A dinâmica clínica, teoria e pesquisa.* São Paulo, SP: Edunisc, Sociedade Brasileira de Neuropsicologia.

Capovilla, A.G.S., Capovilla, F.C., Silveira, F.B., Vieira, R. and Matos, S.A. (1998) Processos fonológicos em paralisia cerebral: Efeitos de treino sobre a consciência fonológica, leitura e escrita. [Phonological processing in cerebral palsy: Effects of training upon phonological awareness, reading and spelling.] *Ciência Cognitiva: Teoria, Pesquisa e Aplicação,* 2(3), 209–252.

Capovilla, A.G.S., Machalous, N. and Capovilla, F.C. (2002) Efeito das ortografias portuguesa e alema sobre as estrategias de leitura de crianças bilingues. [Effect & Portuguese and German orthographies upon reading strategies by bilingual children.] In E.C. Macedo, M.J. Gonçalves, F.C. Capovilla and A.L. Sennyey (eds), *Tecnologia em (re)habilitação cognitiva: Um novo olhar para avaliação e intervenção.* São Paulo, SP. Sociedade Brasileira de Neuropsicologia, Edunisc.

Capovilla, A.G.S., Smythe, I., Capovilla, F.C. and Everatt, J. (2001) Adaptação brasileira do International Dyslexia Test: Perfil cognitivo de crianças com escrita pobre. [Brazilian adaptation of International Dyslexia Test: Cognitive profile of children with poor writing.] *Temas sobre Desenvolvimento,* 10(57), 30–37.

Capovilla, F.C. (2002) Processamento auditivo central: Demonstrando a validade de uma bateria de triagem para crianças de 6 a 11 anos. [Central auditory processing: Demonstrating the validity of a screening battery for children aged 6–11.] In F.C. Capovilla (ed.), *Neuropsicologia e aprendizagem: Uma abordagem multidisciplinar.* São Paulo, SP: Sociedade Brasileira de Neuropsicologia, Scortecci.

Capovilla, F.C. (ed.) (2003) *Enciclopédia da Língua de Sinais Brasileira: O mundo do surdo brasileiro em Libras* (Vol. 1–19, 9000 pp.). [Encyclopaedia of Brazilian Sign Language: The Brazilian Deaf World in Libras]. 2nd edn. São Paulo, SP: Feneis, Imprensa Oficial.

Capovilla, F.C. and Capovilla, A.G.S. (1999) Phonological awareness training: Effects on metaphonological, reading and spelling skills in Brazilian children. *Brazilian Journal of Dysmorphology and Speech-Hearing Disorders,* 3, 45–66.

Capovilla, F.C. and Capovilla, A.G.S. (2001a) Compreendendo a natureza dos problemas de aquisição de leitura e escrita: Mapeando o envolvimento de distúrbios cognitivos de discriminação fonológica, velocidade de processamento e memória fonológica. [Understanding the nature of reading and spelling acquisition problems: Mapping the involvement of phonological discrimination, processing speed, and phonological memory.] *Cadernos de Psicopedagogia*, 1(1), 14–37.

Capovilla, F.C. and Capovilla, A.G.S. (2001b) Compreendendo o processamento do código alfabético: Como entender os erros de leitura e escrita de crianças surdas. [Understanding alphabetic code processing: How to understand reading and spelling errors by deaf children.] In F.C. Capovilla and W.D. Raphael (eds), *Dicionário enciclopédico ilustrado trilíngüe da Língua de Sinais Brasileira*. Volume II: *Sinais de M a Z* (Vol. 2, pp. 1497–1516). 2nd edn. São Paulo, SP: Edusp, Fapesp, Fundação Vitae, Feneis, Brasil Telecom.

Capovilla, F.C., Capovilla, A.G.S. and Macedo, E.C. (2001a) Comunicação alternativa na USP na década 1991–2001: Tecnologia e pesquisa em reabilitação, educação e inclusão. [Alternative communication at the University of São Paulo from 1991 to 2001: Technology and research in rehabilitation, education and inclusion.] *Temas sobre Desenvolvimento*, 10(58–59), 18CE–42CE.

Capovilla, F.C., Capovilla, A.G.S. and Macedo, E.C. (2001b) Rota perilexical na leitura em voz alta: tempo de reação, duração e segmentação na pronúncia. [Perilexical processing during reading performance: Effects upon reaction time, duration and segmentation of utterances.] *Psicologia: Reflexão e Crítica*, 14(2), 409–427.

Capovilla, F.C., Macedo, E.C. and Capovilla A.G.S. (2002a) Tecnologia para análise de emissões vocálicas em nomeação e leitura oral nas afasias e dislexias. [Technology for analysing temporal parameters of pronunciation during reading aloud by aphasics and dyslexics.] In F.C. Capovilla (ed.), *Neuropsicologia e aprendizagem: Uma abordagem multidisciplinar*. São Paulo, SP: Sociedade Brasileira de Neuropsicologia, Scortecci.

Capovilla, F.C., Macedo, E.C. and Capovilla, A.G.S. (2002b) Usando testes computadorizados de competência de leitura silenciosa e em voz alta para mapear desenvolvimento de rotas de leitura, e testes de compreensão auditiva e de leitura para diagnóstico diferencial da dislexia. [Assessing silent reading, reading aloud, auditory comprehension and reading comprehension for differential diagnosis of dyslexia.] In F.C. Capovilla (ed.), *Neuropsicologia e aprendizagem: Uma abordagem multidisciplinar*. São Paulo, SP: Sociedade Brasileira de Neuropsicologia, Scortecci.

Capovilla, F.C., Macedo, E.C., Capovilla, A.G.S. and Charin, S. (1998) Competência de leitura: Modelos teóricos e sistemas computadorizados para avaliação de leitura silenciosa e em voz alta. [Reading competence: Theoretical models and computerized systems for assessing reading aloud and silent reading.] *Ciência Cognitiva: Teoria, Pesquisa e Aplicação*, 2(4), 597–676.

Capovilla, F.C., Macedo, E.C. and Charin, S. (2001) Tecnologia e modelos na avaliação de compreensão em leitura silenciosa e de reconhecimento e decodificação em leitura em voz alta. [Technology and models for assessing comprehension in silent reading and phonological decoding in reading aloud.] In M.T.M. Santos and A.L.P. Navas (eds), *Distúrbios de leitura e escrita: teoria e prática*. São Paulo, SP: Manole.

Capovilla, F.C. and Nunes, L.R.O.P. (2001) A memória de trabalho no paralisado cerebral: Procedimento para avaliar habilidade e processos subjacentes. [Working memory in cerebral-palsy: Procedure for assessing skill and underlying processes.] *Revista Brasileira de Educação Especial*, 7(1), 1–23.

Capovilla, F.C. and Raphael, W.D. (2001) *Dicionário enciclopédico ilustrado trilíngüe da Língua de Sinais Brasileira*. Volume I: *Sinais de A a L* (Vol 1, pp. 1–834), Volume II: *Sinais de M a Z* (Vol. 2, pp. 835–1620). [Illustrated Encyclopaedic Dictionary of Brazilian Sign Language. Volume I: Signs from A to L (Vol. 1, pp. 1–834), Volume II: Signs from M to Z (Vol. 2, pp. 835–1620).] São Paulo, SP: Edusp, Fapesp, Fundação Vitae, Feneis, Brasil Telecom.

Capovilla, F.C. and Viggiano, K. (2003) *Compêndio de avaliação do desenvolvimento da linguagem escolar no surdo*. [Compendium of language development assessment in the deaf.] São Paulo, SP: Edusp, Vitae, Feneis, Imprensa Oficial.

Caramelli, P., Parente, M.A.M.P., Hosogi, M.L., Bois, M. and Lecours, A. R. (1994). Unexpected reading dissociation in a Brazilian Nisei with crossed aphasia. *Behavioural Neurology*, 7, 156–164.

Cardoso-Martins, C. (1991) Awareness of phonemes and alphabetic literacy acquisition. *British Journal of Educational Psychology*, 61, 164–173.

Cardoso-Martins, C. (1995) Sensitivity to rhymes, syllables, and phonemes in literacy acquisition in Portuguese. *Reading Research Quarterly*, 30(4), 808–828.

Cartery, M.T. and Parente, M.A.M.P. (1998a) Dissociações nas disgrafias adquiridas. [Dissociation in acquired dysgraphia.] *Anais do XXX Congresso Brasileiro de Neurologia*, São Paulo, SP.

Cartery, M.T. and Parente, M.A.M.P. (1998b) Estudo de casos de disgrafia central. [Case studies on central dysgraphia.] *Arquivos de Neuro-Psiquiatria*, 56(1), 27.

Chermak, G.D. and Musiek, F.E. (1997) *Central Auditory Processing Disorders: New Perspectives*. San Diego, CA: Singular Publishing.

Dunn, L.M., Padilla, E.R., Lugo, D. and Dunn, L.M. (1986) *Test de Vocabulario en Imágenes peabody: Adaptación hispanoamericana*. [Peabody Picture Vocabulary Test: Hispano-American version.] Circle Pines, MN: American Guidance Service.

Ellis, A. and Young, A.W. (1988) *Human Cognitive Neuropsychology*. London: Lawrence Erlbaum Associates.

Fok, Y.Y.A. and Bellugi, U. (1986) The acquisition of visual-spatial script. In H. Kao, G. van Galen and R. Hoosain (eds), *Graphonomics: Contemporary Research in Handwriting*. Amsterdam: North Holland: Elsevier.

Frith, U. (1985) Beneath the surface of developmental dyslexia. In K. Patterson, J. Marshall and M. Coltheart (eds), *Surface Dyslexia: Neuropsychological and Cognitive Studies of Phonological Reading*. London: Lawrence Erlbaum Associates.

Frith, U. (1990) *Dyslexia as a Developmental Disorder of Language*. London: MRC: Cognitive Development Unit.

Hosogi, M.L. and Parente, M.A.M.P. (1995) As dislexias adquiridas por utilização da via perilexical: Manifestações das dislexias do Português. [Acquired dyslexia in which there is use of the perilexical route: Manifestations of dyslexia in Portuguese.] In B.P. Damasceno and M.I.H. Coudry (eds), *Temas em neuropsicologia e neurolingüística*, vol. 4. São Paulo, SP: Sociedade Brasileira de Neuropsicologia.

Keith, R.W. (1986) *SCAN: A Screening Test for Central Auditory Processing Disorders*. San Antonio, TX: The Psychological Corporation.

Khomsi, A. (1997) A propósito de estratégias de compensação nas crianças disléxicas. [On compensatory strategies used by dyslexic children.] In J. Grégoire and B. Piérart (eds), *Avaliação dos problemas de leitura: Os novos modelos teóricos e suas implicações diagnósticas*. Porto Alegre, RS: Artes Médicas.

Klima, E.S. and Bellugi, U. (1979) *The Signs of Language*. Cambridge, MA: Harvard University Press.

Klima, E.S., Bellugi, U. and Poizner, H. (1988) The neurolinguistic substrate for sign language. In L.N.M. Hyman and C.N. Li (eds), *Language, Speech and Mind*. London: Routledge.

Kraus, N., McGee, T., Carrel, T., Zecker, N., Nicol, T. and Koch, D. (1996) Auditory neurophysiologic responses and discrimination deficits in children with learning problems. *Science*, 273, 971–973.

Lemle, M. (1991) *Guia teórico do alfabetizador*. [A guide to theory for teachers devoted to reading acquisition.] São Paulo, SP: Editora Ática.

Mody, M., Studdert-Kennedy, M. and Brady, S.A. (1997) Speech perception deficits in poor readers: Auditory processing or phonological coding? *Journal of Experimental Child Psychology*, 64, 199–231.

Morais, J. (in press) Estudo comparativo das representações fonológicas e metafonológicas nos iletrados e nos disléxicos. [Comparative study of phonological representations in illiterates and dyslexics.] In F.C. Capovilla (ed.), *Neuropsicologia cognitiva da leitura: Modelos teóricos e tecnológicos, e implicações diagnósticas e de tratamento*. São Paulo, SP: Sociedade Brasileira de Neuropsicologia.

Parente, M.A.M.P (1994) O enfoque cognitivo na avaliação das dislexias adquiridas e o sistema ortográfico do Português. [The cognitive approach in the assessment of acquired dyslexia and the Portuguese orthographic system.] In B.P. Damasceno and M.I.H. Coudry (eds), *Temas em neuropsicologia e neurolingüística*, Vol. 4. São Paulo, SP: Sociedade Brasileira de Neuropsicologia.

Parente, M.A.M.P. (1997) Eficácia da terapia na reabilitação de um cliente portador de alexia pura. [Efficacy in rehabilitation therapy of a pure alexia case.] *Distúrbios da Comunicação*, 9(1), 35–52.

Parente, M.A.M.P. and Hosogi, M. (1999) Acquired dyslexia in a Nisei patient: Repercussion of brain lesion in different writing systems. (XVIII Brazilian Congress of Neurology, São Paulo). *Acta Psychiatrica Brasileira*, 6, 255.

Parente, M.A.M.P., Rocchi, H. and Vieim, I. (1999) Efeitos de escolaridade e idade no estoque fonológico e em mecanismos de retroalimentação. [Effects of schooling and age upon phonological storage and feedback mechanisms.] In *Libro de Resumenes VI Congreso Latinoamericano de Neuropsicología*. Havana, Cuba: Centro de Neurociências de Cuba, vol. l, 146–147.

Pinheiro, A.M.V. (1994) *Leitura e escrita: Uma abordagem cognitiva*. [Reading and writing: A cognitive approach.] Campinas, SP: Editorial Psy.

Pinheiro, A.M.V. (1995) Reading and spelling development in Brazilian Portuguese. *Reading and Writing. Special issue on Literacy Acquisition*, 7(1), 111–138.

Pinheiro, A.M.V. (1996) *Contagem de freqüência de ocorrência e análise psicolingüísticas de palavras expostas a crianças na faixa pré-escolar e séries iniciais do 1° grau*. [Word frequency count and psycholinguistic analysis of words that pre-schoolers and first graders are exposed to.] São Paulo, SP: Associação Brasileira de Dislexia.

Pinheiro, A.M.V. (1997) Análise cognitiva da dislexia do desenvolvimento: Um estudo translingüístico. [Cognitive analysis in development dyslexia: A cross-linguistic study.] Unpublished thesis. Universidade Federal de Minas Gerais. Belo Horizonte, MG.

Pinheiro, A.M.V. and Parente, M.A.M.P (1999) Estudo de caso de um paciente com dislexia periférica e as implicações dessa condição nos processamentos. [A case study in peripheral dyslexia and its implications for reading processing.] *Pró-Fono: Revista de Atualização Científica*, 11(1), 115–123.

Portugal, A.C. and Capovilla, F.C. (2002) Triagem audiológica: Efeitos da perda auditiva sobre vocabulário, consciência fonológica, articulação de fala e nota escolar em escolares de primeira série. [Auditory screening: Effects of auditory loss upon vocabulary, phonological awareness, speech articulation and school grades in first graders.] In F.C. Capovilla (ed.), *Neuropsicologia e aprendizagem: Uma abordagem multidisciplinar*. São Paulo, SP: Sociedade Brasileira de Neuropsicologia, Scortecci.

Rego, M.G.S. and Parente, M.A.M.E. (1999) Hiperlexia: Uma análise cognitiva em síndrome de Asperger. [Hyperlexia: A cognitive analysis in Asperger´s syndrome.] In *Libro de Resumenes VI Congreso Latinoamericano de Neuropsicología*. Havana: Centro de Neurociências de Cuba, vol. l.

Salles, Parente, M.A.M.P., Motta, M.B. and Cechella, C. (1999) Estudo da memória operacional em crianças de primeira e segunda séries e sua relação com a consciência fonológica. [Operational memory in first and second grade children and its relationship to phonological awareness.] In *Libro de Resumenes VI Congreso Latinoamericano de Neuropsicología*. Havana: Centro de Neurociencias de Cuba, vol. l.

Share, D. (1995) Phonological recoding and self-teaching: sine qua non of reading acquisition. *Cognition*, 55(2), 151–218.

Silveira, A. and Parente, M.A.M.P (1995) Leitura tetra-por-tetra: Uma dislexia periférica? [Letter by letter reading: A peripheral dyslexia?] In B.P. Damasceno and M.I.H. Coudry (eds), *Temas em neuropsicologia e neurolingüística*, vol. 4. São Paulo, SP: Sociedade Brasileira de Neuropsicologia.

Smythe, I. and Everatt, J. (2000) Dyslexia diagnosis in different languages. In L. Peer and G. Reid (eds), *Multilingualism, Literacy and Dyslexia*. London: David Fulton Publishers.

Vidigal, B.M. and Parente, M.A.M.E (1995) As dislexias por utilização da via lexical: Manifestações das dislexias profunda e fonológica. [Dyslexia by the lexical route: Manifestations of deep dyslexia and phonological dyslexia.] In B.P Damasceno and M.I.H. Coudry (eds), *Temas em neuropsicologia e neurolingüística*, vol. 4. São Paulo, SP: Sociedade Brasileira de Neuropsicologia.

Vidigal, B.M. and Parente, M.A.M.P. (1999) A influência de fatores visuais e lingüísticos nos processamentos iniciais de leitura: Dois estudos de case de portadores de dislexia de negligência. [The effect of visual and linguistic factors in the initial reading processing: Two case studies in neglect dyslexia.] In *Libro de Resumenes VI Congreso Latinoamericano de Neuropsicología*. Havana: Centro de Neurociências de Cuba, vol. l.

Zaidan, E. (2001) Desenvolvimento de uma bateria de testes de triagem da função auditiva central em pré-escolares e escolares na faixa de 6 a 11 anos. [Development of a battery for screening central auditory function in pre-schoolers and first graders aged 6–11 years.] Unpublished thesis. Universidade de São Paulo, SP, Brasil.

17

PROBLEMS OF DYSLEXIA IN RUSSIAN

Olga Inshakova

INTRODUCTION

There has been much research into dyslexia in the past decade and a considerable volume of theoretical and practical material has been generated. As a consequence, two basic theories of developmental dysgraphia and dyslexia with children have been developed. The first is the theory of phonological deficit with a core of difficulties being experienced by children with speech processing difficulties. The second theory is concerned with visual disorders due to the presence of anomalies within the visual system. Both theories have been comprehensively studied and the evidence suggests that elements of both theories plausibly account for some of the difficulties.

Dyslexia studies in Russia have their old traditions differing from the Western ones. These are mainly associated with ideas of Luria, Vinarskaya, Vygotsky and Levina. Two types of dyslexia are traditionally considered: primary or secondary. Primary dyslexia refers to specific reading difficulties. Secondary dyslexia occurs as a consequence of mental deficiency, disturbed hearing, vision, locomotor system and peculiarities in manifestation, and is singled out as a separate group for studies. Reading (dyslexia) and writing (dysgraphia) disorders are studied separately, although these processes arc closely connected to each other in ontogenesis. Many researchers suggest that dysgraphias are not always associated with serious reading disorders. Published Russian studies assign a major role to dysgraphias, since writing disorders of Russian children occur two to three times more frequently than reading disorders (Inshakova, 1995; Kornev, 1997; Sadovnikova, 1995). According to Kornev, who studied the writing and reading of 186 1st form pupils, dyslexia was found in 10 per cent of children (including minor forms thereof), while dysgraphia was found in 21 per cent of children. Although dyslexia is studied separately (Altukhova, 1995; Kornev, 1995, 1997), sometimes it is considered a synonym of the notion of a 'reading disorder', i.e., without considering difficulties between specific and non-specific mistakes in reading.

Authors undertaking studies in Russia (Andreopoulou and Bogiotopolou, 2000) and in

International Book of Dyslexia: A Cross-Language Comparison and Practice Guide. Edited by Ian Smythe, John Everatt and Robin Salter.   ISBN 0471498416   © 2004 John Wiley & Sons, Ltd.

Greece obtained confirmation of data that reading is an easier skill to acquire in countries with a phonetic principle of writing, and dyslexia is less common there. Reading is a more complex skill in countries with a traditional (historically formed) principle of education (English, French), where a break has occurred between changed spoken language and historical spelling.

Skills of phonemic analysis develop quicker in children of countries where the phonetic principle of writing prevails, since ratios between sound and letter and between pronunciation and spelling are reasonably stable. Teaching by the analytical-synthetic method also plays a certain role in this regard. That is why Russian children make fewer mistakes in writing pseudowords than English children do (Inshakova and Boldyreva, 1998). On the other hand, mistakes are more frequent in reading pseudowords, since regular relations between sound and letter obstruct the integral capture of the read word, especially if the English model of the pseudoword is used in the test. The given result conforms to the data supplied by D. Shankweiler and Landerl *et al.* (1997).

Several major areas of research studying children's dysgraphia and dyslexia exist: clinical-psychological, psyschological-pedagogical and neuropsychological. The clinical-psychological direction is mainly represented by the studies of Isayev (1982) and Kornev (1995, 1997), and Mastyukova, where these authors summarize numerous data of various clinical, clinical-dynamic, electrophysiological and neuropsychological studies in order to understand the mechanisms of dyslexia and dysgraphia. This allowed them to conclude that dyslexia is a polyfactorial model of disorder.

The psychological-pedagogical approach to studies of dysgraphia pathogenesis of schoolchildren is the most common at present. Many authors (e.g. Levina, Spirova, Tokareva, Sadovnikova, Lalayeva) have accumulated a sufficient quantity of data concerning symptoms of specific writing disturbances. In the opinion of the majority of these authors, speech disturbance is the primary reason for dysgraphia.

However, certain authors disagree with such an opinion. They consider that speech disorders are part of the dyslexia syndrome and are caused in certain cases by the same reasons as writing and reading disorders. These cannot be viewed as due to the same causes. If symptoms of dyslexia combine with speech disorders or underdevelopment, then we may refer to a specific form of dyslexia and dysgraphia in such cases. Representatives of the psychological-pedagogical direction associate the onset of the children's dysgraphia with disorder or non-formed higher psychic functions that support the writing process. However, it is impossible to analyse the ratio of specific writing mistakes to visual-spatial, verbal, cognitive and other disturbances within the framework of such an approach. Thus it does not allow us to determine the relationship between dysgraphia with inadequacy or disturbance of certain higher psychic functions. The neuropsychological approach, however, permits us to do so.

Akhutina *et al.* (2001) identified two groups of children with different dyslexia manifestation with the aid of the neuropsychological approach to dyslexia studies. Certain peculiarities are found in the handwriting of the former group of children, manifested in the domination of omissions and confusion of consonants over omissions and confusion of vowels (between 25 per cent and 10 per cent), a considerable number of confused paired unvoiced and voiced consonants in strong position (9 per cent), and an equal number of substitutions of voiced consonants by paired unvoiced ones, and unvoiced by voiced consonants, as well as in the high number of specific mistakes in one script (3.84 on average). The speech of such pupils is not characterized by expressed difficulties with expression programming. Text fragment losses during narration are observed in 33 per cent of children. Inversion is observed in 14 per cent of children. The narrative of children from this group consists on average of 3 simple and 1.55 complex sentences. Their average sentence length is equal to 6.36 words. However, these are associated with the trend of substituting significant parts of speech by pronouns (pronominalization index totalled 0.69). Articulation disturbance is found in 33 per cent of schoolchildren within this group. Another 33 per cent had such disturbances earlier, but these were eliminated during logopaedic training. Disturbances of word sound and syllabic structure are observed in 52 per cent of children. Mistakes of phonetic analysis are more frequent (70 per cent of children) than mistakes of phonetic synthesis (43 per cent of children). Difficulties in information receiving, processing and keeping the left hemispheric principle may explain the existing writing and speech mistakes of such children.

A completely different group of schoolchildren is distinguished against the background of the group described above. They are characterized by prevalence of omissions and confusions of vowel letters over omissions and confusions of letters symbolizing consonant sounds (23 per cent to 14 per cent). There are many mix-ups of letters symbolizing vowel sounds in strong position (9 per cent) and there is discovered a trend to vocalize unvoiced consonants in strong position within the word. The number of specific mistakes in one written work is much higher (4.57 on average).

Omissions of text fragments occur in 67 per cent of children during oral narratives. Other mistakes are rare. These children use on average 2.72 simple sentences and 1.44 complex ones during narration. Sentences developed by these pupils are found to be reasonably long in this case – 6.58 words in average and the pronominalization index is equal to 0.59 for the group on average. Some 78 per cent of children have no articulation disturbances. Distortions of sound-syllabic structure of words occur in 44 per cent of schoolchildren. Phonetic analysis mistakes were found in 89 per cent of children, although phonetic synthesis mistakes occurred in 7.2 per cent of children in this group.

Cognitive differences of children in this group have a different nature. Disturbances of a right hemispheric strategy nevertheless prevail when disorders occur with left hemispheric information processing strategy. This allows us to presume that the peculiarities of speech and specific writing and reading disorders of such children are due to right hemispheric differences. The given example proves that the neuropsychological approach in dyslexia studies is the most helpful since it is based upon fundamental theoretical provisions regarding system composition of higher psychological functions, and studies writing and reading as a complex functional system (Tsvyetkova, 1997; Semenovich, 2001).

DYSGRAPHIA AND DYSORTHOGRAPHY

Dysgraphia is a phenomenon occurring as a result of the disturbed forming of the phonetic principle of writing, based upon the skills of listening and outlining sounds of written words, followed by recording the same by appropriate letters. It is manifested in substitutions, confusions, omissions and inserts of letters in strong positions in words only. Researchers distinguish different kinds of dysgraphia based on the underlying driving mechanism. Writing disorders of Russian children are not restricted to dysgraphic mistakes only. Virtually all researchers suggest that dysgraphia is followed by dysorthographic and agrammatic mistakes in writing.

Dysorthography is presently the least researched writing disorder. Dysorthography means substitutions of letters in the weak position in a word. It is related to the violation of the morphologic principle contemplating a more complex relationship between phoneme and grapheme. The point is that each significant part of word is always written similarly, irrespective of its articulation. Naturally, sound analysis also exists here but morphological analysis, which is impossible without developed vocabulary and syntax, occupies a special place.

Publications by Komarova *et al.* (1992) and Pritshepova (1994, 2001) reveal the presence of a relationship between dysgraphic and dysorthographic mistakes. Medium and severe degree dysgraphia causes spelling errors of similar severity, which are also persistent. According to Pritshepova (2001), dysorthography is present in 80 per cent of children in the second form and 90 per cent of children in the third form among primary schoolchildren with speech disorders. The study in a special school for children with severe speech disorders revealed the presence of dysgraphia in 100 per cent of schoolchildren.

In the opinion of Kornev (1997), unformed metalanguage skills are the basis of dysgraphia and dysorthography. Agrammatical writing disorders remain virtually unexplored.

VISUAL DISTURBANCES

The analysis of the literature in Russia shows that the visual deficit of children with dysgraphia and dyslexia has remained practically unexplored in Russia. However, the study by Levashov (2001) deserves attention. It is dedicated to peculiarities of visual recognition of incentives by children with dyslexia. The study experimental group showed the worst result when naming in sequence four incentives, presented to them vertically, and then horizontally. However, children in the experimental group were capable of laying out the presented sequence in vertical and horizontal directions with the aid of cards, as the control group did. The experimental group encountered huge difficulties when naming incentives horizontally. Therefore, the ability of the experimental group of schoolchildren to track moving incentives in left–right and right–left directions was studied further. It was revealed as a result of a performed study that children with dyslexia discerned incentives moving from the right to left more quickly and with higher accuracy.

EARLY DETECTION

This problem is especially acute at present. Several Russian procedures for early detection (Mishakova, Ogarkina, 2001; Kornev, 1999; Tsvyetkova, 1996) are presently known. The majority of authors consider that speech is the primary representative criterion of early detection. These procedures are used during examination of children aged 5–6 years old, presently in special kindergartens for children with severe speech disturbance and during examination of 6-year-old children joining school. If the greatest risk of dyslexia is found in the child, then he or she is directed to study in a special school for children with speech disturbances. If the risk is small, then a child will go to an ordinary school but must attend lessons with a school speech therapist three times per week.

REMEDIATION

Corrective work is performed in state establishments, such as school speech therapy units and special departments in hospitals for children with speech disorders.

The most efficient treatments by Efimenkova (1997) and by Sadovnikova (1995) are used in the prevention of dyslexia. These procedures comprise several successive stages. Each stage deals with an appropriate assigned task. The tasks are correction of articulation and development of phonetic apprehension and other cognitive functions at the first stage, work with vocabulary and syntax and analysis of polymodal information at the second stage, and development of coherent pronunciation at the third stage.

Procedures by other authors (Lalayeva, Loginova and Pritshepova) are the most frequently used for dyslexia correction with children studying in Grades 2–4. Apart from state establishments, corrective work is carried out with reasonable success in special private institutions. A considerable number of them have been opened recently.

REFERENCES

Akhutina, T.V., Inshakova, O.B. and Velichenkova, O.A. (2001) *The Complex Approach to the Analysis of Specific Mistakes in the Writing of Young Schoolboys*. Moscow, School of Health.

Altukhova, T.A. (1995) Correction of disorders of reading at pupils of primary school for children with severe disorders of speech. Dissertation thesis. Moscow University.

Andreopoulou, A. and Bogiotopoulou, V. (2000) *The writing disorders for school in Greece*. In Proceedings, 25th World Congress of the International Association of Logopedics and Phoniatrics, Montreal (published in CD-ROM).

Inshakova, O.B. (1995) Disorders of writing and reading in right-handed and left-handed pupils. Dissertation thesis, Moscow University.

Inschakova, O. and Boldyreva, M. (1988) *Oshibki napisaniya psevdoslov u uchashckikhsya s digrafiyey. Nauchnye trudy MPGU*. Moscow: Prometey.

Inshakova, O.B. and Ogarkina A.V. (2001) *Sostoyaniye vyerbalnykh i nevyerbalnykh vysshikh psikhicheskikh funktsiy u doshkolnikov, imeyushchikh raznuyu stepen predraspolozhennosti k disleksii*. Moscow: MSPI, Izd-vo NPO MODEK.

Isayev, D.N. (1982) *Psikhologicheskoye nedorazvitiye u detey*. Leningrad: Meditsina.

Komarova, V.V., Milostivyenko, L.G. and Sumchenko, G.M. (1992) Sootnosheniye disgraficheskikh oshibok i orfograficheskikh oshibok u mladshikh shkolnikov s narusheniyami rechi. In *Patologiya rechi: istoriya izucheniya, diagnostika, preodoleniye. Mezhvuzovskiy sbornik nauchnykh trudov /RGPU im. A.I. Gertsena*. St Petersburg: Obrazovaniye.

Kornev, A.N. (1995) *Disgraphia and Dyslexia in Children*. St Petersburg: Gippokrat.

Kornev, A.N. (1997) *Disorders of Reading and Writing in Children*. St Petersburg: Id MIM.

Kornev, A.N. (1999) *Psikhologicheskiy analiz orfograficheskikh navykov pravopisaniya bezudarnykh glasnykh na nachalnom etape ikh formirovaniya. Problemy detskoy rechi. Materialy Vserossiyskoy konferentsii*. St Petersburg: Izd-vo RGPU im. A.I. Gertsena.

Lalayeva, R.I. (1983) *Narusheniya protsessa ovladeniya chteniyem u shkolnikov*. Moscow: Prosvyeshcheniye.

Levashov, O.V. (2001) Disorders of visual-motor functions in dyslexia: Review of new experimental techniques. *The Letter and Reading: Difficulties of Training and Correction*. Moscow: MPSI.

Levina, R.Y. (1961) *Narusheniya pisma u detey s nedorazvitiyem rechi*. Moscow: Izd-vo APN RSFSR.

Loginova, Y.A. (2001) Osobennosti korrektsii disgrafii u uchashchikhsya s zaderzhkoy psikhicheskogo razvitiya. In *Pismo i chteniye: trudnosti obucheniya i korrektsiya. Uchebnoye posobiye*. Moscow: MPSI.

Pritshchepova, I.V. (1994) Osobennosti leksiki mladshikh shkolnikov, stradayushchikh disorfografiyey. In *Metody izucheniya i preodoleniya rechevykh rasstroystv. Mezhvuzovskiy sbornik nauchnykh trudov*. St Petersburg: Izd-vo RGPU im. A.I. Gertsena.

Pritshepova, I.V. (2001) Regarding a technique of correction disorthography in young schoolboys with general undeveloped speech. *The Letter and Reading: Difficulties of Training and Correction*. Moscow: MPSI.

Sadovnikova, I.N. (1995) *Disorders of Written Speech and their Overcoming in Young Schoolboys*. Moscow: Vlados.

Semenovich, A.V. (2001) Aktualnye problemy neyropsikhologicheskoy kvalifikatsii otklonyayushchegosya razvitiya. In *Aktualnye problemy neyropsikhologii detskogo vozrasta*. Moscow: MPSI.

Spirova, L.F. (1959) Sootnosheniye mezhdu nedostatkami proiznosheniya chteniya i pisma. In *Voprosy logopedii*. Moscow: Izd-vo APN RSFSR, 75–134.

Tokareva, O.A. (1969) Rasstroystva chteniya i pisma (disleksii i disgrafii). In S.S. Lyapidevskogo (ed.), *Rasstroystva rechi u detey i podrostkov*. Moscow: Izd-vo MGPI im. V.I. Lenina.

Tsvyetkova, L.S. (1996) *Metodika diagnosticheskogo neyropsikhologicheskogo obsledovaniya detey*. Moscow: Akademiya.

Tsvyetkova, L.S. (1997) *Neyropsikhologiya scheta, pisma i chteniya: narusheniye i vosstanovleniye*. Moscow: Izd-vo Yurist.

Yefimenkova, L.N. (1977) *Korrektsiya narusheniy pismennoy rechi u mladshikh shkolnikov*. Moscow: Prosvyeshcheniye.

18

DYSLEXIA IN SPANISH

Almudena Giménez de la Peña

READING IN SPANISH

The conceptual framework for studying the process of reading has shifted from a general, very inclusive approach to a more specific one. From this latter point of view, reading is conceived as a complex process that requires cognitive and linguistic abilities (see Abu-Rabia, Goswami, this volume). The idea that perceptual or motor skills influence reading acquisition has been abandoned, the causative factors of the performance in reading tasks are focused on linguistic (semantic, syntactic knowledge), and metalinguistic abilities (graphemic knowledge, phonemic awareness), and knowledge of the world (conceptual knowledge). A number of studies provide empirical support for this approach. While little or no improvement in reading has been found after perceptual and motor training (Jiménez and Artiles, 1990), training directed at phonological awareness (i.e. phoneme identification, segmentation or manipulation) has proved to be very successful for learning, remediation (González-Portal, 1984; Jiménez and Artiles, 1990), and to prevent learning disturbances (Claros et al., 1999). Results from different research point to the relevance of the abilities to analyse the structure of language for learning to read, specially phonological awareness (Alegría, 1985; Morais, 1994; Schulte-Körne, Goswami, both this volume).

Reading means the access to the meaning of a word from the recognition of print patterns. The reader can access meaning using two different strategies or routes. One of these routes is called phonological because it works by translating graphemes into phonemes so the reader is able to recognize the word by its phonemic structure. When considered in detail, this procedure implies, at least, three mechanisms (Coltheart and Jackson, 1987): (1) the analysis and recognition of graphemes; (2) grapheme into phoneme conversion; and (3) the assembly of phonemes to produce the word when reading aloud.

The involvement of phoneme processing/manipulation in this route, plus the orthographic regularity of Spanish, have driven the assumption of a strong link between phonological skills and performance in reading tasks (Morais et al., 1987; Defior et al., 1998).

International Book of Dyslexia: A Cross-Language Comparison and Practice Guide. Edited by Ian Smythe, John Everatt and Robin Salter.   ISBN 0471498416   © 2004 John Wiley & Sons, Ltd.

There is accumulated evidence supporting the use of the phonological route when reading in Spanish (similar results have been found in other languages with a shallow orthography such as German, Finnish or Greek, see the corresponding chapters for more detail). For example, findings for a negative relationship are consistent with the importance of grapheme–phoneme conversion during reading between word length and performance (Cuetos, 1989; Valle, 1996). Children commit more errors when reading long rather than short words (Sebastian and Parreno, 1995; Defior *et al.*, 1996), and their reaction times in lexical decision tasks increase with the number of letters (Dominguez and Cuetos, 1992; Jiménez and Hernández, 2000).

However, despite the transparency of the language, there is also solid evidence favouring the idea that readers of Spanish, in spite of its being a completely transparent language, take advantage of a lexical strategy based on the direct access of the meaning from the written form. One source of support for the use of the visual route in Spanish comes from the fact that words are easier to read than pseudowords (Dominguez and Cuetos, 1992; Defior *et al.*, 1996), and the increase of labialization errors with age (Sebastian and Parreno, 1995; Valle, 1996). It is argued that pseudowords are read by the identification of segments and their transformation into sounds. Once the reader has acquired the set of grapheme to phoneme conversion rules, and uses them skilfully, there is no possibility of improvement, and a stabilization of performance is expected. Regarding pseudoword reading, Sebastian and Parreno (1995), and Valle (1996) found that first graders committed more errors than older children. However, after the age of 12, the number of correct answers did not show any significant increase. On the contrary, word frequency continued to show effects on word processing even at the older ages. One plausible interpretation may be that as the number of mental representations of words increase with age and experience, then reading through a lexical route becomes more probable. However, it is not possible to have mental representations of pseudowords. This would explain the lack of improvement in reading pseudowords.

Of interest is the effect of syllable frequency. In transparent languages, such as Spanish, the facilitation produced by frequent syllables was interpreted as evidence that readers take advantage of the syllable as a unit for access (Jiménez and Rodrigo, 2000). An increase in the syllable length has been associated with a higher number of errors (Defior *et al.*, 1996). Nevertheless, this effect could be due to long syllables being very infrequent in Spanish. Controlling the frequency of syllables Jiménez *et al.* (1997) found, using a lexical decision task, that 6–7-year-old children were faster at reading words and pseudowords when frequent syllables were avoided. Surprisingly, this effect is the opposite of what was found with adults. Children's answers showed longer latencies when words were formed by high frequency syllables. These data were interpreted as evidence that the syllable is treated as a phonological variable, and does not connect directly to the lexicon, as happens with adults. The syllable facilitation, then, could be due to the dominance of phonological strategies in the first stages.

The results from such research are consistent with a developmental transition from an analytical reading to a more global strategy (Sebastian and Parreno, 1995). In the beginning, children learn to segment words and to identify graphemes in order to find the corresponding phoneme. As they get older, they become familiar with some letter strings that are kept in memory and treated as a unit. This is shown by the effect of word knowledge on word recognition. In other words, reading performance is mediated by the size of their visual lexicon. Evidence for this assumption comes from the increase with age of substitutions of infrequent for frequent words, or pseudowords for words, which is called labialization (Sebastian and Parreno 1995), the increase in correct answers when reading frequent words (Valle, 1996; Defior *et al.*, 1996, 1998), or quicker lexical decisions for words than for pseudowords (Dominguez and Cuetos, 1992; Jiménez *et al.*, 1997).

In summary, these results provide strong evidence of the use of both routes in Spanish (Sebastian, 1991; Dominguez and Cuetos, 1992; Jiménez and Hernández, 2000). They support the idea that the mechanisms of reading are not exclusively, nor mainly, attached to the transparency of the orthography. On the contrary, these studies in Spanish suggest that reading mechanisms are extendable to different orthographies, and their selection depends on the readers' ability. Expert readers are characterized by their flexibility in using one or the other strategy depending on the requirements of the task, while learners are conditioned by the extent of their graphic vocabulary, and their mastery of the conversion rules.

POOR VERSUS GOOD READERS

The definition of the mechanisms of reading has been of considerable help in interpreting children's difficulties in learning to read, and has provided a successful rationale for the design of intervention techniques. The empirical data from the comparison between good and poor readers have also provided positive evidence of the reliability of this approach.

The dominant idea supported by most of the research is that children with reading difficulties (RD) present a deficit in the process of phonology. This research points to the lack of ability to use the rules for Grapheme to Phoneme Conversion (henceforth GPC) as the main cause of RD.

In a follow-up study, Bravo *et al.* (1996) found that children with RD maintained lower scores than normal readers in a reading test after four courses of education. Only a subgroup of RD children showed an improvement in their performance. The children in this group obtained better scores in the phonological tasks. In addition, Dominguez and Cuetos (1992) argued that poor readers exhibit a deficit in the phonological analysis of printed words and found a similar association with phonological abilities. Their worse scores corresponded to the reading of the pseudoword, a task that requires the use of the GPC rules, and in which visual strategies have no effect. In a recent study, Jiménez and Hernández (2000) obtained similar results. Children with RD achieved lower scores both in naming and lexical decision tasks when pseudowords were implied. These data were also interpreted as evidence that children with RD have difficulties in learning the GPC rules (Valle and Cuetos, 1988; Defior *et al.*, 1996).

A number of studies provide strong support for the relationship between phonological awareness and reading performance. Phonological awareness refers to the ability to recognize that words are decomposable and to carry out mental operations with their segments (Alegría, 1985; Morais, 1994). It has been stated that phonological awareness has several components (Carrillo, 1994), which could have different effects on reading acquisition depending on the transparency of the language (Morais, 1995; Jiménez 1997). Jiménez (1997) looked at the issue of whether children with RD differed from their normal control age and reading level-matched counterparts in phonological awareness. The results showed differences between normal and poor readers in phonological awareness.

However, their scores were equivalent to those obtained by the reading level-match group in an odd-word-out task, but lower in tasks where phoneme monitoring was required. Consequently, there is a causal relationship between phonological awareness and reading difficulties. Such findings allow the interpretation of the poorer performance of children with RD when they have to read by the phonological route (Dominguez and Cuetos, 1992; Jiménez and Hernández, 2000).

Important evidence for the dissociation between the phonological and lexical mechanisms comes from the different pattern produced when word frequency is manipulated. Children with RD were better at reading words than pseudowords, they produce more lexicalizations (Jiménez and Hernández, 2000), and differences between poor and normal readers tend to disappear with age and in tasks that involve frequent words (Dominguez and Cuetos, 1992; Defior *et al.*, 1996). These results suggest that the continuous exposure to printed words helps children to compensate for their phonological deficits by the use of a visual strategy. Children with RD take advantage of the visual route to gain access to their mental lexicons, but their poorer level is found when the task requires phonological awareness.

It is worth noting the parallel between normal and poor readers' development. Although poor readers' scores on reading tasks are lower, their performance follows the same pattern as that of normal readers. Both use the same mechanisms. However, while normal readers take equivalent advantage of both routes, poor readers have limited phonological resources. Education received at school may improve their performance, probably caused by the increase in their visual lexicon, but differences from normal readers still remain. Only specific instruction on phonological abilities would allow poor readers to overcome their deficits.

DYSLEXIA

As stated earlier, the cognitive approach has become the most promising for the explanation of reading alterations. The aim of cognitive psychology is to outline the functional structure of the reading process. It is assumed that processes are not unitary, but composed by a set of subprocesses that are highly specialized (Sánchez Bernardos, 1992; Cuetos, 1999). Thus, there are a number of identifiable components involved in the process from printed words to meaning. A second assumption concerns the independence of these subprocesses. Their contributions take part in a sequence of independent operations. In the case of reading, visual recognition activates letter identification; this could initiate grapheme to phoneme conversion, and so on, before gaining access to the lexicon. All the components contribute to achieve the final result, therefore the alteration could be caused by a single element not working properly, while the others operated correctly. Independence and sequentiality are the essential cues to understanding reading alterations.

The disturbances showed by some children are characterized by a general difficulty in assigning the sound of the word. They have difficulties in segmenting the word into phonemes or manipulating them (Valle and Cuetos, 1988; Cuetos, 1999). The most common errors children make are confusions between phonemes that share many phonetic features like /m/ and /b/, /p/ and /b/ or /g/ and /j/. Therefore, some words are mistaken for others similar in sound, but not in meaning: *baja* ('short') for *paja* ('straw'). As it is very exceptional to find a complete division between reading and writing skills, children with reading disabilities may produce equivalent errors when writing. Therefore, they could mistake graphemes whose corresponding phonemes have phonetic similarities.

Other dyslexic children's mistakes are focused on the orthographic structure of the word. They seem to have problems distinguishing words with similar orthography. As an example they can read *cine* ('cinema') as *cena* ('dinner'), or mistake words with the same pronunciation, but different spelling as *ola* ('wave') and *hola* ('hello') or as *vaca* ('cow') and *baca* ('support'). These children produce persistent misspellings in writing. In Spanish some phonemes can be represented by more than one grapheme: for instance /b/ by b or v, or /χ/ by g or j. Since there are no rules to specify the correct orthography, the only way is to keep it in memory, and this is exactly what dyslexics are not able to do.

Nevertheless, these two routes are not so clear-cut in practice, mainly in the case of developmental dyslexia. Most children show both types of errors, and the diagnosis should be made as a function of the number of times a type of error is present (Cuetos, 1999; Montfort, 2000). Some authors have assumed that the phonological deficit is the core of any reading difficulty, and lexical errors are a consequence of it (Bradley and Brian, 1983; Morais, 1994; Snowling, 1998). There is abundant evidence of the impact of the phono-logical mechanism on reading acquisition (Jiménez and Artiles, 1990), reading develop-ment (Cuetos, 1989; Valle, 1996), reading difficulties (Defior *et al.*, 1996; Snowling, 1998; Jiménez and Hernández, 2000), and in remediation (Valle and Cuetos, 1988; Rueda *et al.*, 1990; Rueda and Sánchez, 1996).

One tentative explanation is that the core of reading is the identification of segments and their correspondence to sound patterns. This mechanism makes it possible to read any word, known or unknown. When the mechanism fails, children make many mistakes and have to rely on memory and analogical strategies (Sebastian and Parreno, 1995). Their reading performance depends on the mental representation of visual words, and the ability to recognize similarities in written strings. Furthermore, the fact that poor and good readers' visual lexicons develop in parallel while their phonological mechanisms do not progress at the same level could be due to the specificity of phonological abilities and their dependency on training. Although some phonological abilities are ready before children receive instruction (i.e. rime, alliteration), it is the acquisition of literacy that constitutes the main driving force in the development of phonological awareness (Carrillo, 1994; Rueda and Sánchez, 1996). An amount of evidence for the facilitation of phonological awareness for reading has identified word segmentation and the lack of ability in the use of GPC rules as a causative variable of reading difficulties (Dominguez and Cuetos, 1992; Defior *et al.*, 1996). However, although phonological segmentation has been demonstrated to be a central resource in improving children's performance, which is generalized to non-taught tasks (Rueda *et al.*, 1990), the improvement is limited to writing tasks, showing little effect on reading performance (Rueda and Sánchez, 1996). It seems to suggest that reading is a complex process that involves the concurrent function of several mechanisms. In this sense, although phonological segmentation is an effective mechanism, reading also involves mechanisms required to recover the whole structure of the word, the use of GPC rules, syntactic analysis, and the other resources for text comprehension (Coltheart and Jackson, 1987; Cuetos, 1999). Admitting that at present we have no empirical data to assess the contribution of different mechanisms on reading, given the facilitation of phonologi-cal training, we propose the integration of different strategies to plan the intervention, and a detailed evaluation to determine individual patterns of alteration.

READING METHODS

There has been intense debate concerning the choice of the most suitable method of learning to read and its adequacy to the orthographical system adopted by a language. As a general description, global or analytic methods start by making the child familiar with some words, leaving the identification of segments to a second stage. On the other hand, synthetic methods aim at the instruction of the codification of the alphabetic units. Thus, the child is instructed in sound–letter correspondence, and practice with all possible combinations of consonants and vowels.

Studies performed in order to contrast the effect of the methods have shown that children will extend the strategy biased by the method. Thus, children who learnt by an analytic method show a tendency to read by a visual strategy, while segmentation strategies are more frequently adopted by children who were trained by a synthetic method. In addition, children are more efficient in phonological tasks when their learning has been oriented to the alphabet: they are less dependent on contextual variables, and get better results reading pseudowords (Leybaert and Content, 1995; Jiménez et al., 1997). Nevertheless, differences disappear after school training. It indicates, on the one hand, that independent of the method, teachers should teach phonological decodification and, on the other, that in the absence of difficulties children can acquire phonological awareness with maturation (Claros et al., 1999).

The facilitation shown by the phonological methods is congruent with the research reported earlier. If reading involves identification of segments, and identification of letter–sound correspondences, a method specially designed to teach these abilities should be successful. The benefits should be more evident in a transparent orthography.

In Spain, many teachers have adopted a method called 'Erase una vez . . .' (Once upon a time . . .), which is providing very good results. Structured as a story where letters have the main roles, the method instructs children in the mechanisms of reading by identifying letters and their peculiarities. Easy to comprehend, and attractive enough for children, it constitutes an appropriate method to improve phonological skills.

CONCLUSION

The research reported here has shed light on the effect of phonological awareness, the skill in the use of conversion rules, and lexical strategies in learning to read and reading difficulties (see also Goswami, Schulte-Körne, in this volume). When considered in detail, reading is a complex process that proceeds from print pattern to meaning following a number of steps. A direct assumption is that the source of disturbance could come from any of these steps. It is the task of the expert to determine the scope of the disorder presented by the dyslexic patient.

Developmental dyslexia involves an extensive set of symptoms (Ellis, 1993), but none of them serves as a critical feature to delimit its diagnosis. Rather it is the constellation of symptoms that allows a child to be considered as dyslexic (Shallice and Warrington, 1980; Ellis and Young, 1988). On the other hand, as the failure could be in any of the abilities or mechanisms involved in reading, patients are characterized by their lack of similarity. Furthermore, children with reading disabilities differ not only in symptoms, but also in their severity. As can be observed, many issues still await future research. One issue is to determine the contribution of any of the components involved in the process of reading to acquisition failures. Another challenge is to evaluate whether the phonological awareness involved in reading is related to more general phoneme monitoring skills that also affect lexical processing (Goswami and Bryant, 1990). The comparative analysis of the learning progress in different languages could help to channel the research to these critical points and provide tools for evaluation and detection of reading deficits, and design methods for intervention.

REFERENCES

Alegría, J. (1985) Por un enfoque psicolingüístico del aprendizaje de la lectura y sus dificultades. *Infancia y Aprendizaje*, 29, 79–94.

Bradley, L. and Brian, P.E. (1983) Categorizing sounds and learning to read. A causal connect. *Nature*, 271, 246–247.

Bravo, I., Bermeosolo, J., Pinto, A. and Oyarzo, E. (1996) Seguimiento de niños con retraso lector severero. *Infancia y Aprendizaje*, 76, 3–12.

Carrillo, M. (1994) Development of phonological awareness and reading acquisition. *Reading and Writing*, 6, 279–298.

Claros, R.M., Guerrero, D., de la Torre, C., Giménez de la Peña, A. and Conde, M.I. (1999) *Análisis léxico y facilitación de la lecto-escritura*. Madrid: Congreso Iberoamericano de Psicología.

Coltheart, M. and Jackson, N.E. (1998) Defining dyslexia. *Child Psychology and Psychiatry Review*, 3, 12–16.

Cuetos, F. (1989) Lectura y escritura de palabras a traves de la ruta fonológica. *Infancia y Aprendizaje*, 45, 71–84.

Cuetos, F. (1999) *Evaluación y Rehabilitación de las Afasias*. Madrid: Científica-Médica.

Cuetos, F., Aguado, G. and Caramazza, A. (2000) Dissociation of semantic and phonological errors in naming. *Brain and Language*, 75(3), 451–460.

Cuetos, F., Dominguez, A., Mira, G. and De Vega, M. (1997) Diferencias individuales en el procesamiento léxico. *Estudios de Psicología*, 57, 15–27.

Cuetos, F., Valle Arroyo, F. and Suárez, M.P. (1996) A case of phonological dyslexia in Spanish. *Cognitive Neuropsychology*, 13, 1–24.

Cuetos, P. and Ellis, A.W. (1999) Visual paralexias in a Spanish-speaking patient with acquired dyslexia: A consequence of visual and semantic impairments? *Cortex*, 35, 661–674.

Defior, S., Justicia, F. and Martos, F.J. (1996) The influence of lexical and sublexical variables in normal and poor Spanish readers. *Reading and Writing*, 8, 487–497.

Defior, S., Justicia, F. and Martos, F. (1998) Desarrollo del reconocimiento de palabras en lectores normales y retrasados en función de diferentes variables lingüísticas. *Infancia y Aprendizaje*, 83, 59–74.

Dieguez Vide, F., Boehm, P., Gold, A., Roche Lecours, A. and Pena Casanova, J. (1999) Acquired dyslexias and dysgraphias: II. Clinical protocol for the assessment and analysis of reading and writing disorders in Spanish. *Journal of Neurolinguistics*, 12, 115–146.

Dominguez, A. and Cuetos, F. (1992) Desarrollo de las habilidades de reconocimiento de palabras en niños con distinta competencia lectora. *Cognitiva*, 4(2), 193–208.

Ellis, A.W. (1993) *Reading, Writing and Dyslexia: A Cognitive Analysis*. Hove: Lawrence Erlbaum Associates.

Ellis, A.W. and Young, A.W. (1988) *Human Cognitive Neuropsychology*. London: Lawrence Erlbaum Associates.

González-Portal, D. (1984) El diagnóstico precoz como medida preventiva de las dificultades de aprendizaje de la lectura. *Revista de Psicología General y Aplicada*, 39(1), 59–73.

Goswami, U. and Bryant, P.E. (1990) *Phonological Skills and Learning to Read*. Hillsdale, NJ: Lawrence Erlbaum Associates.

Jiménez, J.E. (1997) A reading-level match study of phonemic processes underlying reading disabilities in a transparent orthography. *Reading and Writing*, 9, 23–40.

Jiménez, J.E. and Artiles, C. (1990) Factores predictivos del exito en el aprendizaje de la lecto-escritura. *Infancia y Aprendizaje*, 49, 21–36.

Jiménez, J.E., Guzman, R. and Artiles, C. (1997) Efectos de la frecuencia silabica posicional en el aprendizaje de la lectura. *Infancia y Aprendizaje*, 9, 3–27.

Jiménez, J.E. and Hernández, I. (2000) Word identification and reading disorders in the Spanish language. *Journal of Learning Disabilities*, 33, 44–60.

Jiménez, J.E. and Rodrigo, M.J. (1997) Is it true that the differences in reading performance between students with and without LD cannot be explained by IQ? *Journal of Learning Disabilities*, 27, 155–163.

Justicia F., Defior, S., Pelegrina, S. and Martos, F.J. (1999) Sources of error in Spanish writing. *Journal of Research in Reading*, 22, 198–202.

Leybaert, J. and Content, A. (1995) Reading and spelling acquisition in two different teaching methods: A test of the independence hypothesis. *Reading and Writing: An Interdisciplinary Journal*, 7, 65–88.

Montfort, M. (2000) Dyslexia: Oral and written language disorder: A new look at old links. *Folia Phoniatrica et Logopaedica*, 52, 7–13.

Morais, J. (1994) *El arte de leer*. Madrid: Visor.

Morais, J. (1995) Do orthographies and phonological peculiarities of alphabetically written languages influence the course of literacy acquisition? *Reading and Writing*, 7, 1–7.

Morais, J., Alegría, J. and Content, A. (1987) The relationship between segmental analysis and alphabetic literacy. *Cahiers de Psychologie Cognitive*, 7, 415–438.

Rueda, M. and Sánchez, E. (1996) Relación entre conocimiento fonémico y dislexia: Un estudio instruccional. *Cognitiva*, 8(2), 215–234.

Rueda, M., Sánchez, E. and González, L. (1990) El análisis de la palabra como instrumento para la rehabilitación de la dislexia. *Infancia y Aprendizaje*, 43, 39–52.

Sebastian, N. (1991) Reading by analogy in a shallow orthography. *Journal of Experimental Psychology: Human Perception and Performance*, 17, 471–477.

Sebastian, N. and Parreno, A. (1995) The development of analogical reading in Spanish. *Reading and Writing*, 7, 23–38.

Shallice, T. and Warrington, E.K. (1980) Single and multiple component in central dyslexic syndromes. In M. Coltheart, K.E. Patterson and J.C. Marshal (eds), *Deep Dyslexia*. London: Routledge & Kegan Paul.

Snowling, M. (1998) Dyslexia as a phonological deficit: Evidence and implications. *Child Psychology and Psychiatry Review*, 3, 4–11.

Valle, F. (1996) Dual route models in Spanish: Developmental and neuropsychological data. In M. Carreiras, J.E. Garcia Albea and N. Sebastian (eds), *Language Processing in Spanish*. Hillsdale, NJ: Lawrence Erlbaum Associates.

Valle, F. and Cuetos, F. (1988) La dislexia desde el enfoque neurocognitivo. *Revista de Neurología de San Pau*, 10, 9–19.

19

DYSLEXIA IN SWEDISH

Ingvar Lundberg

READING INSTRUCTION IN SWEDEN

Before we discuss the problem of dyslexia, the teaching of reading will briefly be described. A more thorough review has been presented in Lundberg (1999a). The relatively shallow Swedish orthography has led to the inclusion of phonics elements in the early reading instruction. Attempts are made to keep a balance between analytic and synthetic methods. Listening, speaking, reading and writing are integrated from the start, which is in contrast to many other countries where writing is typically introduced later in the programme. In Sweden, writing is supposed to support the acquisition of reading and facilitate the task of breaking the alphabetic code. Phonemic segmentation and sound blending are emphasized early by the majority of teachers. A whole language approach has inspired many teachers but they still insist on giving explicit instruction in the alphabetic principle.

There is no officially adopted or accepted definition of dyslexia in Sweden. The practice varies from completely denying the existence of the condition to an over-application of the label. Medical doctors and psychologists tend to take their diagnosis from DSM-IV. In particular, they want to emphasize the discrepancy definition where dyslexia is defined as a marked (not specified) discrepancy between IQ (instrument not specified) and reading achievement (neither instrument, nor aspect of reading specified). Among some psychologists this practice might be defended by reference to the fact that only psychologists have the right to assess IQ and thus only psychologists are qualified to diagnose dyslexia.

On the other hand, more and more practitioners and researchers in Sweden have come to realize the basic shortcomings of the discrepancy definition. They have assimilated the message from Linda Siegel, Keith Stanovich, Jack Fletcher and others concerning the limited validity of a discrepancy definition of dyslexia (Fletcher et al., 1994; Siegel, 1989; Stanovich and Siegel, 1994; Lundberg, 1999b). They have also been influenced by our Norwegian-Swedish textbook on dyslexia (Höien and Lundberg, 1991) where we suggested a definition of dyslexia very similar to the one proposed by the International

International Book of Dyslexia: A Cross-Language Comparison and Practice Guide. Edited by Ian Smythe, John Everatt and Robin Salter.   ISBN 0471498416   © 2004 John Wiley & Sons, Ltd.

Dyslexia Association several years later. We emphasized word identification as the core problem in dyslexia, a problem in most cases based on poor phonological processing. Our definition states:

> Dyslexia is a disturbance in certain linguistic functions which are important in using the alphabetic principle in the decoding of language. The disturbance first appears as a difficulty in obtaining automatic word decoding in the reading process. The disturbance is also revealed in poor writing ability. The dyslexic disturbance is generally passed on in families and one can suppose that a genetic disposition underlies the condition. Another characteristic of dyslexia is that the disturbance is persistent. Even though reading ability can eventually reach an acceptable performance level, poor writing skills most often remain. With a more thorough testing of the phonological abilities, one finds that the weakness in this area often persists into adulthood. (Höien and Lundberg, 2000)

THE PREVALENCE OF DYSLEXIA

As the concept of dyslexia has been used in different ways, it is not possible to estimate the prevalence of dyslexia in a reliable way. If we restrict the term to apply to serious reading and spelling problems based on difficulties at the word level, often caused by phonological problems, it seems as if many Swedish experts agree on an estimate of 4–8 per cent of the school population. On average, you will then find one or two cases of pure dyslexia in each school class.

Among adults estimation is more difficult. In the Swedish part of the International Adult Literacy Study (IALS; OECD, 2000) the self-reported incidence of dyslexia amounted to only 1.5 per cent which probably reflects under-reporting. The proportion of Swedes who only reached the lowest proficiency level was much higher than 1.5 per cent. In fact, only 18 per cent of the group reaching the lowest literacy level reported dyslexic problems. As already mentioned, Level 1 on the IALS scale is certainly a very low level, and one would expect that the majority of the Swedes at that level suffer from dyslexia. The low proportion of self-reported dyslexia might then reflect compliance or social desirability during the interview but also the fact that a high proportion of low-achieving Swedes have immigrant status.

When discussing the prevalence of dyslexia we should remember that a low level of literacy does not in itself necessarily reflect dyslexic problems. Linguistic, cultural, social, motivational and instructional factors may be important reasons for low achievement.

The many problems in comprehending a text might thus be caused by a number of factors. Poor motivation, poor cognitive functioning, limited vocabulary and limited world knowledge are not necessarily basic dyslexic factors. As our definition suggests, the current conception of dyslexia rather points at word decoding and phonological problems as the core symptoms of dyslexia. However, this does not prevent secondary effects occurring at other levels of processing. Thus, it might sometimes be difficult to isolate dyslexia as such; it may well co-occur with a large number of other functional disturbances, such as ADHD, general cognitive problems, specific language impairments, sensory handicaps, emotional disturbances and social and cultural deprivation (see also Samuelsson *et al.*, 2000b).

In Swedish society a vast majority of people grow up in environments where there is at least the potential for rich literacy stimulation (environmental print, pre-school settings, literate adult models, newspapers, magazines, books, libraries, etc.). Children, almost regardless of social background, have thus a rich potential, an abundant source for 'niche picking' in a society where literacy skills have long been highly valued (see Lundberg, 1991). However, children with a less favourable genetic disposition may avoid the benefits of rich environmental stimulation. Thus, in highly literate societies with well-developed educational systems like Sweden, individual differences in literacy skills may be more related to genetic factors than to a lack of opportunity to learn.

PHONOLOGICAL AWARENESS AND READING DISABILITY

The concept of dyslexia as a phonological deficit has guided much Swedish dyslexia research. The strong relationship between phonological awareness and later success in reading acquisition was demonstrated quite early by Lundberg *et al.* (1980). Their results have been replicated over and over again across languages, ages, and tasks used to measure phonological awareness (see Höien and Lundberg, 2000, for a review).

One distinctive advantage in doing research on the relationship between phonological awareness and reading in Sweden has been the late school start. Until recently most children did not start school before the age of 7. Thus, one can find perfectly healthy and cognitively well-developed children who, by the age of 7, know only a few letters and cannot read a single word (except for a few logographs). The main reason for this state of affairs is the simple fact that they have not yet enjoyed the benefit of explicit reading instruction. This situation makes it possible to avoid the confounding effects of reading skill and reading instruction when the critical role of phonological awareness is examined. It is also possible to clarify the role of general cognitive development.

READING DISABILITY CAN BE PREDICTED
AND PREVENTED

In our research we have attempted to answer a number of questions discussed in the current literature on the relationship between phonological awareness, reading acquisition and dyslexia.

A commonly held view is that reading instruction is necessary for the development of phonemic awareness. However, we have demonstrated that phonemic awareness can be developed among Scandinavian pre-schoolers outside the context of formal reading instruction without the use of letters or other elements of early reading instruction. Lundberg *et al.* (1988) designed a Danish programme based on earlier Swedish work which required daily games and exercises in group settings over a full pre-school year. The programme included listening games, rhymes and ditties, playing with sentences and words, discovering the initial sounds of words and finally carrying out full segmentation of words into phonemes. (An American version of this programme is now available; Adams *et al.*, 1998.)

The effects of this programme were very clear and it could be concluded that phonemic awareness can be developed among pre-schoolers by training, without introducing letters or written text. A more crucial element seems to be the explicit guidance of children when they are trying to access, attend to and extract the elusive, abstract, and implicit segments of language.

The crucial question now is whether explicit training in pre-school also facilitates later reading and spelling acquisition in school. The pre-school children studied by Lundberg *et al.* (1988) were followed up through four school years, and reading and spelling were assessed on several occasions. The trained group outperformed the control group on each of 12 points of measurement, indicating the beneficial effect of the pre-school programme.

Lundberg (1994) presented data from children in pre-school with a high risk of developing reading disability as revealed in a pre-test on phonological awareness and general language development. Risk children who were involved in the training programme had fairly normal reading and spelling development, whereas the control children showed the expected poor literacy development. Thus, it seems to be possible to prevent the development of reading and spelling disabilities in school by a carefully designed pre-school programme which brings the children to a level of phonological awareness that is sufficiently high to meet the demands involved in the alphabetic system. The children at risk who did not enjoy the benefit of such training seemed to face serious obstacles on their way to literacy.

Olofsson (1999) followed up a group of students 20 years after their first diagnosis as dyslexics by the age of 8. In comparison with a control group, they had clear and persistent problems in tasks involving phonological processing demands, although their reading comprehension was not significantly inferior to the control subjects.

In another longitudinal study Jacobson and Lundberg (2000) followed the reading development of 90 dyslexic students from Grade 2 to Grade 9 and analysed their growth curves. Some 25 per cent of the variance of the individual slopes could be explained in a multiple regression where intelligence and phonological factors made a significant contribution. This kind of analysis deserves more attention since it can answer the critical question of which factors determine individual success. Knowledge of these factors would have important implications for remedial work in special education.

NEURO-BIOLOGICAL PERSPECTIVES

A step in the direction of finding a neurological correlate to the phonological problems was taken by Larsen *et al.* (1990) in a study of 15-year-old dyslexics in Stavanger. Brain scans (MRI) revealed that the planum temporale tended to be of equal size in the two hemispheres more often among dyslexics than among normal controls. More specifically, however, all dyslexics with severe phonological problems had symmetry of the plana temporale. We still do not know, however, how this deviation from the normal pattern in the language cortex affects the development of phonological coding and other processes necessary for fluent reading.

It would be tempting to look for a clear-cut dyslexia diagnosis by using brain imaging and referring people with symmetric plana to the dyslexic category. Even if one ignores the discouraging costs, such a procedure is not feasible. It would certainly be very difficult to reliably assess the symmetry of individual cases. Individual variability is considerable. One can also find individuals with strong indications of dyslexia based on other criteria but with perfectly normal asymmetry of planum temporale as well as non-dyslexic individuals with symmetry.

An interesting case of developmental surface dyslexia has been reported by Samuelsson

(2000). The child had a very early acquired and well localized brain damage in the occipital region which might explain her inability to use an orthographic or logographic strategy in reading and spelling.

Functional studies will certainly reveal more about the neurobiological basis of dyslexia in the near future. Martin Ingvar and Torkel Klingvall in Stockholm are Swedish brain scientists who have already significantly contributed to a deeper neurobiological understanding of dyslexia.

PSYCHOLOGICAL AND SOCIAL DIMENSIONS OF READING DISABILITY

The failure to learn an important skill in school, such as reading, will certainly have profound effects on an individual, far beyond a circumscribed disturbance of the phonological module. The social perspective on reading disabilities is provided by studies of the long-term unemployed, prisoners and inmates in institutions for juvenile delinquents.

A study of the long-term unemployed

Lindgren and Ingvar (1996) found in a study of the population of people who had been unemployed for more than 12 months that at least one out of five had serious reading and spelling problems. The test battery primarily captured manifest reading ability without going beneath the surface and investigating word recognition and phonological processing. Thus, the prevalence of dyslexia in a more restricted sense cannot be estimated. However, this conclusion is important. A strategic measure to be taken for many long-term unemployed individuals must involve intense training of reading and writing skills.

The prison population

Recently, two studies have been conducted in Sweden, reporting high frequencies of dyslexic problems in different samples of prison inmates (Alm and Andersson, 1997; Jensen *et al.*, 1998). Alm and Andersson (1995) found that 39 out of 61 prison inmates (64 per cent) exhibited reading and writing skills that were below average for Grade 6 children (12 year olds); they also concluded that 19 out of 61 inmates (31 per cent) in their sample showed reading and writing deficits attributable to dyslexic problems. Jensen *et al.* (1998) reported similar findings. They found that 26 out of 63 inmates could be diagnosed as dyslexics (41 per cent) and that an additional 10 cases were borderline cases (10 per cent). However, there are methodological drawbacks associated with these Swedish studies, involving high attrition rates and lack of relevant control groups together with controversial assessment methods. Information on distinguishing between poor reading caused by lack of educational opportunity and poor reading caused by phonological coding deficits has not been reported.

The first step to overcome some of the problems mentioned was taken in a study by Samuelsson *et al.* (2000b), where we estimated that about 10 per cent of the prison population suffered from dyslexic problems, that is, just a slightly higher prevalence than in a normal population and far below earlier estimates. The extensive literacy problems observed among the inmates were interpreted as based on social, cultural and educational deprivation rather than constitutionally based dyslexia.

In a study in progress we have a more extensive battery of tests, questionnaires and interviews with a total testing time of about four hours for each participant. We have also two comparison groups, one group of younger individuals matched on reading level and one group of adult readers matched on educational level and reading habits.

Institutions for juvenile delinquents

Studies by Svensson *et al.* (2000) have attempted to estimate the prevalence of literacy problems in the population of juvenile delinquents in Swedish institutions. The picture turned out to be more complex than had been reported earlier. Literacy problems are certainly common among the inmates, but a surprisingly large number of pupils show adequate reading and spelling skills. In the poorly achieving group (about 25 per cent) immigrant youngsters are highly over-represented. Immigrant pupils often show adequate word reading ability but fail in text comprehension tasks. Dyslexia in the restricted sense (word recognition problems based on deficit phonological coding) was not more frequent among the inmates than in the normal population (6–8 per cent).

DYSLEXIA AND CREATIVITY

Our main focus so far has been on dyslexia as a serious handicap in the current knowledge society. However, there might be another side to the coin. Studying dyslexia is not just a question of identifying disabilities. Equally important may be looking for abilities. It has been suggested that dyslexics sometimes show uncommon gifts, skills, and talents in fields like creative arts, architecture, construction, handicraft, design, etc. (see West, 1997). Systematic studies of this assumption are few, however. An attempt at clarification has recently been made by Wolff and Lundberg (2000). We studied a sample of students in creative arts and photography and compared them with a sample of students in business school. Both types of higher education have very restricted admission policies with about 10 per cent selection rate. Among the art students close to 30 per cent showed dyslexic tendencies. In contrast, such tendencies were almost completely absent among the students in business school. Further studies on this issue are under way.

REFERENCES

Adams, M.J., Foorman, B.R., Lundberg, I. and Beeler, T. (1998) *Phonemic Awareness in Young Children*. Baltimore, MD: Brookes.

Alm, J. and Andersson, J. (1997) A study of literacy in prisons in Uppsala. *Dyslexia*, 3, 245–246.

Fletcher, J.M., Shaywitz, S.E., Shankweiler, D., Katz, L., Liberman, I., Stuebing, K.K., Francis, D.J., Fowler, A. and Shaywitz, B.A. (1994) Cognitive profiles of reading disability: Comparisons of discrepancy and low achievement definitions. *Journal of Educational Psychology*, 86, 6–23.

Gustafson, S., Samuelsson, S. and Rönnberg, J. (2000) Why do some resist phonological intervention? A Swedish longitudinal study of poor readers in grade 4. *Scandinavian Journal of Educational Psychology*, 44, 146–162.

Höien, T. and Lundberg, I. (1991) *Dysleksi*. Oslo: Gyldendal.

Höien, T. and Lundberg, I. (2000) *Dyslexia. From Theory to Practice*. Dordrecht: Kluwer Academic Publishers.

Jacobson, C. and Lundberg, I. (2000) Early prediction of individual growth in reading. *Reading and Writing: An Interdisciplinary Journal*, 13, 273–296.

Jensen, J., Lindgren, M., Wirsén-Meurling, A., Ingvar, D. and Levander, S. (1999) Dyslexia among inmates in relation to neuropsychology and personality. *Journal of the International Neuropsychological Society*, 5, 452–461.

Larsen, J.P., Höien, T., Lundberg, I. and Ödegaard, H. (1990) MRI evaluation of the size and the symmetry of planum temporale in adolescents with developmental dyslexia. *Brain and Language*, 39, 289–301.

Lindgren, M. and Ingvar, D. (1996) Reading and writing disabilities in Swedish unemployed adults. Assessment and remediation. (Submitted paper.)

Lundberg, I. (1991) Reading as an individual and social skill. In I. Lundberg and T. Höien (eds), *Literacy in a World of Change*. Stavanger: Center for Reading Research/UNESCO.

Lundberg, I. (1994) Reading difficulties can be predicted and prevented: A Scandinavian perspective on phonological awareness and reading. In C. Hulme and M. Snowling (eds), *Reading Development and Dyslexia*. London: Whurr.

Lundberg, I. (1999a) Learning to read in Scandinavia. In M. Harris and G. Hatano (eds), *Learning to Read and Write. A Cross-Linguistic Perspective*. Cambridge: Cambridge University Press.

Lundberg, I. (1999b) Towards a sharper definition of dyslexia. In I. Lundberg, F.E. Tönnessen and I. Austad (eds), *Dyslexia: Advances in Theory and Practice*. Dordrecht: Kluwer Academic Publishers.

Lundberg, I., Frost, J. and Petersen, O.-P. (1988) Effects of an extensive program for stimulating phonological awareness in preschool children. *Reading Research Quarterly*, 33, 263–284.

Lundberg, I., Olofsson, Å. and Wall, S. (1980) Reading and spelling skills in the first school years predicted from phonemic awareness skills in kindergarten. *Scandinavian Journal of Psychology*, 21, 159–173.

Miller Guron, L. and Lundberg, I. (in press) Dyslexia and second language reading. A second bite at the apple. *Journal of Research in Reading*, 26, 69–82.

OECD (2000) *Literacy, Economy and Society*. Paris: OECD.

Olofsson, Å. (1999) Early reading problems: A follow-up 20 years later. In I. Lundberg, F.E. Tönnessen and I. Austad (eds), *Dyslexia: Advances in Theory and Practice*. Dordrecht: Kluwer Academic Publishers.

Samuelsson, S. (2000) Converging evidence for the role of occipital regions in orthographic processing: A case of developmental dyslexia. *Neuropsychologia*, 4, 351–362.

Samuelsson, S., Finnström, O., Leijon, I., and Mård, S. (2000a) Phonological and surface profiles of reading difficulties among very low birth weight children: Converging evidence for the developmental lag hypothesis. *Scientific Studies of Reading*, 4, 197–214.

Samuelsson, S., Gustavsson, A., Herkner, B. and Lundberg, I. (2000b) Is the frequency of dyslexic problems among prison inmates higher than in a normal population? *Reading and Writing: An Interdisciplinary Journal*, 13, 297–312.

Siegel, L.S. (1989) IQ is irrelevant to the definition of learning disabilities. *Journal of Learning Disabilities*, 22, 469–479.

Stanovich, K.E. and Siegel, L.S. (1994) The phenotypic performance profile of reading-disabled children: A regression-based test of the phonological-core variable-difference model. *Journal of Educational Psychology*, 86, 24–53.

Svensson, I., Lundberg, I. and Jacobson, C. (2000) The prevalence of reading disabilities among inmates at Swedish institutions for juvenile delinquents. (Paper submitted.)

West, T.G. (1997) *In the Mind's Eye*. New York: Prometheus Books.

Wolff, U. and Lundberg, I. (2000) Dyslexia and creativity. Paper presented at the International Dyslexia Association conference in Washington, DC, Nov. 2000.

20

ISSUES IN THE ASSESSMENT OF READING DISABILITY IN SECOND LANGUAGE CHILDREN

Esther Geva and Lesly Wade-Woolley

INTRODUCTION

In the past, minority children in certain immigrant groups were discriminated against and regarded as educationally inferior, and were much more likely to be identified as slow learners and placed in special education classes (Cummins, 1984, 1989). Some have argued that in Western countries psychological assessments were (mis)used to legitimize the 'educational disabling' of immigrant and minority children (Cummins, 1989; Ogbu, 1978). Arguments were made that minority and immigrant children with limited proficiency in the language of the majority are over-represented in programmes designed for the learning disabled and language handicapped (Benavides, 1989; Ortiz and Ramirez, 1989). The main concern was that observations made about the learners' less than perfect oral language proficiency were taken as evidence for a learning problem, and that professionals often have little understanding of issues related to limited English proficiency, leading to misinterpretation of data gathered as part of the referral and assessment process, and erroneous decisions to delay further assessment.

In response to these concerns, current approaches to ESL literacy acquisition encourage teachers to consider the gap between the development of everyday highly contextualized language use, which emerges quickly, and decontextualized, school-like, academic language, which takes much longer to develop in English as a second language (ESL) children (Cummins, 1984). Ironically, Limbos and Geva (2001) found that teachers in multi-ethnic multi-lingual classrooms are highly sensitive to equitable teaching practices, and perhaps for this reason, they tend to withhold judgement about ESL children who may show similar warning signs to those noted in at-risk first language (L1) children.

International Book of Dyslexia: A Cross-Language Comparison and Practice Guide. Edited by Ian Smythe, John Everatt and Robin Salter. ISBN 0471498416 © 2004 John Wiley & Sons, Ltd.

Limbos and Geva (2001) report that a higher number of primary level ESL children who were at-risk were never referred for assessment, though teachers had a higher 'hit rate' in correctly identifying L1 children who were at-risk. Further, teachers rated ESL students whose oral language skills were good as being adequate readers despite evidence that some of these children had poor reading skills. These results and those of others (e.g., Cline and Frederickson, 1999) indicate that teachers of young school children tend to rely on oral language fluency in ESL students as an indicator of acceptable progress in the development of reading skills.

In this chapter we discuss key issues in the research literature on the development of second language (L2) reading skills in young school children. Our objective is to tie this research to potential implications for assessment. At the same time, we wish to emphasize that while there is a vast amount of research on children learning to read in their L1, less is known about the dimensions which distinguish children who learn to read in their L2 with little difficulty and children whose L2 literacy development is effortful and frustrating.

ASSESSMENT IN THE L1

As a response to concerns about the over-representation of minority children in special education classes, various approaches gradually emerged for alternative, culturally sensitive assessment procedures which included the use of principles of dynamic assessment, reliance on curriculum-based assessment, and a careful pre-referral process (e.g., Campione, 1989; Cline and Frederickson 1996; Cole, 1996; Dao, 1991; Duran, 1989; Figueroa, 1989; Gavillan-Torres, 1983; Oller and Damico, 1990; Samuels Tzuriel and Halloy-Miller 1988). One strong alternative assessment procedure that gained popularity is the notion that if a bilingual or ESL child does not make adequate progress in spite of instruction, assessment should take place in the Ll as well as in the child's L2 (Chamberlain and Medeiros-Landurand, 1991; Gopaul-McNicol and Thomas-Presswood, 1998; Ortiz and Ramirez, 1989). The rationale behind this is that assessment in the child's Ll may provide more complete and valid information about the child's 'true' strengths and weaknesses. Indeed, researchers and practitioners tend to assume that if assessment of a bilingual learner does not include data based on the child's Ll, it is unreliable, if not just plain 'biased' (Hamayan and Damico, 1990; Holtzman, Jr. and Wilkinson, 1991). In spite of good intentions, assessment in the Ll may be problematic, unfeasible, or perhaps unnecessary because of a variety of reasons such as:

- lack of trained professionals who can carry out assessments in the child's L1;
- lack of adequate reliable and valid assessment instruments in the child's home language (Sattler, 1992);
- Ll language loss and less than optimal conditions for maintaining and/or facilitating age-appropriate Ll language and literacy skills (Sattler, 1992; Schiff-Myers, 1992);
- the inadequacy of Ll instruments and norms developed in the home country to evaluate in a reliable and valid manner the cognitive and linguistic abilities and the educational achievement of children in immigrant communities (Geva 2000; Sattler, 1992).

It is clear from the above that assessment in the child's Ll is not a panacea for ensuring a valid assessment. In fact, an examination of new research on the development of L2 reading skills in bilingual and L2 children suggests that while assessment in the Ll can be useful in the data gathering process, it may be possible to assess accurately even when assessment in the Ll is not possible, or when it provides only partial information.

THE ROLE OF L2 ORAL LANGUAGE PROFICIENCY

Another issue involving the assessment of reading disabilities in L2 children concerns the role of oral language proficiency (OLP) in L2 reading, and the extent to which the development of L2 reading skills depends on adequate L2 linguistic proficiency. There are three groups of studies that help to understand the relation between OLP and reading in L2 children. One group pertains to reading comprehension processes, another pertaining to word recognition processes and the third relating to the relationships between word recognition and reading comprehension.

Ll-based research supports the existence of a positive relationship between OLP and reading comprehension in elementary school children (Chall, 1996; Scarborough, 2001). The available research on L2 also supports the idea that comprehension-based aspects of reading, including reading fluency, are facilitated by increasing levels of L2 oral proficiency. There is ample research evidence that a better command of elements of spoken language such as vocabulary, grammatical knowledge and discourse related knowledge is crucial for L2 text comprehension, and learning from text. Indeed, Chall (1996) underscores the importance of exposing L2 learners to enriched language programmes early on. In general, studies targeting students in higher grades find positive correlations between L2 proficiency and L2 reading comprehension (Anderson and Roit, 1996; Fitzgerald, 1995). Studies targeting primary level and junior level children (e.g., Chitiri Sun, Willows and Tylor, 1992; Gersten and Geva, 2003; Geva and Clifton, 1993; Geva, Yaghoubzadeh, and Petrulius-Wright, under review; Geva and Ryan, 1993; Verhoeven, 2000) also support the idea that various aspects of reading comprehension depend on increasing levels of OLP.

Another group of studies pertains to the role of OLP in the development of word-based reading skills in L2 children. Recent research has shown that the development of word recognition (that is, the ability to recognize printed words out of context) in children learning to read in their L2 is not tied as closely to OLP. For example in a well-known study, Durgunoglu Nagy and Hacin (1993) found that OLP in the L2 (English) did not predict basic reading skills (i.e., word recognition, pseudoword reading) in young Latino school children, while phonological processing skills did. Other studies involving a variety of L2 learning contexts (e.g., French immersion, bilingual programmes, ESL programmes) and a variety of writing systems being learned as L2 (e.g., English, French, Hebrew, Farsi) have found only weak relationships between L2 proficiency and performance on measures of word recognition, pseudoword decoding and spelling in the L2 (Chiappe and Siegel, 1999; Commeau, Cormier, Grandmaison and Lacroix, 1999; Geva, Wade-Woolley and Shany, 1993; Gholamain and Geva, 1999; Gottardo Siegel and Wade-Woolley, 2001). Based on results of a longitudinal research of ESL children, Geva, Yaghoubzadeh, and Schuster (2000) report that children with English as Ll were more proficient than ESL children on a variety of tasks used to assess their language proficiency in English. However, the ESL children and the children with English as L1 did not differ on basic reading skills such as word cognition and decoding skills.

In other words, while L2 reading comprehension is related to L2 oral language proficiency, the research on young bilingual children does not support a strong version of this belief when it comes to word-based reading skills (Geva, 2000). Instead, it appears that, provided that children have attended school on a regular basis, and have been already exposed to appropriate and systematic literacy instruction in the L2, there is no compelling reason to attribute persistent difficulties in developing basic word recognition and spelling skills to a less-than-optimal level of L2 language proficiency.

The third group of studies that needs to be considered concerns the relationship between word recognition processes and reading comprehension. Some ESL educators and researchers focus on the development of reading comprehension in ESL learners, and tend to minimize the role of word recognition processes in reading comprehension. They tend to attribute poor reading comprehension difficulties in L2 children to the children's OLP level. Even though the need to continue developing OLP is not disputed, recent research has shown that such difficulties may be related to problems with word recognition skills. Moreover, recent research has shown that in spite of limited OLP, with adequate instruction children can learn to carry out with accuracy word-based processes such as decoding and spelling words (e.g., Durgunoglu *et al.*, 1993; Geva *et al.*, 2000; Geva and Siegel, 2000; Geva and Wade-Woolley, 1998; Geva Wade-Woolley and Shany, 1997; Gholamain and Geva, 1999; Gottardo *et al.*, 2001; Wang and Geva, 2003). Moreover, there is evidence that normally achieving (NA), Primary Level ESL children can develop concurrently their language and literacy skills, and show increasing success in comprehending texts (Geva and Clifton, 1993; Geva *et al.*, under review; Willows and Dixon, 1998), in story writing, and in reading texts fluently (Geva and Yaghoubzadeh, 2003, under review). Some ESL children may have a specific disability involving difficulty in learning to decode and spell words, and accompanying, perhaps causal, difficulties in component skills such as phonological awareness. The tendency to withhold assessment and remediation until OLP has reached some (unspecified) optimal level may result in cumulative deprivation and unjustly withheld services.

Careful and reliable assessment of ESL children as being reading disabled is a complex task (Geva *et al.*, 2000). Geva, Yaghoubzadeh and Petrulius-Wright (under review) report that while listening comprehension, a measure of OLP, correlates with reading comprehension, a much more accurate picture of variation in reading comprehension is achieved when, along with oral language indices, factors such as decoding skills, phonological processing skills, and speed of letter naming are taken into account. Persistent difficulties on these latter tasks, in spite of adequate instruction, indicate that the problem may be caused by difficulties in developing prerequisite skills necessary in learning to read, and not merely underdeveloped OLP (Geva, 2000; Geva *et al.*, 2000; Geva *et al.*, under review). This research has shown that regardless of children's Ll background (e.g., Punjabi, Tamil, Portuguese, Cantonese) within each language group, the profiles of the at-risk ESL children included persistent low scores on word recognition and spelling tasks, as well as poor performance on phonological processing and speed of naming tasks (see below). Indeed, on the basis of longitudinal research of ESL children at the primary level, Geva (2000) proposes that a noticeable gap between listening comprehension and reading comprehension (with a pattern favouring listening comprehension over reading comprehension), and persistent poor word recognition skills in spite of adequate OLP development can be highly suggestive of reading disability in L2 children. A similar procedure was proposed by Stanovich (1991) with regard to Ll children.

COGNITIVE AND LINGUISTIC PROCESSES IN L2 READING

A number of processes that have been studied in Ll reading research have also been the target of L2 investigations The findings of these studies indicate that there are both factors that are common to all languages and language-specific factors that underlie the development of successful reading in L2. Of the processes associated with reading development and reading difficulties that have been most heavily researched, two are phonological processing and rapid naming.

There has been extensive research on the importance of phonological processes in the acquisition of reading in Ll children (Adams, 1990; Stanovich and Siegel, 1994). In addition to skills such as the knowledge of letter names (Chall, 1996; Ehri, 1991), phonological processing is one of the chief skill sets necessary for the mastery of the sound–symbol relationship basic to alphabetic writing systems. Phonological processing skills are often defined as phonological awareness, phonological memory, and phonological mediation in word retrieval (Wagner and Torgesen, 1987), although the latter, also known as rapid naming, is conceptualized by some scholars as lying outside, but interacting with, the phonological module. Phonological awareness comprises the ability to reflect on and manipulate units of spoken language smaller than the word, such as syllables, onset-rime constituents, and phonemes. This skill may be measured by counting, deleting, substituting, blending or segmenting elements (Yopp, 1988; Stanovich, 1993; Shankweiler, 1999). Young children who find it difficult to conceptualize spoken language as consisting of isolatable elements often experience trouble in acquiring reading skills (e.g., Ehri, 1998; Elbro, 1996; Shankweiler, 1999; Torgesen, 1999). This difficulty is particularly marked in the acquisition of word identification and decoding skills (e.g., Adams, 1990; Elbro *et al.*, 1998; Shankweiler, 1999; Snowling, 1995; Stanovich, 2000; Stanovich and Siegel, 1994; Swan and Goswami, 1997; Torgesen, 1999).

Investigations of normal word reading development in first and second languages have shown remarkable parallels. These parallels hold for comparisons across languages that are strikingly different, such as Punjabi-English (Chiappe and Siegel, 1999; Wade-Woolley and Siegel, 1997), Farsi-English (Gholamain and Geva, 1999), English-Hebrew (Geva *et al.*, 1993), Cantonese-English (Gottardo *et al.*, 2001), French-English (Bruck and Genesee, 1995; Comeau *et al.*, 1999), English-Spanish (Cisero and Royer, 1995; Durgunoglu *et al.*, 1993), and Turkish-Dutch (Verhoeven, 1994).

Phonological awareness studies have demonstrated that the awareness of individual sounds of speech in Ll and L2 correlate with each other and can predict reading and spelling development across languages, in both Ll and L2. The robustness of these findings is strengthened by the variety of populations that have been studied in this line of research. For example, Comeau *et al.* (1999) have investigated phonological awareness of English-speaking children learning to read in a French immersion programme, finding that phonological awareness in French and English was strongly predictive of word decoding in both languages. Chiappe and Siegel (1999) showed that phonological awareness and phonological decoding discriminated between Punjabi-speaking children who were good and poor readers of English. In an investigation comparing the English-spelling skills of English-speaking children and Punjabi- and Chinese-speaking children, Wade-Woolley and Siegel (1997) found that phonological awareness in English predicted a significant amount of the variance in both Ll and L2 groups. In a study investigating parallel processes in both L1 and L2, Gottardo *et al.* (2001) found that phonological skills were correlated across languages, and that these skills in both L1 and L2 were correlated with L2 reading ability for Chinese-speaking children learning English.

Rapid naming, an index of speed of access to the representations of words in the 'mental dictionary', has also received some attention by researchers interested in its relation to reading in L2 contexts. Although in some studies L2 learners are found to be slower at naming than their L1 counterparts, their naming speed improves and catches up with their L1 counterparts (e.g., Geva *et al.*, 2000). Importantly, individual differences in L2 naming speed appear to be predictive of reading development in L2, as is the case for L1 naming speed. This finding holds for diverse language groups, such as Farsi-speaking children learning English (Gholamain and Geva, 1999), and English-speaking children learning Hebrew (Geva, under review). Gholamain and Geva (1999) showed that speed of naming colours and letters in Farsi predicted the English reading skills of Farsi-speaking children, and that parallel tasks in English predicted word-based reading in Farsi. In the work of Geva (2000), Grade one children's speed of naming objects, letters and colours was a significant predictor of basic reading skills in both English and Hebrew. Geva *et al.* (2000) found that individual differences in speed of letter naming in English, the L2, predicted word recognition and pseudoword decoding of ESL children and children of their counterparts who had English as their L1.

In addition to patterns that are common across languages, studies that have looked at specific elements of phonological processing and rapid naming have generally found patterns of behaviour that are language-specific. Languages vary along a number of dimensions, relating both to oral and written aspects of languages, and some of these differences have significant implications for the processes involved in reading. In terms of writing systems, alphabetic languages differ in orthographic depth, or the regularity of correspondence between letters and sounds. Some languages, such as Spanish and German, are associated with orthographies that are 'shallow', that is, they are transparent and easy to decode. Other languages, such as English, are associated with 'deeper' orthographies, where the relations between symbols and sound are less regular and more idiosyncratic. Children learning to read in a shallow orthography may learn the sound–symbol code more rapidly and attain high rates of accuracy earlier than young readers of a deeper orthography, as Geva and her colleagues found in studies of young children learning to read in Hebrew and English concurrently (Geva, under review; Geva and Siegel, 2000; Geva and Wade-Woolley, 1998). Languages may differ in the contents of their phonemic and syllabic repertoires. This can be illustrated in a comparison of Chinese and English. Consonant clusters, such as 'tr' and 'st', and phonemes such as /θ/, the first sound in 'thick', appear only in English, but tones appear only in Chinese. Wang and Geva (2003) report that young school ESL children with Cantonese as their L1 experienced difficulties in spelling words containing the /θ/ phoneme, but did not differ from English as L1 children in their spelling of words which contained familiar phonemes. Another dimension along which differences are found is that of morphology. Hebrew represents prepositional phrases as one word (e.g., /babayit/, meaning 'at home'), while in Turkish, post-inflections and vowel harmony are reflected in word spellings.

Cognitive and linguistic processes that are associated with reading acquisition may also show different patterns of relationships in different languages. For example, phonological awareness appears to maintain a predictive relationship with word recognition in deep orthographies longer than in shallow orthographies. Geva (under review) reports that although both phonological awareness and rapid naming were predictive of basic reading skills in English, the L1, and Hebrew, the L2, the phonological awareness measures were strongly associated with accuracy in English, while speed of naming was more strongly associated with development of basic reading skills in Hebrew. For shallow orthographies, therefore, speed of naming appears to be a more robust predictor of reading success (de Jong and van der Leij, 1999; Wimmer, Mayringer and Landerl, 2000) and of reading failure (Wimmer *et al.*, 1998; Wolf, Pfeil, Lotz and Biddle, 1994). While the relative contribution of phonological awareness and naming speed may vary among languages, evidence from many languages suggests that both are implicated in successful reading acquisition.

READING DIFFICULTIES IN L2 LEARNERS

Research with children learning a second language indicates that processes such as phonological awareness, speed of naming and verbal memory are sources of individual differences in reading development in L2, just as they are in Ll. Furthermore, these skills transfer from Ll to L2. Two important implications of these findings are clear. First, these cognitive processes may be good indices of reading development in L2 children. Second, individual differences in these underlying abilities may be more reliable predictors of the course of reading disability than other, more global measures of L2 OLP or general intelligence (Geva *et al.*, 2000).

A current controversy surrounds the requirement in many jurisdictions that children demonstrate a significant discrepancy between assessed intellectual functioning and academic achievement in order to be considered reading disabled or dyslexic. Children who experience reading difficulties without such a discrepancy may be considered 'garden-variety' poor readers (Stanovich, 1988), and as such may not be eligible for the same special education services which are available to those children who meet the criteria. The discrepancy requirement is currently under attack by researchers for a number of reasons. First, the symptoms associated with a reading disability in young children are identical for both discrepant and non-discrepant poor readers, and research evidence points to the same underlying cause, which is an impairment in the phonological processing module (Stanovich and Siegel, 1994; but see Fawcett Nicolson and Maclagan, 2001). Second, evidence also suggests that reading-disabled and garden-variety poor readers benefit equally from the same type of remediation. Third, as Stanovich (1986) has shown, Matthew effects, in which 'the rich get richer and the poor get poorer', manifest themselves as children get older. In this case, because early experiences with reading are difficult and unrewarding, poor readers read less and acquisition of knowledge that typically occurs through reading is deficient. These children, who may initially show a discrepancy, eventually manifest a more general cognitive deficit due to their lack of reading experience. Fourth, intelligence is only weakly associated with the acquisition of basic decoding skills in young readers, unlike phonological processing, which shows a very strong, causal relationship. The research evidence suggests that these considerations apply to all readers, regardless of their language background.

For L2 readers, however, there is another compelling reason to avoid the use of the discrepancy criterion. The difficulties in the use of standardized intelligence measures with linguistically diverse populations is usually presented in terms of arguments about the validity of the obtained scores. This is compounded when the scores are a necessary component of the definition of reading disability and decisions about who is entitled to remediation services. Because L2 children are in the process of developing L2 proficiency, it may be difficult to attain a verbal score that is high enough to establish a discrepancy.

While a possible solution to this is to rely on non-verbal intelligence to establish the discrepancy, this solution is more apparent than real, since the concerns about the application of L1 norms to an L2 population remain. Likewise, available evidence questions the predictive validity of non-verbal intelligence in the development of basic reading skills in L2 learners (Geva and Siegel, 2000; Geva et al., 2000). The cognitive and linguistic processes discussed above appear to transfer from Ll to L2, and to be effective indices of basic reading skills. Other factors that are more global in nature, such as oral language proficiency and general intelligence, may be more subject to influences of exogenous variables, such as cultural knowledge, socio-economic factors, and the social context of language acquisition. In sum, underlying cognitive processes which have been shown to be important sources of individual differences in L2 reading acquisition, should be targeted for early identification and programming endeavours.

SUMMARY AND IMPLICATIONS

The available research on L2 reading development in school children suggests that, as is the case with children who learn to read in their L1, some L2 children may read with difficulty not merely because they require more time to gain sufficient language proficiency in the L2 (though they may continue to benefit from language instruction), but because they have problems with the acquisition of basic reading skills. The available research on L2 reading development in children has also shown that for children who learn to read concurrently in Ll and L2, there is positive and significant correlation between parallel component reading skills and predictors of successful reading development in the Ll and the L2. Other research has shown that it is possible to evaluate such skills even when OLP is still developing. Individual differences in basic components of reading in the L2 correlate with performance on higher level aspects of reading comprehension as well. This line of research has shown that it is possible to evaluate adequate performance in reading and on reading components even when OLP is not fully developed, that parallel skills correlate in the child's L1 and L2, and that measures of general ability are not that useful in identifying reading disability in L2 children. It follows that if a child who has had adequate instruction in the L2 continues to do poorly in the L2 and to lag behind other children from the same ethnic/linguistic background, it is possible to predict that this child will continue to have difficulties and that this child is likely to experience similar difficulties in the L1 as well. One of the practical outcomes of this body of research is that it may not be necessary or ethically justifiable to withhold assessment and intervention from L2 learners who show the warning signs of reading disability.

Research on the development of reading skills in children learning to read in L2 and on reading disabilities in L2 children is still in its infancy. Many questions about the normal course of L2 reading development and about the most effective assessment and remediation related issues remain unanswered. However, on the basis of the available research a few practical recommendations for clinicians and educators can be made. These are summarized below:

Do
- assess as many of the areas known to be related to dyslexia as possible;
- assess in English and the home language where possible;

- monitor progress and learning over time;
- look beyond oral language proficiency;
- provide direct instruction in reading skills;
- provide language enrichment opportunities;
- consider the transfer of specific skills from the first language.

Do not
- wait or delay assessment until oral language proficiency has reached an 'appropriate' level;
- assume that word recognition and word attack skills are unimportant;
- assume persistent language and reading difficulties will 'catch up' if ignored;
- seek to establish a discrepancy in order to justify a label of reading disability;
- assume that persistent difficulties across-the-board merely reflect 'negative' transfer from the first language;
- use test norms based on the child's first language.

REFERENCES

Adams, M.I. (1990) *Beginning to Read: Thinking and Learning about Print.* Cambridge, MA: MIT Press.

Anderson, V. and Roit, M. (1996) Linking reading comprehension instruction to language development for language minority students. *Elementary School Journal*, 96, 295–310.

Benavides, A. (1989) High-risk predictors and prereferral screening for language minority students. In A.A. Ortiz and B.A. Ramirez (eds), *School and the Culturally Diverse Exceptional Student: Promising Practices and Future Directions.* Reston, Virginia: ERIC Clearinghouse on Handicapped and Gifted Children.

Bruck, M. and Genesee, F. (1995) Phonological awareness in young second language learners. *Journal of Child Language*, 22, 307–327.

Campione, J.C. (1989) Assisted assessment: A taxonomy of approaches and an outline of strengths and weaknesses. *Journal of Learning Disabilities*, 22(3), 151–165.

Chall, J.S. (1996) *Stages of Reading Development* (2nd edn). Orlando, FL: Harcourt Brace College Publishers.

Chamberlain, E. and Medeiros-Landurand, P. (1991) Practical considerations for the assessment of LEP students with special needs. In E.V. Hamayan and J.S. Damico (eds), *Limiting Bias in the Assessment of Bilingual Students.* Austin, TX: Pro-Ed.

Chiappe, P. and Siegel, L.S. (1999) Phonological awareness and reading acquisition in English- and Punjabi-speaking Canadian children. *Journal of Educational Psychology*, 9, 20–28.

Chitiri, H.F., Sun, Y., Willows, D.M. and Taylor, I. (1992) Word recognition in second language reading. In R.J. Harris (ed.), *Cognitive Processing in Bilinguals.* North-Holland, Amsterdam: Elsevier Science Publishers.

Cisero, C. and Royer, J. (1995) The development and cross-language transfer of phonological awareness. *Contemporary Educational Psychology*, 20, 275–303.

Cline, T. and Frederickson, N. (1996) *Curriculum Related Assessment in Bilingual Children.* Clevedon: Multilingual Matters Ltd.

Cline, T. and Frederickson, N. (1999) Identification and assessment of dyslexia in bi/multilingual children. *International Journal of Bilingual Education and Bilingualism*, 2, 2, 81–93.

Cole, E. (1996) Immigrant and refugee children and families: Supporting a new road traveled. In M. Luther (ed.), *Dynamic Assessment for Instruction: From Theory to Application.* Toronto: Captus University Publication.

Comeau, L., Cormier, E., Grandmaison, E. and Lacroix, D. (1999) A longitudinal study of phonological processing skills in children learning to read in a second language. *Journal of Educational Psychology*, 91, 29–43.

Cummins, J. (1984) *Bilingualism and Special Education: Issues in Assessment and Pedagogy.* Clevedon: Multilingual Matters Ltd.

Cummins, J. (1989) A theoretical framework for bilingual special education. *Exceptional Children,* 56, 111–119.

Dao, M. (1991) Designing assessment procedures for educationally at risk Southeast Asian-American students. *Journal of Learning Disabilities,* 24(10), 594–601.

de Jong, P.F. and van der Leij, A. (1999) Specific contributions of phonological abilities to early reading acquisition: Results from a Dutch latent variable longitudinal study. *Journal of Educational Psychology,* 91, 450–476.

Duran, R.P. (1989) Assessment and instruction of at-risk Hispanic students. *Exceptional Children,* 56, 154–158.

Durgunoglu, A.Y., Nagy, W.E. and Hancin, B. (1993) Cross-language transfer of phonemic awareness. *Journal of Educational Psychology,* 85, 453–465.

Ehri, L.C. (1991) Learning to read and spell words. In L. Rieben and C.A. Perfetti (eds), *Learning to Read: Basic Research and its Implications.* Hillsdale, NJ: Lawrence Erlbaum Associates.

Ehri, L.C. (1998) Research on learning to read and spell: A personal historical perspective. *Scientific Studies of Reading,* 2, 97–114.

Elbro, C. (1996) Early linguistic abilities and reading development: A review and a hypothesis. *Reading and Writing: An Interdisciplinary Journal,* 8, 453–485.

Elbro, C., Borstrøm, I. and Petersen, D.K. (1998) Predicting dyslexia from kindergarten. The importance of distinctness of phonological representations of lexical items. *Reading Research Quarterly,* 33, 36–60.

Fawcett, A.J., Nicolson, R.I. and MacLagan, F. (2001) Cerebellar tests differentiate between groups of poor readers with and without IQ discrepancy. *Journal of Learning Disabilities,* 34, 119–135.

Figueroa, R.A. (1989) Psychological testing of linguistic-minority students: Knowledge gaps and regulations. *Exceptional Children,* 56, 145–152.

Fitzgerald, J. (1995) English-as-a-second language learners' cognitive reading processes: A review of research in the United States. *Review of Educational Research* 65, 145–190.

Gavillan-Torres, E. (1983) Issues of assessment of limited English proficiency students and of truly disabled in the United States. In N. Miller (ed.), *Bilingualism and Language Disability.* San Diego, CA: College Hill Press, Inc.

Gersten, R. and Geva, E. (2003) Insights into the New Research Base on Teaching Reading to English Learners. *Educational Leadership,* in press.

Geva, E. (2000) Issues in the assessment of reading disabilities in L2 children – Beliefs and research evidence. *Dyslexia,* 6, 13–28.

Geva, E. (under review) L1-L2 transfer and orthographic specificity? – Evidence from phonological processing and rapid automatized naming in young bilingual readers.

Geva, E., Barsky, A. and Westemoff, A. (2000) Developing a framework for interprofessional and diversity-informed practice. In E. Geva, A. Barsky and F. Westemoff (eds), *Interprofessional Practice with Diverse Populations: Cases in Point.* Westport, CT: Greenwood Press.

Geva, E. and Clifton, S. (1993) The development of first and second language reading skills in Early French Immersion. *Canadian Modern Language Review,* 50, 646–667.

Geva, E. and Ryan, E.B. (1993) Linguistic and cognitive correlates of academic skills in first and second languages. *Language Learning,* 43, 5–42.

Geva, E. and Siegel, L. (2000) Orthographic and cognitive factors in the current development of basic reading skills in two languages. *Reading and Writing: An Interdisciplinary Journal,* 12, 1–30.

Geva, E. and Wade-Woolley, L. (1998) Component processes in becoming English-Hebrew biliterate. In A. Durgunoglu and L. Verhoeven (eds), *Acquisition of Literacy in a Multilingual Context: A Cross-Cultural Perspective.* Hillsdale, NJ: Lawrence Erlbaum Associates.

Geva, E., Wade-Woolley, L. and Shany, M. (1993) The concurrent development of spelling and decoding in two different orthographies. *Journal of Reading Behavior,* 25, 383–406.

Geva, E., Wade-Woolley, L. and Shany, M. (1997) The development of reading efficiency in first and second language. *Scientific Studies of Reading,* 1(2), 119–144.

Geva, E. and Yaghoubzadeh, Z. (2003) Rudiments of reading fluency in L1 and ESL children: the role of oral proficiency and underlying cognitive-linguistic processes. Under review.

Geva, E., Yaghoubzadeh, Z. and Petrulis-Wright, J. (under review) The role of English oral language proficiency in the reading development of Ll and L2 primary level children.

Geva, E., Yaghoubzadeh, Z. and Schuster, B. (2000) Understanding individual differences in word recognition skills of ESL children. *Annals of Dyslexia*, 50, 121–154.

Gholamain, M. and Geva, E. (1999) Orthographic and cognitive factors in the concurrent development of basic reading skills in English and Persian. *Language Learning*, 49, 183–217.

Gopaul-McNicol, S. and Thomas-Presswood, T. (1998) Best practices in intellectual/educational assessment. In *Working with Linguistically and Culturally Different Children: Innovative Clinical and Educational Approaches*. Boston: Allyn & Bacon.

Gottardo, A. Yan, B., Siegel, L. and Wade-Woolley, L. (2001) Factors related to English reading performance in children with Chinese as a first language: More evidence of cross-language transfer of phonological processing. *Journal of Educational Psychology*, 93, 530–542.

Hamayan, E.V. and Damico, J.S. (eds) (1990) *Limiting Bias in the Assessment of Bilingual Students*. Austin, TX: Pro-Ed.

Holtzman, Jr. W.A. and Wilkinson, C.Y. (1991) Assessment of cognitive ability. In E.V. Hamayan and J.S. Damico (eds), *Limiting Bias in the Assessment of Bilingual Students*. Austin, TX: Pro-Ed.

Limbos, M. and Geva, E. (2001) Accuracy of teach assessment of second language students at risk for reading disability. Journal of Learning Disabilities, 34(2) (March/April 2001), pp. 136–151.

Ogbu, J.U. (1978) *Minority Education and Caste*. New York: Academic Press.

Oller, J.W. and Damico, J.S.C. (1990) Theoretical considerations in the assessment of LEP students. In E.V. Hamayan and J.S.C. Damico (eds), *Limiting Bias in the Assessment of Bilingual Students*. Austin, TX: Pro-Ed.

Ortiz, A.A. and Ramirez, B.A. (eds) (1989) *School and the Culturally Diverse Exceptional Student: Promising Practices and Future Directions*. Reston, VA: ERIC Clearinghouse on Handicapped and Gifted Children.

Samuels, M., Tzuriel, D. and Malloy-Miller, T. (1988) Dynamic assessment of children with learning difficulties. In R.F. Brown and M. Chazan (eds), *Emotional and allied issues in the field of disability*.

Sattler, J.M. (1992) Assessment of ethnic minority children. In J.M. Sattler, *Assessment of Children* (revised). San Diego, CA: Jerome M. Sattler.

Scarborough, H.S. (2001) Connecting early language and literacy to later reading (dis)abilities: Evidence, theory, and practice. In S. Neuman and D. Dickinson (eds), *Handbook for Research in Early Literacy*. New York: Guilford Press.

Shankweiler, D. (1999) Words to meaning. *Scientific Studies of Reading*, 3, 113–127.

Snowling, M.J. (1995) Phonological processing and developmental dyslexia. *Journal of Research in Reading*, 18, 132–138.

Stanovich, K.E. (1986) Matthew effects in reading: Some consequences of individual differences in the acquisition of literacy. *Reading Research Quarterly*, 21, 360–407.

Stanovich, K.E. (1988) Explaining the differences between the dyslexic and the garden-variety poor reader: The phonological-core variable-difference model. *Journal of Learning Disabilities*, 21, 590–612.

Stanovich, K.E. (1991) Conceptual and empirical problems with discrepancy definitions of reading disability. *Journal of Learning Disabilities*, 14, 269–280.

Stanovich, K.E. (1993) Romance and reality. *The Reading Teacher*, 47(4), 280–291.

Stanovich, K.E. and Siegel, L.S. (1994) The phenotypic performance profile of reading-disabled children: A regression-based test of the phonological-core variable-difference model. *Journal of Educational Psychology*, 86, 24–53.

Stanovich, K.E. (2000) Progress in Understanding Reading: Scientific Foundations and New Frontiers. New York: The Guildford Press.

Schiff-Myers, N.B. (1992) Considering arrested language development and language loss in the assessment of second language learners. *Language, Speech and Hearing Services in Schools*, 23(1), 28–33.

Swan, D. and Goswami, U. (1997) Phonological awareness deficit in developmental dyslexia and the phonological representations hypothesis. Journal of Experimental Child Psychology, 66, 18–41.

Torgesen, J.M. (1999) Phonologically based reading disabilities: Toward a coherent theory of one kind of learning disability. In R.J. Sternberg and L. Spear-Swerling (eds), *Perspectives on Learning Disabilities: Biological, Cognitive, Contextual*. Boulder, CO: Westview Press.

Verhoeven, L. (1994) Transfer in bilingual development: The Linguistic Interdependence Hypothesis revisited. *Language Learning*, 44, 381–415.

Verhoeven, L. (2000) Components in early second language reading and spelling. *Scientific Studies in Reading*, 4, 313–330.

Wade-Woolley, L. and Siegel, L.S. (1997) The spelling performance of ESL and native speakers of English as a function of reading skills. *Reading and Writing: An Interdisciplinary Journal*, 9, 387–406.

Wagner, R.L. and Torgesen, J. (1987) The nature of phonological processing and its causal role in the acquisition of reading skills. *Psychological Bulletin*, 101, 192–212.

Wang, M. and Geva, E. (2003) Spelling acquisition of novel English phonemes in Chinese children. *Reading and Writing: An Interdisciplinary Journal*, in press.

Willows, D. and Dixon, M. (1998) Implementing and maintaining change in a primary literacy program: A longitudinal case study of the Balanced and Flexible Literacy Diet. Paper presented at the National Reading Conference, Scottsdale, AZ.

Wimmer, H., Mayringer, H. and Landerl, K. (1998) Poor reading: A deficit in skill-automatization or a phonological deficit? *Scientific Studies of Reading*, 2, 321–340.

Wimmer, H., Mayringer, H. and Landerl, K. (2000) The double deficit hypothesis and difficulties in learning to read a regular orthography. *Journal of Educational Psychology*, 92, 668–680.

Wolf, M., Pfeil, C., Lotz, R. and Biddle, K. (1994) Towards a more universal understanding of the developmental dyslexias: The contribution of orthographic factors. In V.W. Berninger (ed.), *The Varieties of Orthographic Knowledge I: Theoretical and Developmental Issues*. Dordrecht: Kluwer.

Yopp, H.K. (1988) The validity and reliability of phonological awareness tests. *Reading Research Quarterly*, 23, 159–177.

INDEX